Dru

THE ROUGH GUIDE

There are more than one hundred and fifty Rough Guide travel, phrasebook, and music titles, covering destinations from Amsterdam to Zimbabwe, languages from Czech to Thai, and musics from World to Opera and Jazz

Forthcoming titles include

Dominican Republic • Jerusalem
Laos • Melbourne • Sydney

Rough Guides on the Internet

www.roughguides.com

Rough Guide Credits

Text editor: Jennifer Dempsey
Series editor: Mark Ellingham
Typesetting: Helen Ostick

Publishing Information

This first edition published June 1999 by
Rough Guides Ltd, 62–70 Shorts Gardens, London, WC2H 9AB

Distributed by the Penguin Group:

Penguin Books Ltd, 27 Wrights Lane, London W8 5TZ
Penguin Books USA Inc., 375 Hudson Street, New York 10014, USA
Penguin Books Australia Ltd, 487 Maroondah Highway,
PO Box 257, Ringwood, Victoria 3134, Australia
Penguin Books Canada Ltd, 10 Alcorn Avenue,
Toronto, Ontario, Canada M4V 1E4
Penguin Books (NZ) Ltd, 182–190 Wairau Road,
Auckland 10, New Zealand

Typeset in Bembo and Helvetica to an original design by Henry Iles.
Printed in Spain by Graphy Cems.

Pictures on pp. 8, 23, 47, 72, 81, 91, 93, 98, 101, 106, 123, 130, 219,
223, 253, 275, 278, 283, 334, 360 & 365 © **Alexis Maryon**

A catalogue record for this book is available from the British Library.
ISBN 1-85828-433-3

Drum 'n' bass

THE ROUGH GUIDE

by Peter Shapiro

with pictures by
Alexis Maryon

Contents

Part One: Drum 'n' Bass

Part Two: Down Tempo and Big Beat

Introduction

T he *Rough Guide to Drum 'n' Bass* follows the path of the breakbeat after its arrival on British shores and its subsequent recirculation throughout the world via genres like Jungle, Drum 'n' Bass, Hardcore Techno, Trip-Hop/Down Tempo and Big Beat. Originally the part of late '60s/early '70s records where all the instruments would drop out except for the drums, which would continue the groove rather than solo, the breakbeat formed the foundation of the early hip-hop records (when it was still largely the provenance of guys with "two turntables and a microphone") and of the records made when hip-hop was largely created by the sampler. Now generally defined as almost any rhythm that is not in 4/4 tempo, the breakbeat has become the building block of what is considered the first specifically British strain of dance music, Jungle, and later the crucial aspect of other British mutations of hip-hop – Big Beat and Trip-Hop.

Covering both the innovators and the apprentices of breakbeat science in an encyclopedic format, this book is divided into two sections: one focusing on Drum 'n' Bass/Jungle/Hardcore and the other focusing on Trip-Hop and Big Beat. While combining these somewhat disparate genres under the umbrella of "drum 'n' bass" may be controversial, there is no denying that all these artists belong to the same breakbeat continuum. Of course, as anyone who has ever read an interview in the music press would know, musicians hate to be pigeon-holed, so quibbles over nomenclature shouldn't matter anyway, right?

What does matter is that beginning roughly with the records of Shut Up and Dance in the very late '80s, enterprising British producers started turbo-boosting the low ends of House and Techno with the chest-caving sub-bass and hyper-kinetic breakbeats of hip-hop to create a new form of music known at various times over its progression as rave, Hardcore, Jungle and drum 'n' bass. While it has never had anywhere near the prolonged mainstream acceptance of House, there is no question that drum 'n' bass's mutation of rhythm, celebration of speed, dialectic of ecstasy and come-down, and play of surfaces is potentially the most exciting musical development since the dawn of hip-hop.

Moving in parallel to the evolution of drum 'n' bass, albeit with very different chemical imperatives, artists like Coldcut and DJ Shadow took their cues from the mix-and-match aesthetic of cut 'n' paste legends Double Dee & Steinski and the dusty productions of hip-hop masters the 45 King and DJ Premier to create their own blunted, detached take on aural collage called variously Trip-Hop, Down Tempo or Downbeat. A few years later, as the dividends of abstraction were evaporating, some court jesters with samplers and big record collections remade this minimal music with rock's maximal hedonism in mind to produce Big Beat, the most mindlessly enjoyable music in years.

Although *The Rough Guide to Drum 'n' Bass* is meant to function as a reference book, by no means does it pretend to be objective. The proliferation of electronic dance music has been the biggest breath of fresh air to blow across British and, even if it doesn't necessarily want to admit it, American youth culture in some time. Its greatest failing, though, has been the largely uncritical press that has developed alongside it, which has given the culture extreme delusions of grandeur. While wanting to celebrate the achievements of Jungle, Down Tempo and Big Beat, this book has been written with the full intention of ruffling feathers and provoking debate within a scene that has been too insular for its own good.

Thanks to everyone who loaned me records and photos and divulged info, my editor Jennifer Dempsey and, most of all, to my wife, Rachael, who put up with my bouts of insomnia more than any reasonable person should have to.

Peter Shapiro

drum 'n' bass

A Guy Called Gerald

No other British artist involved in dance music since the Acid House explosion has produced as many important records as A Guy Called Gerald. From "Voodoo Ray" (1989), the song that put British House on the map, to **Black Secret Technology** (1995), the album that definitively showed that Jungle was capable of full-length album statements, Gerald Simpson has consistently explored virgin territory, paving the way for lesser musicians to take the credit.

Like most of his fellow movers on the drum 'n' bass scene, Gerald Simpson was a young Mancunian marking time by listening to David Bowie and Peter Gabriel until the planet-rocking sound of Electro came along and changed his perception of music. Afrika Bambaataa's rewiring of Kraftwerk and novel use of Roland drum machines turned Simpson on to the power of technology and he soon began pushing the parameters of his own rudimentary synths. Experiments with bolstering the Electro records he was playing out as a DJ with a Roland 606 drum machine caused him to ditch DJing in favour of spending all of his time with a vast array of Roland rhythm machines and synthesizers.

The first products of his Roland infatuation were two records that shaped the direction of British House music: his own "Voodoo Ray" and 808 State's "Pacific State" (1989). As is typical of the history of black musical innovation, however, Simpson never saw any of the money that these British Top 20 singles earned. Adding insult to injury, an ill-fated deal with CBS Records stalled the momentum he had generated and left his career in tatters (for more on this phase of his career, see *The Rough Guide to House*).

While taking refuge from the headless chickens of the major label dance departments, Simpson started fooling around with breakbeats and plunging them into the depths of his sampler. The result of this experimentation was a series of ferocious, proto-Jungle 12"s released on his newly formed Juice Box label in 1991 that seemed to express his rage at the mainstream dance scene and exorcised the demons of exploitation in a flurry of gun-play beats and rude bwoy swagger. The following year these singles were compiled on the landmark **28 Gun Bad Boy** album which was criminal-minded years before "Original Nuttah" hit the scene and laid the foundations for Ibiza Records' ragga-chat Jungle and DJ Hype's jump-up sound.

After creating the blueprint for Jungle's most effective dance-floor formula, Gerald made a U-turn and started producing some

remarkably intricate and emotive records, beginning with "Glok Track" in 1993. "Nazinji Zaka" and "Finley's Rainbow" (both 1994) introduced Gerald's new-found predilection for evocative, atomised African rhythms and fazed/phased voices. With its disembodied reggae vocal and parsed drum beat, "Finley's Rainbow" anchored his 1995 album, **Black Secret Technology**. One of the first single-artist drum 'n' bass albums, **Black Secret Technology** expanded on Simpson's idea that the sampler was a time machine by linking ancient African rhythms and more modern funk beats with futuristic breakbeat science to produce "trance-like rhythms [which] reflect my frustration to know the truth about my ancestors who talked with drums". "Energy", co-produced with Goldie, sounded like Jamaican nyabinghi drummers jamming in an anti-gravity chamber, while its bird calls referenced "Pacific State" which had since become a favourite sampling tool of the "intelligent" drum 'n' bass brigade.

Scandalously, the album was virtually ignored upon release, but was re-released in 1997 with the addition of the classic "Aquarius Rising", which featured vocals from former Deee-Lite siren Lady Miss Kier. Unfortunately, the apotheosis of the clinical Techstep sound seemed to leave Gerald in a creative bind and the "Radar System/The Fallen Prince of Heaven" (1998) single sounded like he was merely keeping up with the Joneses. Hopefully, the dissolution of his Juice Box label and a relocation to New York will re-ignite the musical ferment that has made A Guy Called Gerald the standard bearer for British dance music. Beginning its life with an excellent three-CD collection of material from his archives called **Cryogenics** (1999), Gerald's new Rotary Code label has taken a large first step towards that end.

◐ 28 Gun Bad Boy   Juice Box, 1992

An essential document of urban malevolence, gangster posturing and skull-snapping beats that is a genuine landmark. Even so, it is next to impossible to find.

◐ Black Secret Technology   Juice Box, 1995

Although it is less visceral than its predecessor, it's equally moody and it's still the most satisfying of drum 'n' bass' single-artist albums.

A-Sides

As drum 'n' bass producers flee from the jungle in droves, Jason Cambridge hasn't forgotten that drum 'n' bass is solely about the rhythm and the subsonic frequencies. Beginning his career in 1992 with "Expressions" on IE Records, Cambridge was one of the leading producers of early breakbeat Hardcore with tracks like "It's Not Over" (1993) and "Jurassic Park" (1993) recorded as Citadel of Chaos for the Boombastic Plastic label.

Hooking up with fellow Essex lad Mark Ryder of the Strictly Underground organization, Cambridge became one of the mainstays of the label, producing tracks as Dub Technicians and collaborating with Uncle 22 on the awesome "Six Million Ways to Die" (1993). He was also responsible for such floor-fillers as Gangster Sound's "Amen" cut-up, "Selector" (1994), and A-Sides' "Kid Caprice" work-out, "Illusions" (1995). Not content with producing almost half of Strictly Underground's records, A-Sides was also one of the resident DJs at their Ravelation events at Wembley Arena.

In 1996 he set up his own label, East Side, which debuted with A-Sides' stunning collaboration with Cool Hand Flex, "Uptown/After Dark". Nothing but bass sine waves, a hip-hop sample and snapping drums, "Uptown" laid down the label's crowd-pleasing, jump-up blue-print. The formula was perfected by Fate's (A-Sides and Majistrate) "The Shuffle/Get the Formula" (1997), Mikey James' "From Da East" (1997), Flava Unit's (James) "The Playa" (1997) and Uncle 22's "Wu Tang Sword" (1997).

A-Sides' biggest anthem, though, was "Punks" (1997) on Strictly Underground. Sampling Redman's famous boast "The funk phenomenon/ I'm bombing you like Lebanon", "Punks" was similar to

Armand Van Helden's House classic "Funk Phenomenon", but with even more of a bottom end. His collaboration with Randall, "Idle" (1997), introduced steel drums into his sound palette, while "Calibre" and "Melt" (both 1997), which were released on Metalheadz, featured more mechanical sounds. His sub-label, Fuze, was responsible for acidic drum 'n' bass like "Time" (1997), "Emunation/Doodle Bug" (1998) and "Orbiter" (1998). Unlike most drum 'n' bass producers, even when A-Sides goes technoid, however, he never loses the hip-hop feel that makes his records so effective. As drum 'n' bass shifted its focus towards a loose-limbed funk feel at the end of 1998, Embee's "The Chase/The Hog" (1999) capitalised on this love affair with all things '70s with a Rhodes-infested blaxploitation jam.

⊙ Various Artists – East Side Mixed By A-Sides   East Side, 1998

An impressive mix compilation of A-Sides' jump-up label that doesn't let its guard slip for one second.

Adam F

More than anyone, Adam F represents the upwardly mobile tendency of drum 'n' bass. Granted, LTJ Bukem created the cool-jazz sound that initially gentrified Jungle, but as the son of glam-rocker Alvin Stardust, a former keyboardist for fey rockers The Moody Blues, someone who doesn't detest Phil Collins and a committed pursuer of the live drum 'n' bass ideal, Adam F is the epitome of Jungle's worrying ability to attract the staunch believers in tasteful musicality who have colonised drum 'n' bass. For all of that, however, Adam F is

responsible for one of drum 'n' bass' finest moments, "Metropolis".

Born in Liverpool, Adam Fenton was introduced to music at a very young age and was a professional, gigging musician by the time he was a teenager. His earliest Jungle tracks, "Sea of Destiny" and "Light Years" (both 1994), were released on the Lucky Spin label, but didn't attract much attention. With a sample of Boogie Down Productions' "Criminally Minded", "Criminal Active/Enchanted" (1994) was more developed and was played by Fabio and Bukem. "Lighter Style" (1995) followed suit in a similar mock bad bwoy style, but Adam F wouldn't find his sound until his third release for Section 5.

The fusion mantra "Circles" (1995) sounded just like its title with its five-note arrangement and became one of the year's biggest across-the-spectrum tunes. "Circles" was followed by the almost as success-ful "Aromatherapy" (1995), which set new lows in both its title and its wispy nonentity of a production, and "F-Jam" (1995), which owed a great deal to Rose Royce's "Love Don't Live Here Anymore" and fea-tured MC Conrad on vocals.

Adam F momentarily broke away from his jazz obsession with the remarkable "Metropolis/Mother Earth" (1996) which was his debut for Metalheadz. The swarming background drone and paranoiac atmos-pherics of "Metropolis" did not sound as if it was made by the same producer who made the spineless "Aromatherapy", but the razor-sharp details were the mark of someone who prizes craftsmanship above all else. It was a stunning record, and followed "Circles" as an award winner.

After a car accident, Adam F re-emerged with the very disap-pointing **Colours** (1997) album. Retreating from the darkness of "Metropolis", **Colours** returned to the palliative vibes of his nu-fusion tracks. "Music in My Mind" and "Dirty Harry" epitomised what jour-nalist Simon Reynolds called "fuzak", while the collaboration with Everything But the Girl's Tracey Thorn, "The Tree Knows Everything", was simply a mess. He redeemed himself, though, with the awesome "Brand New Funk" (1998), which constructed a clarion call for the funk to return to the Jungle with a wah-wah snippet from Rhythm Heritage's "Theme from SWAT", a mammoth breakdown featuring old-schooler Spoonie Gee and a blaxploitation fanfare that collapsed into a grinding, unresolved bassline and ticking time-bomb drums.

⦿ Colours   Positiva, 1997

With major-label backing, this should be easy to find, but there are really only two worthwhile tracks, "Circles" and "Metropolis", both of which are available as singles.

Air

In 1992 the French newspaper *Le Figaro* ran a headline that read: "Thirty Years of French Rock 'n' Roll And Still Not One Good Song". Since that article ran, however, a host of Gallic musicians have emerged to make the bad taste of Johnny Hallyday, Magma and Indochine distant memories. While the French may still be incapable of making a decent rock record, the influx of dance music and hip-hop into France in recent years has meant that French music is no longer simply a parade of jailbait nymphets singing Eurovision cannon fodder or kitsch hymns to the latest tropical dance craze. The latest in a long line of post-hip-hop artists, Air mix the traditional Gallic virtues of Françoise Hardy-style breathiness, Serge Gainsbourg-style seediness and Jacques Brel-style melancholia with an almost-British religious devotion to pure pop and a deep affection for ancient American analogue electronics.

Jean-Benoit Dunckel and Nicolas Godin were high school friends from Versailles who, after a few years of teaching mathematics and architecture, decided to rekindle the spirit of their old high school band, Orange. Instead of picking up their old guitars and David Bowie records, they picked up a cheap vocoder and dusted off some Nina Simone and Debussy records. Their first single, "Modular" (1996), was originally released on the Source label and then licensed to Mo' Wax in the UK where the slow and low emotionalism of its Gainsbourgian groove was welcomed with open arms by a Down Tempo scene bored with its own pot-fuelled anaesthesia. "Casanova 70" (1996) and "Le Soleil Est Près de Moi" (1997) followed suit with re-tooled Easy Listening floating on top of dreamy atmospheres and gossamer textures.

After contributing the Nina Simone-sampling "Soldissimo" to the excellent **Super Discount** (1997) compilation, Dunckel and Godin quickly became the darlings of the British music press with their debut album, **Moon Safari** (1998). Capitalising on the vogue for both lounge music ("All I Need" and "Ce Matin Là") and retro-electronics ("Sexy Boy" and "Kelly Watch the Stars"), **Moon Safari** perfectly encapsulated the underground's nostalgia for a semi-remembered time in the past when technology was fun rather than leading humanity down an Orwellian path to enslavement. In other words, it was retrograde pop fluff with a sun tan and continental flair that seemed positively revolutionary compared to the cheap and clumsy oafs churned out by the British star machine.

◉ Moon Safari   Virgin, 1998

Not as awesome as a jaded music press would have you believe, but an enjoyable record that doesn't take itself too seriously.

Aphrodite

With a succession of sample-heavy, low-riding, dancefloor-friendly tunes from the beginning of the rave era to the present, Aphrodite is the man who put the bass in drum 'n' bass. Never forgetting that dance music is supposed to be fun, Aphrodite has eschewed obvious experimentation and jazzy seriousness in favour of a boombastic bass aesthetic that marks him out as Jungle's greatest populist. The easy, body-moving groove of Aphrodite's tracks belies the fact that he has consistently introduced new sounds and techniques to the drum 'n' bass palette. That he has never achieved the celebrity of media stars like Goldie or LTJ Bukem is down to a blink-ered mainstream press who can only see innovation on "intelligent Jungle's" pretentious surface.

Aphrodite was christened Gavin King and his *nom de disque* came from the Aphrodite club that he ran in Leamington Spa during Acid House's summer of love in 1988. Testament to his House roots appears on the track that first attracted attention his way, 1992's "Some Justice". Working with Mickey Finn and Claudio Guissani as Urban Shakedown, Aphrodite speeded up a sample of Ce Ce Rogers' House classic, "Someday", and welded it to sparse bass oscillations, video game rapid-fire effects and scatter-shot drum breaks to create one of Hardcore's most affective anthems.

The following year Aphrodite started his own label, Aphrodite Recordings, with the release of "Raw Motion" and **The Vine** EP. The hallmark Aphrodite sound was introduced in 1994 with the gut-wrenching bottom end of "Cocaine" and perfected with his 1995 land-mark "Bass Light". With chopped-up drum breaks, flatulent bass riffs and clever rap samples, Aphrodite tracks like "Bass Light", "Bomber" and "Listen to the Rhythm" became staples of the hip-hop-heavy jump-up style of Jungle popularised by DJs like Hype and Mickey Finn.

During this time, Aphrodite was one of the main DJs on the London pirate radio station Pulse FM which played a large part in spreading the sound of Hardcore and Jungle across the capital. At Pulse he met Tony B, with whom he would collaborate as Amazon II to release dancefloor phenomena like 1995's "Beat Booyaa!" and 1996's "King of the Beats" which heralded one of Aphrodite's most successful devices: the half-speed build-up before the bassline kicks in. Aphrodite has also collaborated with Mark QED as Aladdin to pro-duce hyper-kinetic tracks like "Mash Up You Know" and the stunning

"Woman That Rolls!" (both 1995).

As Jungle moved away from the grapeshot snares that marked its '93–'95 golden age towards the streamlined drum sounds of both Alex Reece and Ed Rush, Aphrodite followed suit with more brittle drum programming, but retained the funk by making his basslines even more wobbly and queasy. He also adopted Josh Wink's crowd-pleasing tricks of long intros and snare rolls to create the tension essential to good dance music that drum 'n' bass producers seemed to have forgotten on tracks like "Summer Breeze", "Tower Bass!" and "Style From the Dark Side" (all 1996). With its snare rolls, impossibly catalytic bassline, superfly hip-hop samples and bongo break, "Style From the Dark Side" might be his best, as well as his most complex, track.

Aphrodite renewed his partnership with Mickey Finn in 1997 with Urban Takeover's sublime "Bad Ass!/Drop Top Caddy" 12". Aphrodite had always pilfered from old-school breakbeats, but he reached a funk epiphany with "Bad Ass!"'s groove which was lifted wholesale from New Birth's rare groove classic "Ain't No Change". With the success of "Bad Ass!", Aphrodite and Finn started the Urban Takeover label which has developed such up-and-coming jump-up talent as Natural Born Chillers and Mulder. After years of making some of

Jungle's most compelling music, Aphrodite finally made the charts again with his remix of the Jungle Brothers' "Jungle Brother" which hit the British Top 20 in 1998.

⊙ Aphrodite Recordings   Aphrodite, 1997

A towering monument to the bass, compiling some of the best of King's output as Aphrodite, Aladdin and Amazon II.

Aquasky

O riginally from Bournemouth, Aquasky epitomise the post-LTJ Bukem trend that has transformed drum 'n' bass from a kinetic re-invention of hip-hop into a soothing balm. With wind chimes, cooing mermaid divas, whirlpool synths and unctuous basslines, Aquasky's music isn't so much oceanic as it is palliative.

Dave Wallace and Brent Newitt were chums as toddlers and when they met up again years later they realised they shared similar tastes in music and haircuts. The duo made smarmy jazz-funk as Jazziac Sunflowers for Bob James' Black on Black label, and along with Kieron Bailey they made a demo of drum 'n' bass tunes which Moving Shadow released under the name Aquasky. "Images/Dezires" (1995) was everything the title would lead you to expect: a gurgling jacuzzi of lite jazz sounds, textures that were as cool and wet as a puppy's nose and a new age aura that should've alienated all but the most ardent of Mike Oldfield fans.

Dave Wallace's "Expressions" (1996) followed suit with Vince Guaraldi piano lines, a streamlined beat and Steve Winwood middle-of-the-road synth noodlings. More drum 'n' bass destined for luxury sedan adverts came in the form of Aquasky's "Tranquility/Kauna" (1996) which sounded as if it had wafted in on a Polynesian tradewind. Brent Newitt's outings for Reinforced as Spacelink ("Timezone/Offset Jazz" [1996]) and Immortal Minds ("Pinnackle Vision" [1996]) similarly oozed astral vibes that congealed immediately upon impact.

Despite the embarrassing title, Aquasky's "Nylon Roadster/Cosmic Glue" (1996) was probably their most listenable record because of the slightly harsher textures and a low end that bordered on the funky. Wallace reverted back to form, however, on "Flight/Waves" (1996) which moved all the wrong chakras with its "All that we are and seem is but a dream within a dream" vocal sample. Wallace's Soul Motive project for House label Nuphonic and Newitt's Skin Divers releases on R&S were similarly fey.

Forming their own Passenger label in 1997, the trio took a few more risks on their **Orange Dust** (1997) album. The gushing synth-scapes were still present, but on "Raw Skillz" they hooked up with hip-hoppers Big Kwam and the Scratch Perverts to prove that they could strut as well as stroke crystals.

◉ Orange Dust   Passenger, 1997

If you like jazzy drum 'n' bass, then this will do fine. "Raw Skillz" might take you by surprise, though.

Arcon 2/Leon Mar

Trying to find some kind of rapprochement between the air-brushed smoothness of fusion-influenced drum 'n' bass and the sharp angles of Techstep, producers like Leon Mar (aka Arcon 2) have developed a claustrophobic, clinical, highly detailed sound that often feels like David Banner's laboratory just as all hell is about to break loose. Even when he was exploring HAL's psyche after the *2001* computer turned evil, Mar coloured his angry tech-beats with the jazz-funk of a Johnny Hammond or a Weather Report turned compulsive.

After a decade of dance music productions, Mar's first drum 'n' bass release, "Release the Love" (1996), appeared on Reinforced and followed a fairly standard fusion-Jungle formula. He wouldn't stake a claim on virgin territory until the sci-fi synth explorations of "Liquid Earth Parts 1 & 2" (1996) which was released under his Arcon 2 guise. "The Beckoning/Skyland" (1996) was another Martian melt-down of the "Apache" break and showed Arcon 2 to be the most musical of the Techstep practitioners.

"Zorak/90:90" (1997) featured sonic-boom basslines, mangled vocals and impossibly dense percussion that briefly opened up for a tempestuous breakdown before clenching up again. "Zorak" was included on his **Beckoning** album (1997) which set stormtrooper Techno against galactic jazz to create a combination that seemed to sum up Reinforced's first seven years.

The graceful, dubadelic "Confessions" (1996) and "Running" (1997), released as Leon Mar, were more explicitly soulful, but still had vortices of spiralling drums that felt like high school science experiments. "Address Unknown", from Reinforced's **Enforcers: The Beginning of the End** (1997) compilation, was one of the more quiet passages from Miles Davis' **Dark Magus** set to a Photekian break of drums, gongs and metal boxes. A more aggressive darkside sound appeared on Arcon 2's "Neut/Shock" (1998) which choreographed a cyborg *capoeira* of rumbling basslines, precision drum breaks and rusting synth lines. "Rezurection/Passing Phases" (1998), a collaboration with Tee-Bone, was more subdued despite its Hardstep bassline and showed that Mar was willing to allow some space to develop within the confines of his drum neurosis.

O Beckoning   Reinforced, 1997

If you like Swiss-engineered watches, than you'll love the clockwork percussion and detailed craftsmanship on display here.

Back 2 Basics Records

"**A**re you ready for some blood-clot Jungle Techno?" Run by Jason Ball from his base in Birmingham, Back 2 Basics specialised in the kind of phat beats and oleaginous basslines that would harden your arteries. Along with label mainstays Lee and Warren Smith (aka Asend & Ultravibe and Dead Dred), Ball kept the faith in Jungle's two commandments – blitz the bass and spray the drums – while all around him were succumbing to the cult of "intelligence".

Emerging just as Hardcore was mutating into Jungle, Back 2 Basics lived up to the label's name with stripped-down tracks like "Back 2 Basics" (1993) and "Horns 4 '94" (1994). Evoking both the vogue for air horns and Tim Taylor's rave classic "Egyptian Horn Track", "Horns 4 '94" in particular set the dancefloors alight and marked breakbeat music's new minimalism. Even better, though, was DJ Taktix's stunning "The Way" (1994) which was an incredibly rough cut-up track that sounded like a Junglist version of Afrika Bambaataa's **Death Mix**.

Asend & Ultravibe's "What Kind of World" (1994) juxtaposed scatter-shot breaks with mournful synth washes and a wistful reggae vocal sample, creating a lament for the Junglist bad bwoys. Ultravibe's "Guardian Angel" and Asend & Ultravibe's "Real Love" (both 1995) continued the wistful vibe with slightly muted beats, minor key piano samples and melancholy diva vocals. "Real Love", though, also seemed to undercut the eulogising with gunshot sounds and thoroughly menacing bass bombs. The JB's "Back 2 Life" and "Crazy Feeling" (both 1995) accomplished the same thing by defiling samples of Soul II Soul and Debbie Malone with searing "Amen" breaks and overmodulated basslines.

Dred Bass' "Smokin' Cans" (1995) did away with any ambivalence and absolutely tore it up with some straight-up gangsta business. The JB's awesome "Rockin' With the Best" (1996) "put some karate in your body" with one of Jungle's best ever intros (courtesy of the Real Roxanne). With its obvious Jimmy Castor via NWA sample, his "Go Back, Way Back" (1996) was rather less inspired, even if the low end kicked just as hard. As Bad Behaviour, Ball's hip-hop samples and an incredibly evil bassline kicked out a weakling House intro on the excellent "Bust This" (1996).

While Back 2 Basics laid the foundation of jump-up's G-Funk obsession, the label also went deep into the heart of the bass with sparse bottom-end tracks like Dred Bass' "World of Music" and Northern Connexion's "The Bounce" (both 1995). Back 2 Basics' sub-label, Second Movement, continued in this vein with NC & Ultravibe's "Take Your Soul" and Northern Connexion's "Spanish Guitar" (both 1995). Murphy's Law's "20 Seconds" (1996) was one of the label's most militant tracks to date as it had no hook other than sinister vocoded vocals. Swoosh's "Ya Rockin'" (1997) was a rare example of enthusiasm in a scene wallowing in a miasma of technoid grumbling, but as Dred Bass' disappointing **World of Music** (1998) proved, the label was seemingly forced to abandon the breakbeat mania of old in favour of the new school's rigidity.

⊙ **Various Artists – Explicit Bass**   Back 2 Basics, 1996

Although it has less than ideal mixes of some of the label's best tracks, this is the only comprehensive compilation.

Nicky Blackmarket

Setting up the Hardcore section at the London record shop he co-owns, Nicky Blackmarket is one of the most important men in drum 'n' bass. Black Market has become the focal point of London's drum 'n' bass scene, but Nicky Blackmarket's profile is fairly low-key despite a constantly packed DJ schedule that included Kool FM in addition to landmark clubs like Thunder and Joy.

Although he is more known for Black Market and his DJing, his records for Reinforced were almost as important. As Nick O.D., his **Spam Volume 1** EP (1992) was classic breakbeat Hardcore with tracks like "Jazzy Hardcore" and "Ruff Dub" bringing in new sounds to the genre. **Spam Volume 2** (1993) followed the Darkcore vogue with heaving synths and manic breaks on tracks like "(Non)Sense" and "Distance (I Need You)". The **Tearin'** EP (1994) featured up-to-date remixes of "(Non) Sense" by Tek 9 and his own reworkings of "Jazzy Hardcore" and "Distance (I Need You)" that transformed them into Junglist floor-fillers.

He formed his own label, Gyroscope, and its biggest track was Nicky Blackmarket's "Geese Toon" (1994), which layered a sample of honking bird calls over tearing drum beats. Blackmarket's other label, Kartoonz, releases sure-fire, floor-filling jump-up anthems that concentrate on crashing percussion beats. After concentrating on his DJing, he returned to production with a major label remix of TDF's "Seven" (1997), which rolled out the breaks over the top of the original's guitar licks. A reasonable facsimile of his DJing skills could be heard on the nostalgia compilation **The Old Skool Masters – Ratpack Vs. Nicky Blackmarket** (1998), where he mixed up classic tracks from the likes of Omni Trio and Doc Scott.

⊙ **Nick O.D. – Spam Volume 1**   **Reinforced, 1992**

Certainly not the best of Reinforced's early releases, but this is still classic Hardcore from its golden age.

Blame & Justice

B lame (aka Conrad Shafie) began his journey through the artier end of drum 'n' bass when he met up with longtime collaborator Justice while studying in Luton during the second wave of rave. Under the influence of Mantronix and LFO, the duo started up a small label, Death Row, to release their experiments in breakbeat-driven House. One of these Death Row records, "Music Takes You" (1992), was picked up by Moving Shadow on the strength of its double-time shuffling rhythm and Seal sample. Even better, though, was Rob Playford's "Two Bad Mice Take You" remix which did away with the uncleared Seal sample in favour of a surging mutation of Loleatta Holloway, scratching and a half-speed reggae bassline of which Sly Dunbar would have been proud.

Blame kept the bubbling momentum going with the effervescent "Feel the Energy" and "This Piano Track" (both 1993). After "Sykological Hostage/A21" (1993), however, Blame & Justice seemed to forsake hip-hop's fractured logic in favour of the breezy vibes of Lonnie Liston Smith on their "Essence/Anthemia" (1994) 12". Inspired by the cosmic aura of LTJ Bukem's "Music", mixes of "Essence" and "Anthemia" were subtitled "The Jazz Testament" and "Heaven" in a clear signal of the forthcoming wave of Ambient and intelligent Jungle. Their "Nocturnal/Nightvision" (1994) continued to stir up Jungle's version of quiet storm R&B, while Blame's **Sub Committee** EP (1995) would undercut the balmy zephyrs of jazziness with gusts of disorienting drum programming.

The skittering dynamics of "Planet Neptune"'s (1996) drum machine extended **Sub Committee**'s inventive low-end manipulations, but Blame's collaboration with Deep Blue, "Transitions" (1996), was as breathtakingly naff as its title. This fusion-based serenity was massaged into plasma on the Icons album, **Emotions With Intellect** (1996), that Blame recorded with Justice and released on Justice's Modern Urban Jazz label. Justice beefed up the jazz influences with an explicitly Electro feel on records like "Aquisse/Feverish" (1996) for the Basement label and "Savage Times/Tension" (1997) on DJ Pulse's Creative Wax label.

Even more harp murmurs, aqueous textures, heart beats, flutes and saxes floated through the soundfield of Blame's mix compilation for Good Looking, **Logical Progression Level 2** (1997). Blame's move from Moving Shadow to Good Looking entailed a less attractive shift towards chord progressions and complex time signatures on tracks like "360 Clic/Overhead Projections" and "J. Walkin'" (both 1997). "Visions of Mars/Centuries" (1998), however, was like Techstep written by Burt Bacharach – the more melodic side of malfunctioning machines. Further collisions of agreeability and metal were engineered by Odyssey who recorded "Expressions/Rituals" (1997) and "Object" (1998) for Blame's 720 Degrees imprint.

Justice, meanwhile, hooked up with the Moving Shadow exiles at Partisan for the synth pulsations of "Mauve Flow/Switch" and "Sequence" (both 1998). His **Viewpoints** album (1998) on Recordings of Substance took melodic Techno's obsession with deep sea diving and astral travelling on a breakbeat cruise through soaring synths and plunging basslines. Blame's **Between Worlds** EP (1998) achieved a similar feat, although with a slightly less agreeable blend of machine and nature.

◉ Icons – Emotions With Intellect   Modern Urban Jazz, 1996

It verges on new age spinelessness, but if you like your drum 'n' bass to sound like live musicians, then this is the record for you.

Boymerang

L ike Spring Heel Jack's John Coxon, Boymerang hung out on the fringes of indie rock for several years until it became apparent that the old behemoth had completely run its course. From 1988 until 1994 Graham Sutton dabbled in post-Can, Talk Talk-influenced guitar soundscaping with experimentalists Bark Psychosis. When the group dissolved at the 1994 Phoenix Festival, this ex-raver returned to breakbeat music for solace and inspiration. Unlike other lapsed indie kids who have made drum 'n' bass safe for middle-class cultural tourists, however, Boymerang isn't interested in being quirky and "complex". Instead, Boymerang has started to use the scene's ver-

nacular, ditched the Doc Martens in favour of aerodynamic trainers and been taken under the wing of Grooverider whose imprimatur has allowed Boymerang to enter drum 'n' bass' inner sanctum.

Boymerang's self-titled debut EP (1995) for Tony Morley's Leaf label still had echoes of the post-rock navel gazing of old, but "The Don" was a Down Tempo cut-up of his own voice and opiated, impressionistic synth patterns and "Theme From Boymerang" had breathy sighs over a scruffy but mellow break. The **Pro-Active** EP (1995) was a combination of an avalanche of "Amen" drums on one side ("Getting Closer") with soothing jazz ripples and the "Kid Caprice" break on the other ("Autumnal"). His most notable track, though, was his remix of MLO's "Revolutionary Generation" (1995) which was Jungle made by, and for, someone who had spent a lot of time listening to the anti-social punk rock of Big Black.

Boymerang has talked about connecting with "the post-E mentality" of Techstep and the low-end rumble of his "Still" (1996) 12" which appeared on Grooverider's Prototype label was about as far from the "peace and loveism" of rave as you could get. "Still" was featured, along with the dancefloor smash "Soul Beat Runna" (1997), on his **Balance of the Force** (1997) album which seemed to suggest that he was a jack of all trades, but a master of none. Conceived as a "proper" album that progressed from one element to the next, **Balance of the Force** flitted from unconvincing menace to panoramic, astro-jazz noodlings without ever staking any claims or exploring any new territory. There were some nice sounds and an obvious attention to detail, but no real fire and it ended in the worst way imaginable – with the sounds of waves lapping against the shore.

Since **Balance of the Force**, Boymerang has remixed Ed Rush and Nico's "Technology", but given that he has insisted that his tracks take two months of almost constant work to create, we probably won't hear from him again until the next millennium.

◉ Balance of the Force   Regal, 1997

Although it was meant to, the album doesn't make a grand statement, but it's worth owning for "Soul Beat Runna" and "Still" which are both fine singles.

Breakbeats

Although breakbeats have probably existed since jazz pioneers Jelly Roll Morton and Bunk Johnson first started to play with drummers in New Orleans at the turn of the century, the idea of isolating the part of the record where the rest of the band "gives the drummer some" didn't occur to anyone until Kool DJ Herc first tapped into the New York City power supply at a Bronx block party in the early '70s.

Herc was a Jamaican DJ who had emigrated to the US in 1967 and set up his own sound system in the Bronx. When his reggae records failed to move the crowd at the block parties, he turned to funk, but the only part of the records he would play was the short section where all the instrumentalists dropped out except for the percussionists. The "break" was the part of the record that the dancers wanted to hear anyway, so he isolated it by playing two copies of the same record on two turntables – when the break on one turntable finished, he would play it on the other turntable. Herc's breakbeat style of DJing was much in demand and soon enough other DJs like Grandmaster Flash, Afrika Bambaataa and Grand Wizard Theodore emerged playing a similar style of music, but with greater skill and more technological sophistication.

The breakbeat was music's great equaliser – nearly every record no matter how unsavoury its provenance had two or three seconds that made it worthwhile. Herc's biggest record was a 1973 cover of Jorgen Ingmann's "Apache" by Michael Viner's Incredible Bongo Band that featured the cheesiest organ and horn fills ever recorded on top of a chorus of massed bongos. Apparently, Viner was a friend of the music industry's Mike Curb, and was the director of entertainment for Richard Nixon's second inaugural party. So, hip-hop's national anthem and probably the most famous breakbeat of all time was not only originally a hit for Cliff Richard & the Shadows, but also the product of a record that was probably designed to appease a family values crusader like Mary Whitehouse. Hip-hop's cult of the break could redeem anything: breaks by Neanderthal metal acts like Billy Squier,

Aerosmith and Thin Lizzy and schlock jazz-lite artists like Bob James became the basis of records by everyone from Run DMC to the Wu Tang Clan.

As British Hardcore started to develop out of Hip-House and Belgian Techno in the early '90s, the breakbeat was again the core of the record. Shut Up and Dance stole beats from Suzanne Vega and Def Jam records, while 4 Hero's "Mr Kirk's Nightmare" (1991) took a snippet from the Isley Brothers' b-boy classic "Get Into Something". In 1993 LTJ Bukem instigated the use of what may be the most used breakbeat ever. His single "Music" was based around the drum solo from The Winstons' version of the gospel staple "Amen Brother". Previously used by Mantronik in a chopped-to-bits form on "King of the Beats", the "Amen" break was generally too fast for hip-hop records, but its searing momentum was perfect for a genre exploring the outer reaches of the bpm speed limit. "Amen" has since been used on literally thousands of records, outdoing even the king of the break, James Brown.

Of course, Brown's beats like "Funky Drummer" and "Give It Up or Turn It Loose" have been used by everyone from Kicks Like a Mule to Aphrodite and Wax Doctor. In drum 'n' bass, the Godfather's most used break comes from one of his side productions, Lyn Collins' "Think (About It)". Easily identifiable by the high-pitched hiccup in the background (which is Brown saying either "You're bad sister" or "You're bad Hank"), "Think" has graced records by Origin Unknown, DJ SS and Jonny L among countless others.

As hip-hop-derived genres, Down Tempo and Big Beat are also completely reliant on the break. Portishead's breakthrough was largely on the back of samples of Lalo Schifrin and Isaac Hayes, while the Chemical Brothers and Fatboy Slim owe debts to jazz organist Jimmy McGriff and soulster Edwin Starr. Two and a half decades after its development, the term "breakbeat" has since come to signify a separate genre of (quasi-) funky drum beats with squelchy Techno effects on top, while "a break" has come to signify any short instrumental passage, drums or otherwise, that can be sampled and chopped up. However you want to define it, the logic of the breakbeat is hip-hop's gift to the world and the most crucial development in popular music since James Brown almost invented the "give the drummer some" interlude.

⊙ Various Artists – Ultimate Breaks and Beats
Vols. 1–25   Street Beat, 1985–1990

They may be of questionable legality, but these 25 volumes are collectively the Bible of breakbeat and represent some of the greatest and most vital musical scholarship ever undertaken. Volume 1 features the "Amen" beat.

⊙ Various Artists – Kurtis Blow Presents
the History of Hip-Hop Vol. 1   Rhino, 1997

One of the few entirely legal collection of classic breakbeats, this excellent collection features "Apache", Jimmy Castor's immortal "It's Just Begun", Baby Huey's "Listen to Me" and Dennis Coffey's "Scorpio".

Congo Natty/Rebel MC

O ne of Jungle's unsung heroes, Michael West began his career as Rebel MC with Brit rappers Double Trouble and the bubblegum pop hit "Street Tuff". After leaving Double Trouble in 1990, he released **Black Meaning Good** (1991), an album that featured ragga stars like Barrington Levy, Tenor Fly and Dennis Brown crooning and toasting on top of reggae-House riddims. **Word, Sound and Power** (1992) was a further exploration of roots electronica that mashed up Techno, House, reggae, ragga and hip-hop. Forming the Tribal Bass label, Rebel MC released "Tribal Bass" (1992) and the Demon Boyz' "Dett" (1992) and "Jungle-ist" (1993) which were Hip-House tracks borrowing a vibe from the Yard that heralded the emergence of Jungle.

The X-Project label followed shortly with the "Old School Ting" (1993) single. As Conquering Lion, West, with help from DJ Ron and Jumping Jack Frost, released the sound system mash-up "Lion of Judah/Innah Sound/Dub Plate Special" (1993). With vocals from Supercat and more gun shots than a Sam Peckinpah flick, Conquering Lion's massive "Code Red/Phenomenon" (1994) caught the attention of 4th & Broadway who re-released the track along with "Rastaman/Word, Sound and Power/Code Black" (1995).

Moving back underground, West started the Congo Natty label with Black Star's "Champion DJ" (1995). With tearing breaks that sought to link Jungle's bottom end with roots reggae's militancy and dancehall toasting from Top Cat, "Champion DJ" was a dancefloor anthem that created the Congo Natty blueprint. Sweetie Irie and Tenor Fly followed Top Cat out of the dancehall on to the Junglist dub plate on Black Star's "Get Wild" and "Alaska Ride" (both 1995). Tribe of Issachar continued setting dancefloors alight with the enormous "Junglist" (1996) which featured vocals from Peter Bouncer. With vocals from Bounty Hunter, Lion of Judah's "Emperor Selassie I" (1996) was not only one of the label's biggest records, but its most effective combination of roughneck and roots.

DJ Kane's brilliant mix of Black Star's "Radical" (1997) was based around a killer KRS-One loop, while Tribe of Issachar's "War Dance" (1997) set a new standard of rawness for the label. The jump-up jeremiads continued on Lion of Judah's tearing "Exodus/Mystic Vibration" (1998) which sampled both Bob Marley's "Iron Lion Zion" and Martin Luther King on top of one of the most invigorating basslines ever. "Jungle Souljah/Rasta Music" (1998) was less intoxicating, but remixes of Tribe of Issachar's "Fever" and "Junglist" (both 1998) rode samples of Craig Mack and Public Enemy into jump-up heaven.

⊙ **Conquering Lion – "Code Red"**   4th & Broadway/X-Project, 1994

Sirens, gun shots, dub basslines, rude boy vocals, scatter-shot breakbeats, what more could you ask for?

DJ Crystl

Like most of the first wave of Hardcore/drum 'n' bass producers, Danny Chapman was a b-boy and graffiti artist who was turned on to the possibilities of rave at the beginning of the '90s. A former DJ with British hip-hop crew The Brotherhood, DJ Crystl combined his old-school breakbeat sensibilities with unexpected influences from Future Sound of London and The Orb to help initiate the brief flourishing of Ambient Jungle.

Crystl's first single was the frenzied breakbeat mechanics of "Suicidal/Drop Ecstasy" (1992) which instigated his relationship with the Lucky Spin and Dee Jay labels. With the darkside in vogue, his next release was the ornery synth menace of "Dark Crystl" (1993). Although it was less oppressive, "Warpdrive" (1993) managed to sound even more sinister because it was more subtle – its evil intentions crept up on you from out of nowhere. With an insistent and eerie metallic loop slicing through the vortex of fissile snares, "Warpdrive" sounded like a Junglist version of Louis and Bebe Barron's soundtrack for the '50s sci-fi flick *Forbidden Planet*.

Later in the year, though, he had lightened up considerably. "Meditation" (1993) found Crystl floating on an ethereal, dreamy vibe which took him to the forefront of the emerging Ambient Jungle scene. "Your Destiny" and "Sweet Dreams" (both 1994) followed suit with textures that were more cinematic than somatic. "Let It Roll" (1994) was a bit rougher in the bottom end, but still displayed a concern for delicacy.

The remix of "Let It Roll" (1995) brought Crystl back to his b-boy roots with tearing snares, chest-puncturing bass and a Big Daddy Kane sample exhorting you to "Let it roll". "Perpetual Motion" (1995), a collaboration with New York rappers Headrush, tried to bring Big Apple hip-hop into Britain's Jungle and was hailed as the future on its release, but the reality was that the two elements sat uncomfortably next to one another. A far more successful rapprochement between hip-hop and Jungle was Crystl's remix of DJ Krush's "Meiso" (1996). A bare-knuckled knock-about that managed to go with the flows of MCs Malik and Black Thought, Crystl's mix reproduced the choked, asthmatic atmosphere of the original with its clenched rhythm track and burnt-out dynamics. "183" (1997), however, didn't seem to know whether it wanted to be hip-hop or drum 'n' bass and just sat impassively in an unattractive middle ground.

⊙ "Warpdrive"   Dee Jay, 1993

It didn't express the pharmaceutical holocaust that many of its contemporaries did, but "Warpdrive"'s baleful textures and rhythms made it clear that all was not right with the world. (Available on **Drum & Bass Selection 1**).

D'Cruze

One of the true drum 'n' bass survivors, Jay D'Cruze has prowled the shadows of the breakbeat scene since its inception in the early '90s. As a teenager hanging around Romford's Boogie Times record store, D'Cruze hooked up with owner Danny Donnelly's Suburban Base label and released his debut single "World Within a World/I Believe" in 1993. He swiftly followed this with the distinctive dark remake of the "Hot Pants" beat on "Bass Go Boom/Want You Now" (1993). But he really made his name with his collaboration with Q Bass as Boogie Times Tribe on the classic "Real Hardcore/Dark Stranger" (1993). Perhaps a bit over the top, "Dark Stranger" sampled a documentary about the making of Francis Ford Coppola's *Dracula* and made losing control seem fun. With centrifugal drums and shivering synth motifs, Q Bass' remix made the track's death drive much more apparent.

A transitional track between Darkcore and Jungle, "Watch Out" (1994) was a splintery masterpiece of drum shards, Belgian sinewaves, the haunted-house synth from Michael Jackson's "Thriller" and ragga roughness. "Lonely" (1994) and "Are We In/Heaven" (1995), on the other hand, went for the cocooning approach with symphonic spirals and warm synth washes that only detonated the breaks towards the end of the track. **Control** (1995), D'Cruze's debut album, featured more polished, late-night, jazzy vibes on tracks like "All Night Groove" and "My Mind".

After a lengthy absence, D'Cruze returned in 1997 with "Land Speeder/Find My Way" which featured vocalist Shelley Nelson, post-"Autobahn" synths out of the Motor City and *de rigueur* cardboard-box drums. Seemingly realising that both he and most of the rest of the drum 'n' bass community were in a terminal holding pattern, he shifted his allegiances towards the jump-up crews and released the killer 12" "The Funk/Bitch" (1997) on A-Sides' East Side label. Moving from summer-breeze flutes to metallic "Think" drums and foghorn basslines, "Bitch" showed that you didn't have to discard Jungle's rollers instinct for the sake of technology. More rapprochements between Grooverider-style cyber-menace and DJ Hype crowd-pleasing occurred on "Importance of Drums/Holocaust" (1998), whose titles said it all.

⊙ Control   Suburban Base, 1995

Made at the height of the intelligent Jungle fervour, this has too much neon warmth for its own good, but it does show off D'Cruze's serious mixing board chops.

Danny Breaks/ Droppin' Science/Sonz of a Loop Da Loop Era

J ust as '60s British blues freaks who knew they couldn't approximate the feel of the real thing turned the blues into an energy music that exuded a casual violence, so '80s British b-boys turned hip-hop into a hyperkinetic music of pure sensation when rave fever hit. Along with fellow speed-freak ex-body-poppers Aphrodite and DJ Hype, Danny Breaks has been involved in all the various permutations of British post-hip-hop since its beginnings as Hardcore.

Born in Southend, Breaks was a typical British hip-hop-obsessed kid who tried his hand at all aspects of hip-hop culture, eventually settling for the RSI-inducing rigours of DJing. After landing a job at the Boogie Times record shop which was owned by Danny Donnelly, he released his debut record, "Far Out" (1992), on Donnelly's Suburban Base label. Recorded under the name Sonz of a Loop Da Loop Era, "Far Out" heard the sounds of '80s New York with a day-glo intensity and the track was all hot flashes and giddy energy that managed to dent the UK Top 40. "Peace & Loveism" (1992) was similarly ecstatic, but with less of the debut's scratchy intensity. There was plenty of scratching on The Flowers In My Garden EP (1993) which featured the stunning "Skratchadelikizm", whose title gave breakbeat Hardcore its most fitting description. The final Sonz of a Loop Da Loop record was the equally breathtaking "What the.../R Yeah" (1993).

Taking its name from a Craig G rap, Breaks started the Droppin' Science label in late 1993. With its gushing, orgasmic diva moans, Vince Clark-like synths and cascading drums, "Droppin' Science Volume 1" was an intermediary track between rave's Ecstasy rush and the more po-faced science of drum 'n' bass's "maturity". "Volume 2" (1994) was something else entirely. A truly mind-bending example of breakbeat manipulation that went off on a hundred different tangents, "Volume 2" sounded like DJ Shadow's Down Tempo journey "In/Flux" played back at twice the speed.

Breaks' hip-hop roots came to the fore on "Volume 3: Firin' Line", "Volume 4: Long Time Coming" (a remix of "Safari Sounds") (both 1994) and the fierce Rakim-sampling "Volume 5: Step Off" (1995). With these records, Breaks added enormous sub-bass noise to his complex breakbeat patterns and re-arranged sample detailing without sacrificing his head-wrecking minimalism.

1996 saw the introduction of Kosmos and Dylan to the Droppin' Science roster with "Tighten Up" and the excellent "Witchcraft/Virus". Breaks contributed one of the few decent tracks on Mo' Wax's **Headz 2** (1996) compilation, "Science Fu Beats", which featured his snapping drum sounds slowed down to half-speed and offered an insight to the layman on drum 'n' bass production. Picking up the tempo, Breaks and Dylan released a couple of mercilessly mechanistic 12"s in 1997–98 in the form of "Conscience/Solar Funk" (1997) and "The Spine/Molecules" (1998), which kept Droppin' Science's computer-literate b-boy vibe alive.

⊙ **"Far Out"**   Suburban Base, 1992

Available on **A History of Hardcore** and **Here Come the Drums: Hip-Hop Drum 'n' Bass**, Breaks' debut remains one of the most exciting visions of an alternate hip-hop ever conceived.

⊙ **"Volume 2"**   Droppin' Science, 1994

Available on Kodwo Eshun's excellent **Routes From the Jungle** compilation, this really is a stunning exercise in breakbeat science from its most consistent laboratory.

De Underground Records

S tarting off life in 1992 by re-releasing Lennie De-Ice's proto-Junglist classic "We Are E", De Underground Records was a label/shop complex that served as East London's Hardstep headquarters. Run by Cool Hand Flex, Randall and Mike Underground, De Underground was one of the few labels that kept the faith in Jungle's original polypercussive tenets while nearly all around them were tempt-ed by the false prophets (and profits) of "intelligent" drum 'n' bass.

Originally released on IE Records in 1991, "We Are E" was a wild-style collage of gun shots from old ska records, two-note synth riffs, a muezzin wail, a ragga bassline and the Funky Drummer that heralded breakbeat as something other than speeded-up Hip-House records. The demand for the track was such that De Underground re-released it and it eventually sold 15,000 copies.

However, this kind of success was short-lived and, despite the presence of major players like Randall and Cool Hand Flex, De Under-ground releases were completely ignored by the time of Jungle's media cross-over. Although the label released records of primitive dreaminess like Uncle 22's "My Love" (1994), De Underground con-centrated on the shattered snares and depth-charge basslines of the deeply unfashionable style that would soon be codified as jump-up. Records like Cool Hand Flex's "Rude Boy Soldier", "Mercy Mercy" (both 1994) and "Cool Run" (1995) were all unpolished, rough-cut mixtures of flailing beats, upfront bass and vocal samples that eschewed the increasingly clinical precision of the mainstream in favour of the teetering-on-the-edge-of-control excitement that characterised Hardcore's golden age.

The store in the Forest Gate area of London, however, acted as a focal point for the simmering Jump-Up scene and records like Cool Hand Flex's "Melody Madness" and "Low Key" (both 1995) and "Sur-vival" (1996) made some in-roads when pushed by DJs like Randall and Hype and showed that dancing to Jungle wasn't a thing of the past.

O Various Artists – Urban Essence   De Underground, 1996

A fine collection of rough and ready tracks from Cool Hand Flex, Uncle 22, Mike Underground and Jon E-2 Bad that proved breakbeat's excitement came from the play of textures and not the craftsmanship.

Dead Dred/
Asend & Ultravibe

While the mainstream dance press fawned over "intelligent" Jungle's embrace of melody, labels like Back 2 Basics and producers like Asend & Ultravibe concentrated on the elements that made Jungle exciting in the first place: the drum and the bass. With a succession of singles that featured murderous bass bombs, flying drum shrapnel and menacing rude bwoy samples, Lee and Warren Smith (the duo behind Asend & Ultravibe and Dead Dred) showed that they liked a bit of rough. Their success on the dancefloor proved that the Smith brothers were not alone in their love of roughneck posturing.

As Dead Dred, the Smith brothers helped Moving Shadow celebrate its fiftieth release with the all-time classic "Dred Bass" (1994). A cauldron of queasy, gut-churning low-end frequencies that was more about power than fluidity, "Dred Bass" inaugurated the my-Roland-weighs-a-ton bass sound that would dominate Jungle for the next couple of years. The wavering quality of the bass was intensified by the threshing snares that hurtled by in waves of descending beat clusters. It didn't even need the reggae DJ samples for the dread vibes, the attitude was all in the bottom end: roll over LTJ Bukem and tell Luke Vibert the news, "Dred Bass" was as complex and intelligent as any drum 'n' bass track ever made.

By contrast, Asend & Ultravibe's rude bwoy elegy, "What Kind of World" (1994), set stuttering funk breaks against a string melodrama to create the Junglist version of Ice Cube's "Dead Homiez". The lamenting continued on Ultravibe's "Guardian Angel" (1995), Basic

Movements' "Jelly" (1995) and Asend & Ultravibe's "Real Love" (1995) which wrapped a sample of an aching Mary J. Blige in a subdued and almost downbeat bassline while the breaks flew by like strangers in a crowd.

A collaboration between Lee Smith and Jason Ball from Back 2 Basics, Dred Bass's awesome "World of Music" and "Smokin' Cans" (both 1995) transported Compton, California to merry olde England and laid down the foundations for the following two years' worth of jump-up with their gangsta samples, Dr Dre keyboards and *Sturm und Drang* basslines that were ridiculously over-the-top.

Dead Dred's "Down With the Sound/Come On Baby" (1996), however, had a laboured feel and a new sound for which they obviously had no affection. Tracks like "New Identity" from Dred Bass's **World of Music** (1998) album showed that the "Dred Bass" tremolo had become a grinding, post-industrial moan devoid of funk.

⊙ **"Dred Bass"**   Moving Shadow, 1994

A genuine drum 'n' bass landmark that linked London's Jungle producers with the low-end theorists of New York hip-hop by indulging in the sphincter-loosening bass mutation pioneered by the likes of Afrika Bambaataa and EPMD.

DJ Dextrous

Despite his relatively low profile, DJ Dextrous has been a prime mover on the Jungle scene since the beginning. One of the first breakbeat DJs to use a live MC during his sets, Dextrous helped pave the way for the ragga influence which moved Hardcore away from the rave and towards the Jungle. Along with his MC, Rude Boy Keith, Dextrous set up the King of the Jungle label in 1993. The label's first release, Dextrous & Keith's "Lovable", was a Junglist anthem that combined Jamaican dancehall chatter with shuffling JB breaks, smooth diva vocals, Deep House keyboard swirls and a wildly distorted "Mentasm" synth stab. At around the same time, Dextrous' other label, Subliminal, was releasing tracks like Tee Bone's "Selectors Roll" (1993).

After the King of the Jungle follow-up to "Lovable", the Horn EP (1994), Dextrous and Keith released the **Da Kings of the Jungle** EP (1994) on Suburban Base. With irresistible ragga samples undercut by drums that seemed to fly off in every direction without establishing a danceable rhythm and almost mournful synth washes, "Time to Move" (1994) seemed as though it was sounding the death knell for the ragga Jungle which had dominated the scene's commercial mainstream. A collaboration between Dextrous and new signings DJ Matt & Dr P, "Legend/Sunny Smiles" (1995) followed the same blueprint with ghostly train sounds and chiming bells.

"Moonlighting" (1995), on the other hand, worked a more soulful vibe than Dextrous had used in the past and his next few releases followed in this more jazzy style. Forming Solid State with some old associates from Kool FM and releasing the **Artefacts** EPs (1997), "Mrs Warren's Profession" (1998), "On the Corner" (1998) and "Street Hustler/Tunes" (1999) on the State of the Art label, Dextrous showed that he was trying to walk the line between ruffness and "intelligence" and became one of the figureheads of drum 'n' bass' new-found love of jazz-funk liquefaction. His best effort at reconciling the delirium of the early days of Hardcore with the technical precision of contemporary drum 'n' bass was "The Deep/This Situation" (1997). The last release on his Subversive label, "The Deep" brought Darkcore's horror movie samples into the Techstep domain with its "Wake up, you've just had a bad dream" refrain, while "This Situation" was a fine jazz-tinged jump-up style workout.

⊙ **"Lovable"**   King of the Jungle, 1993

A strange but very effective tune that flits schizophrenically between straightforward ragga Jungle, lovers' rock, Deep House and Belgian synth terror. (Available on **Drum & Bass Selection 1**).

Digital

F amous for his dub basslines, Steve Carr got his start in music (and his nickname) by helping with his father's reggae sound system. When rave culture hit Digital's native Ipswich, he switched allegiances to breakbeat. A blend of "Amen" beats with techy synth washes, Authorized Riddim's (a collaboration with Danny C) "Split Personality" (1993) was Digital's ahead-of-its-time debut for the local Certificate 18 label.

Hooking up with the Timeless label, Digital released Natural Mystic's "Echoes/Illusions" in 1994 which capitalised on the growing vogue for smooth, ambient styles. The chilled-out vibes of Digital's "Touch Me" and "Take Me Away/Why" (both 1995) followed in similar style, but it was the well-constructed Detroit-jazz textures of "Spacefunk" (1996) that made his name. A 12" on Metalheadz, "Niagra/Down Under" (1996), was his reward and he didn't disappoint with the Techno keyboards subduing an "Amen" break that roiled beneath cooing sirens.

Firmly established in the Metalheadz camp, Digital succumbed to the cult of precision and tracks like "Far Out" and "Metro" (both 1997) were clinical machine nightmares that sounded like every other track making the rounds post-Techstep, although the chopped-up fragment of the "Apache" break gave "Metro" a degree of tension. More "Apache" compression, although in a more delicate context, was to be found on "Express/Reaction" (1998) released on Fabio's Creative Source label. Digital's penchant for rhythmic minimalism was displayed on the cavernous "Lower Depths/Sub Zero" (1998) on Photek Productions, while "Escape/Delight" (1998) was Digital having a drum tantrum. "Chameleon/Control" (1998) was his much-vaunted return to Timeless, but the acid riffs were tired, the rhythms stunted and he made a very unconvincing hard man.

⊙ **Authorized Riddim – "Split Personality"**   Certificate 18, 1993

His first record is probably his best and the slicing steel-blade synths of this were startlingly prescient.

Digital Hardcore Records/Alec Empire

Alec Empire is the exception that proves the rule. Easily the most politically committed musician since the heyday of Red Wedge and Rock Against Racism, Empire is that rarest of musicians: one who is capable of making both great political music and great music. Inspired by both punk rock and Underground Resistance, Empire and the artists on his Digital Hardcore label make the supposedly content-free energy of Techno and breakbeat bristle with a no-compromises, in-your-face intensity.

Developing simultaneously with British Hardcore, Empire released his first record, the **Yobot** EP (1992), on Achim Sczepanski's Force Inc. label. Featuring the notorious "Hetzjagd auf Nazis" ("Hunt Down the Nazis"), the EP made the tacit miscegenation of British Hardcore explicit by positing its promiscuous play of signifiers and breakbeat rhythms as the antithesis of Germany's increasingly whitewashed Trance movement. Turning rave's cheap, kindergarten keyboard riffs into air-raid sirens, sub-bass into depth charges and breakbeats into gun shots, "Hetzjagd auf Nazis" imagined Ecstasy delirium as political fervour.

Of course, no one wanted anything to do with such a record, so Empire's next record, the **Suicide** EP (1992), fed the ravers' apoliticism back to them as a bizarre fantasy of Ecstasy abuse leading to the destruction of the German state because the middle class was addicted to the high and couldn't work and didn't want to eat, thus leading to the collapse of the government, or so he claimed. The record was so lithe that perhaps it worked too well and Empire was back to the rabble-rousing on the **Bass Terror** EP (1993).

Even more upfront was Empire's group, Atari Teenage Riot. After securing a hefty advance from the British Phonogram label, Empire, with a KLF-style marketing scam, Hanin Elias and Carl Crack, released a self-titled debut album in 1993 which set Elias' hoarse attempts to shout down Babylon against overstretched amps and febrile breakbeats. ATR, like most of Empire's projects, were concerned with the notion and sound of overload as an agent provocateur, even if the only political action they ever engendered was thrashing about a crowded club.

With the money ATR wangled from Phonogram, Empire started his Digital Hardcore label in 1994 with his own **Digital Hardcore** EP. DJ Bleed's **Uzi Party** EP (1994) followed with the brutal Amiga thrash of "Deaf, Dumb and Blind", while Sonic Subjunkies' **Suburban Sound-**

tracks Volume 1 (1994) featured clanging industrial noises to go along with the pile-driving breaks. EC8OR, Christoph de Bablon and Shizuo followed suit with EPs and albums of extreme distortion and pneumatic beats, the best of which was Shizuo's pummelling **Shizuo Vs. Shizor** album (1997). A bargain-priced eight track compilation of the label's recent releases, **You've Got The Fucking Power** (1998), collected tracks by Shizuo, Bomb20 and Golden Vampire to become the label's most accessible introduction.

Empire also formed his Riot Beats label in 1994 with his **Destroyer EP**. With a hint of funk creeping into the beats and a judicious use of hip-hop samples, Riot Beats took its lead from Jungle, but only to tear it apart. Brother Crush's "King of the Street" (1996) was the label's high point: instead of the speed-as-release dynamic of drum 'n' bass, "King of the Street" was speed as hostility. With its grim blaxploitation flick sample, several hundred bpms and shitty sub-bass, "King of the Street" was about as ugly as The Exploited's "City Baby Attacked By Rats".

In the meantime, Empire was releasing an array of eclectic records under his own name for Mille Plateaux. Albums like **Limited Editions 1990–94** and **Generation Star Wars** (both 1994) were as raw as his Digital Hardcore albums, but without the shattering breakbeats. **Low On Ice (The Iceland Sessions)** (1995) was a collection of bleak, desolate ambient electronica that was the flipside to his smash-the-state recordings, while **Hyper-Modern Jazz 2000.5** (1996) was both a laugh at the easy listening and jazz fads and an attempt to wind up his fans. Atari Teenage Riot's **Burn Berlin Burn** (1997) album broke the band in the States on a small scale where Digital Hardcore was distributed by the Beastie Boys' Grand Royal label. Meanwhile, Empire set up his Geist label to release the triple-CD retrospective of his solo material, **The Geist of Alec Empire** (1997).

⊙ **Alec Empire – "Hetzjagd auf Nazis"**   Force Inc., 1992

Raw, febrile, brutal – one of the best records of the '90s. (Available on the **Rauschen 10** compilation.)

◎ **Various Artists – Rough and Fast!!**   Riot Beats, 1995

Even though it doesn't include "King of the Street", it does feature much of Empire's best work.

Dillinja

At its best, drum 'n' bass demolishes the often racist notion that funk is somehow "natural". Some of drum 'n' bass' funkiest tracks have been the result of tedious, painstaking craftsmanship, chopping breaks into hundreds of fragments and weaving them into intricate patterns whose flow belies their complexity. One of the acknowledged masters of such devastating beat construction is the south London producer known as Dillinja, who is justly celebrated as an innovator of both ambient drum 'n' bass and Hardstep Jungle.

Karl Francis began his exploration of the depths of bass in 1990 when he built his own sound system at the age of 16. He made his first tune the following year, "Tear Off Your Chest", with DJ Clarky under the name Holy Ghost. Another collaboration with Clarky, Above Average Intelligence's "Steelers Anthem/Sax Into the Night" (1992), set in motion the hip-hop-inspired brutal minimalism that would characterise Dillinja's greatest tracks. "Deadly Deep Subs" (1993) and "Chapter 19/Chapter 20" (1993) (recorded as Trinity) featured enormous bass bombs and unfeasibly polypercussive drum breaks that were at least a year ahead of their time. The flip of

"Deadly Deep Subs" was the Fender Rhodes-tinged "Sovereign Melody" which set the tone for his startling collaboration with Mystery, "Deep Love" (1994). Starting with a swatch of jazzy keyboards courtesy of Lonnie Liston Smith, "Deep Love" then wove a melancholy wah-wah guitar lick over Dillinja's trademark bass subs and a remarkable deconstruction of the "Think" break.

At the same time as he was exploring the astral planes and helping to establish drum 'n' bass' Age of Aquarius, Dillinja was instigating Jungle's gangsta infatuation with hard-stepping tracks like "Lionheart", "Warrior", "Gangsta" (recorded as Trinity) and the awesome "Muthafucka" (all 1994). His staggering, gangster-leaning tower of bass, "Tear Down Da Whole Place" (1994), served as the template for the swaggering, intimidatingly muscular tracks he released as Capone: "Massive" (1995), "Guess Who?/Mysteries of the Deep" (1996) and "Paradise" (1997).

The Angels Fell EP (1994), perhaps his best record, started off with wistful diva vocals, but then collapsed into a dark, gloomy dub chamber of bass and beats that felt stagnant and claustrophobic despite the Brownian motion of the splintered breaks. The flipside, "Ja Know Ya Big/Brutal Bass", continued the sense of dread and defeated possibilities. Bleaker still were Dillinja's tracks on the labels he ran with Lemon D, Valve and Pain. Both "Violent" and "Acid Track" (both 1997) were belching, iron-lunged monsters that presaged the snarling bass ferocity of his Cybotron releases like "Threshold/Got To" (1997) and "Light Years/Revelations" (1998). Like most of drum 'n' bass' big names, Dillinja has inked a deal with a major label (London), who hopefully will not rein in drum 'n' bass' most extreme bottom-end sensibility.

⊙ **The Angels Fell**   Metalheadz, 1994

This dark grotto of bass frequencies is probably his best record, but also seek out his releases on Hard Leaders as Capone (most of which are available on the **Suspect Package** and **Way Out Chapter** compilations).

Doc Scott/
Nasty Habits

Getting his name from the hip-hop tapes he used to distribute to his school friends in Coventry like a medic dispensing prescriptions, Doc Scott quickly moved on to getting a buzz from punishing people with sonic malice. He first came to attention with **The Surgery** EP (1991) which was released on Donovan "Bad Boy" Smith's Absolute 2 label. The title track was little more than a variation on the synth stab from Joey Beltram's "Mentasm", another synth pattern that sounded like a twitching nerve, and a claustrophobic rhythm track that gave "Surgery" a compressed, almost unpleasant feel. Of course, it immediately became a Darkcore standard.

Logically, **The Surgery** EP was followed by the similarly styled **NHS** EP (1992) and the **NHS 2 Remix** EP which featured an even tougher remix of "Surgery" courtesy of Grooverider, who played the track to death at his club night, Rage. The ultimate Rage anthem, however, was "Here Comes the Drumz" from his **As Nasty As I Wanna Be EP** (1992), which Scott released on Reinforced as Nasty Habits. With brutally metallic synths pushing the adrenalised drum break over the edge and Public Enemy's Flavor Flav exclaiming "Confusion!", "Here Comes the Drumz" sounded like James Brown's Funky Drummer playing inside a loaded gun chamber. Almost as good, and almost as vicious, was the EP's other track, "Dark Angel".

The Techno influence moved from the industrial New York/Belgium axis of Joey Beltram and Frank DeWulf to the more melodic Detroit sound of Derrick May and Carl Craig on Scott's "Last Action Hero" (1993). Despite the occasional presence of the trademark kamikaze synths, the track was almost warm – an attribute antithetical to the previous year and a half's worth of dystopic drones – and became a key moment in the growing movement for Hardcore to become more "musical". He continued in the same vein with the swooping "Far Away" (1994), which was a floor-filler in the early days of LTJ Bukem's Speed club.

Scott set up his own label, 31 Records, in 1995 to release his series of **Octave** EPs. 1995 also saw Scott become one of the residing DJs at Goldie's Metalheadz Sunday Sessions and the release

of the awesome "VIP Drumz '95" remix of "Here Comes the Drumz" on the Metalheadz label. With the re-emergence of the gruesome spaceship hums of the Techstep style, Doc Scott re-affirmed his status as the leading light of darkness with "Shadow Boxing" (1997). The definitive two-step track, "Shadow Boxing" was part of a movement that seemed to want to wipe away any sense of warmth or energy out of the music that once epitomised the Ecstasy experience and now seemed to carry the weight of the world on its shoulders.

⊙ **"Here Comes the Drumz"**   Reinforced, 1992

Available on compilations like **Dreamscape Volume 2** and **Here Come the Drums: Hip-Hop Drum 'N' Bass**, this growling but euphoric beast is one of the classics of breakbeat.

Dom & Roland

From his humble beginnings at No U Turn, the label that has more or less created the sound of drum 'n' bass post-1995's media breakthrough, Dominic Angas has quickly become one of the leading names of the new school of dark producers. Born in London in 1974 and then spending five years in Germany, Angas returned to England to follow the standard route of the drum 'n' bass producer from hip-hop teenager to breakbeat twenty-something. After he pestered No U Turn's Nico Sykes to allow him to record a track at his studio, Sykes relented and eventually released Angas' debut 12", which was recorded with Brian Fenner as Current Affairs on Sykes's new Saigon imprint in 1995.

Current Affairs' next 12", "Cutting Edge/Turbulence" (1996), was released on the stalwart Moving Shadow label. With crashing "Amen" and "Think" beats, sirens, trains flying past and a subsonic bass riff placed painfully high in the mix, "Turbulence" ripped dancefloors to shreds and heralded the new age of darkness alongside tracks by Ed Rush and DJ Trace.

Angas' first release as Dom & Roland (Angas and his sampler), "Dynamics/The Planets" (1996), was another landmark in Techstep production with its bruising barrage of grape shot snares and furious two-note bassline. "You're Something Else/Interstellar Jazz" (1996) was a small step backwards, but "The Storm/Sonic Shock" (1996) brought widescreen, cinematic atmospherics to the brutality of the bottom end.

The quality of Angas' productions was affirmed when Moving Shadow's main man Rob Playford chose him to produce the label's hundredth release alongside him and Goldie. The result, Dom & Rob's "Distorted Dreams" (1997), sounded like an adolescent temper tantrum of stroppy bass frequencies and video game violence writ large, as it was meant to see if drum 'n' bass' recent converts were hard enough. The hissy fits continued on Current Affairs' "The Drones" and Dom & Roland's "Resistance/Hydrolics" (both 1997).

Perhaps surprisingly, drum 'n' bass's most fearsome low-end terrorist, Ed Rush, reined in Angas' extremities on "Valves/Terminal" (1997) which the duo released as Neotech. An epic of tension rather than blare, "Valves" was especially notable for its two-second breakdown which consisted of the sound of someone cocking a gun. Angas hooked up with another of the scene's hot producers, Optical, for "Quadrant 6/Concrete Shoes" (1997), but it again tended towards outburst and the metallic textures had seemingly appeared on every record of the previous nine months suggesting that Techstep's store house of production techniques had run dry. With a preponderance of stale two-step beats, Dom & Roland's **Industry** album (1998) did nothing to convince anyone otherwise.

⊙ **"Dynamics/The Planets"**   Moving Shadow, 1996

No less intimidating than most of his other releases, this is probably Angas's best record because the drums have a thrilling violence that grooves without irritating.

Dougal

Cheesy and proud of it, Dougal is surely the most relentlessly uplifting DJ and producer working in dance music. With a penchant for smiley synth riffs that are as cheery and instantly memorable as a Saturday morning theme tune, Dougal's music may veer perilously close to *Stepford Wives* unreality, but his is the sound of the shiny young Britain imagined by Stock, Aitken & Waterman.

Born Paul Clarke in 1975, the Northampton resident became a House DJ in his teens and eventually migrated towards Hardcore as it was splitting from Jungle. With more gratuitous tempo changes than a Def Leppard anthem and more shameless hooks than Sly Stone's "Dance to the Music", the nitrous rush of tracks like Dougal's "Life Is Like a Dance" and "Really Love U" (both 1994), Dougal & Eruption's "Party Time" (1995) and Dougal & Hixxy's "Seven Ways/Innovation" (1995) was pure pop polished to its essence: speed, catch-phrases, gloss and a galvanising riff.

"Seven Ways/Innovation" was the first release on the Essential Platinum label that he co-runs with Hixxy, which has since gone on to become one of the two or three most important Happy Hardcore labels with releases like Hixxy & Sharkey's "Toytown" (1995) and Force & Styles' "Fireworks/Zurich" (1995). Dougal's collaborations with Mickey Skeedale provided some of his most anthemic records with tracks like "On a High" (1995), "Lovetoy/Back to the Future" (1996) and "Got to Go" (1997) all dancefloor stompers.

Even more of a bliss overload were Dougal's tag-team efforts with DNA. "Hornz (Remix)" and "Dream of Heaven/Sometimes" (both 1997) both featured plenty of 4/4 bounce, rising piano lines and cheeky-chappy synth riffs. Teaming up with Innovate, Dougal was responsible for one of 1998's biggest tracks, "Innovate Anthem" (1998), which featured vocals from Happy Hardcore mainstay Jenna.

◉ **Various Artists – Bonkers 5**   React, 1998

Volume 5 of the best-selling Happy Hardcore series features Dougal at the controls with a rousing selection of anthems.

Dream Team/Joker

After an illustrious career producing Hardcore tracks like "Ecstasy Is a Science" and "Total Amnesia" (both 1992) and running his Brain label, veteran producer Bizzy B turned to the hip-hop that originally inspired him to bring the visceral energy that breakbeat music lost when it became infatuated with the power of technology and the polish of studio craftsmanship. Announcing themselves with the undeniable "Stamina" (1995) for Suburban Base, Dream Team (aka Bizzy B & Pugwash) have since become perhaps the leading exponents of jump-up Jungle. With more gratuitous percussion tricks than a Neal

Pert drum solo and a backwards overmodulated bassline, "Stamina" might have been aimed at brooding halls of bass like AWOL, but it was so kinetic that it couldn't have been any further from Jungle's new-found moodiness if it was made by Bobby McFerrin.

Credited to the Dynamic Duo and released on their own Joker label, Bizzy B & Pugwash's "Yeah Man" (1995) was even less subtle. One of the most physically intense Jungle tracks, "Yeah Man" had drums so far up front in the mix that they threatened to take your head off and a bro-ken-rib bassline that didn't let up for a second. Joker's "Raw Dogs" (1996) was far less physical despite the sample's claim of being "raw like *Reservoir Dogs*", but the "Raw Dogs Relik" (1996) mix by Shy FX recti-fied matters with a more insistent tempo and a fatter bassline.

Dream Team's "Just a Little Hip Hop" (1996) started off with Bukem-esque keyboard swatches, but it was just a ruse: the track soon descended into the seventh circle of their usual low-end inferno. By this point, Bizzy B & Pugwash's formula was set in stone: flatulent, sing-song basslines, old-school hip-hop samples and breakbeat fren-zy. It might not have broken any new ground, but the formula was absolutely thrilling on the dancefloor. Tracks like Dream Team's "It's Rollin' Alright", "Check the Teq", "Scandalize" (all 1996), Special K & Dream Team's "All DJs" (1997) and Joker's "Cool Rok Stuff" (1997) were all constructed according to this same blueprint and everyone of them was thoroughly rinsing.

Featuring vocal tunes and productions from the likes of Majistrate, Bizzy B's Brain compilation, **Hoods From Da City** (1996), tried to intro-duce a more spiritual vibe to his usual thrash-about-the-room style, but it was the roughneck tracks that impressed. Dynamic Duo's awesome "The Click" (1996) introduced a more menacing minimalism to their sound without forsaking jump-up's body-moving imperative. Pug-wash's "Star Wars" and Dream Team's "Clear My Throat" (both 1997), however, reverted back to the tried and true. Dream Team's debut album, **The Drum & Bass World Series** (1997), celebrated their label's 25th release, but tried a little too hard to be all things to all people. Surrounding Chuck D and Flavor Flav in a cathedral of squelchy bass, Dream Team's "Public Enemy" (1997) turned Public Enemy's militancy into pure electricity, while "Somebody/Beat of the Year" (1999) pumped up some lovers' rock with distorted low-end mayhem. The splintering angularity with which Bizzy B & Pugwash arranged the samples showed the way out of drum 'n' bass' prison of rigidity. Unfortunately, no one followed them.

⊙ **Dream Team – "Yeah Man"** Joker, 1995

As funky as the Godfather and as mosh-worthy as the Butthole Surfers, this might be the most physical breakbeat track ever. (Available on **DJ Box Volume 1**.)

⊙ **Dream Team – "Public Enemy"** Joker, 1997

Unquestionably the jump-up track of the year, this was one of the few tunes that knew what to do with the de rigueur tantrum beats of 97–98. (Available on **Here Come the Drums**.)

Ed Rush

With beats that are not so much block-rockin' as knock your block off, Ed Rush is probably the undisputed king of the new wave of noir that has swept drum 'n' bass. The brutally industrial sound that he helped bring back into fashion with collaborators DJ Trace and Nico at No U Turn Records ruled drum 'n' bass for the better part of two years and has positioned Ed Rush as one of breakbeat music's leading figures.

Born Ben Settle in west London, the young Ed Rush was a b-boy who, in the usual trajectory, had tuned on to rave because of the breakbeats. He pestered neighbour Nico Sykes, who was an engineer with his own label, to produce tracks with him. The result was "Bludclot Artattack" (1993), a disturbing Darkcore track recorded in Sykes' cramped, collapsing loft that didn't have the pulsating momentum of other dark tracks and marked Jungle's transition away from the Ecstasy rush towards the blunted, bloodshot detachment of marijuana.

After disappearing from the scene for two years, Ed Rush re-emerged as agent provocateur on Trace's epochal "The Mutant" (1995). His return as Ed Rush, "Guncheck" (1995), was characterised by seething gangsta attitude and sneering basslines. The flip, "Force Is Electric", had a nasty snatch of static that sounded like a short-circuiting wire or a mosquito flying into an electric lamp running through the track. His contribution to the scene-defining **Techsteppin'** (1996) compilation, "Check Me Out", had all the ferocity of gangsta Hardstep tracks released by the Dope Dragon and Philly Blunt labels, but it felt sapped of energy, foggy, depleted.

The **Skylab** EP and "Kilimanjaro" (both 1996), released on Metalheadz and Grooverider's Prototype labels respectively, marked the acceptance of his hideously distended distorted bass sounds (achieved by running the synths through a guitar distortion pedal) by the drum 'n' bass mainstream. With rigid drum intros and oppressive, coagulating bass sounds, "Skylab" and "The Raven" (from the **Skylab** EP), in particular, seemed to presage the next two years of drum 'n' bass. The equally dystopic "Mothership" (1996) began like the soundtrack to an Agatha Christie murder-by-the-docks tale and slowly turned into a Dario Argento splatter-fest with punishing drums and a bassline of Rabelaisian proportions.

With its grandiose synth stabs and thunderous bass chorus, "Technology" (1997), which anchored No U Turn's **Torque** compilation, was an almost Wagnerian vision of sonic violence. Ed Rush also contributed a mix session to **Torque** which included his perfectly titled "Comatone" (1997) – the clockwork rhythm and the bass were so claustrophobic and dense that the track was almost desensitising.

By this time Ed Rush was a bona fide star on the scene and he hooked up with another figure who was defining drum 'n' bass' uncompromising new sound, Optical (who had engineered the **Skylab** EP), to form the Virus label. The label's first two releases, "Medicine/Punchbag" and "Zardoz/Satellites" (both 1998), were, despite the bass distortion, marked by the unrelentingly clinical production values and obsessively precise drum programming that was the hallmark of the two-step sound that was moving drum 'n' bass away from its breakbeat roots. These singles, along with tracks like the sort of jazzy "Glass Eye" and the bass-heavy "Slip Thru", were collected on the duo's **Wormhole** album (1998).

⊙ Various Artists – Torque   No U Turn, 1997

An essential collection of bass mutations that includes some of Ed Rush's finest tracks: "Mothership", "Comatone", "Technology" and "Sector 3".

Ellis Dee

The erstwhile Roy Collins took the dodgiest pseudonym in a genre characterised by dodgy pseudonyms during the Second Summer of Love when he ran the Rave at the Cave parties in Elephant & Castle. Quickly becoming one of the biggest names of the early rave circuit, Ellis Dee soon became the main man behind the pop rave act Rhythm Section. "Feel the Rhythm" and the **Midsummer Madness** EP (both 1991) both made the lower reaches of the British pop charts with anthemic combinations of joyful piano riffs and ever-quickening breakbeats.

Tiring of the escalating nursery school vibe of the rave, Ellis Dee hooked up with fellow rave stalwart Swan-E to release the proto-Jungle of "Roughneck Business" (1992). After several years of concentrating on his DJing, Ellis Dee hooked up again with Swan-E to form the Collusion label in 1995. Ellis Dee's "Lockdown" (1996) was a serious DJ Hype-style rinse out of a hip-hop sample eulogising America's ever-growing prison population, while his "The Real Killer" (1996) featured MC Fearless getting busy on top of timestretched kung-fu flick samples and Dr. Dre gangsta boogie keyboards.

At around the same time, Ellis Dee was producing Down Tempo tracks for the obscure American label Kram. With enormous string breakdowns and MC Fats doing his soulful thing, "97 Style" (1997) was a late '90s update of rave dynamics that gave this old-timer his highest profile since the old school was the new school.

⊙ **"The Real Killer"**   Collusion, 1996

An unjustly overlooked jump-up tearer featured on Ellis Dee's half of **World Dance: The Drum + Bass Experience**.

Endemic Void

Drum 'n' bass might be urban music par excellence, but many of the genre's best producers hail from the leafy suburbs of Hertfordshire. Straight outta Harlow, Danny Coffey is one of the few jazzy drum 'n' bass producers whose fusion licks don't emulsify and congeal immediately upon impact.

Born in 1973, Coffey started off recording Ragga Jungle for Labello Blanco as Strictly Rockers in the early '90s. Records like "Strictly Rocking" (1991), the **Murder** EP (1992) and "Lightning and Thunder" (1993) followed the genre's early formula of speeded-up breakbeats fleshed out with samples of toasting dancehall DJs. After a few more mellow releases as Slipstream, Coffey hooked up with former KLF collaborator Tony Thorpe and his newly formed Language label in 1995.

As Endemic Void, Coffey recorded the dark and angular "Subether" for the label's inaugural release, **Miscellaneous** (1995), and established himself as one of the more individualistic producers on the drum 'n' bass scene. Re-inventing himself as a fusioneer influenced by Weather Report, Brothers Johnson and Airto Moreira as well as Roni Size, Coffey's subsequent Endemic Void releases delved further and further into the mesmerising heart of jazz. The **Whole World** EP (1995) represented the middle ground between the jacuzzi jazz that Endemic Void would soon recline in and the droning bass and off-kilter rhythms that characterised "Subether". The easy ambience of "Serious Intent" (1996) heralded the breezier direction of his debut album, **Equations** (1996).

A collaboration with Shogun as Machine on DJ Pulse's Creative Wax label, "Off the Cuff" (1996), took Coffey further into the realm of

LTJ Bukem, while Endemic Void's "Lamentation" (1997) used a live bassline as a nod to Coffey's fusion influences. Jazz-funk's Rhodes infatuation showed up on Coffey's releases as Tertius: "Miracle Switch" and "Vibes" (both 1997) for Renegade, "Wolf/Ninth Episode" (1997) with Professor Smalls for Funk 21 and "Structure/Infra" (1998) for Moving Shadow exiles Partisan. The peripatetic Coffey has also explored chiming complexity as Brasswolf (with Klute) and expressed his inner b-boy as Blades for Smokers Inc.

◉ Equations   Language, 1996

Not as unctuous or as facile as most jazzy drum 'n' bass, this album is the acceptable face of fusion.

Eruption

Encompassing rave promotion and the production of singles and compilations of both Happy Hardcore and Jungle, Chris Brown's United Dance empire is one of the major forces in Hardcore. As a DJ and producer in his own right, Brown is only marginally less influential.

His first record as Eruption and the first release on United Dance was a collaboration with DJ Slam, "In Jeopardy/Hold On" (1994). Eruption and United Dance really made their mark with the Hardcore classicism of "I Need Somebody" (1994) and the collaboration with Sy, "12 Inches of Love/Thunder" (1995). With hurtling snares, a buoyant synth riff, disembodied moans and what sounded like JB's grunts from "Think" speeded up and elongated, "12 Inches of Love" was an undisputed anthem that transcended its wretched punning title. Eruption's "Drop the Beat/Easy Bass" (1995) followed with similar pump-ing-funk dynamics, but his collaboration with Dougal, "Party Time/I.O.U." (1995), was more of a bouncy 4/4 lark about a fun castle.

"Let the Music/Eruption in My Mind" (1996) brought a harder edge to his music with more distorted, trebly synths and mild acid riffs, even though the sing-song melodies were still present and cor-rect. With its big hands-in-the-air breakdown, "Don't You Want to Me" (1996) was another sizeable hit despite its awkward, overly declamatory vocals. "Another Lonely Day" (1997), on the other hand, featured huge acid builds and some hip-hop crowd pumping on top of a stomping 4/4 beat and diva gush. United Dance's biggest hits, though, came from Force & Styles whose "Heart of Gold" and "United in Dance" (both 1997) tore up dancefloors up and down Britain.

⊙ "Another Lonely Day"   United Dance, 1997

A killer slice of pop overload that has way too many hooks competing for space, but since when was too much ever enough?

Essence of Aura/Carlito

A ny form of music that relies heavily on the logic of technology for its force will eventually camouflage itself with the mantle of "craftsmanship". Drum 'n' bass is no different. Artists like Coventry's Essence of Aura were seduced by soft-jazz's illusion of groove and style, civilised the breakbeat and moved it out of the jungle and into a sleek loft conversion decked out with Purves & Purves chairs and well-polished surfaces.

James Mitton-Wade, Ian Scott and Tim Grantham started to make drum 'n' bass upwardly mobile in 1994 with "Or 04", a white-label 12" that betrayed the influence of LTJ Bukem. Released on Moving Shadow, their follow-up, "Northern Lights" (1995), was an affecting blend of subdued dynamics, buried diva vocals and rico-cheting drums that set them apart from the paint-by-numbers ambience of the rest of the drum 'n' bass "intelligentsia". By the time of their next release, "Let Love Shine Through/So This Is Love" (1995), however, the similarities between Essence of Aura's sound and the lowest-common-denominator button-pushing of Progressive House were laid bare as "Let Love Shine Through" sampled an old Junior Boys Own track.

Essence of Aura disbanded in 1995 when Scott relocated to the US and Mitton-Wade adopted a new alias from Brian De Palma's gangster flick, *Carlito's Way*. Recording for Fabio's new label Creative Source, Carlito continued down the same path he forged with Essence of Aura: "Carlito's Way/Heaven" (1995) was a sickly unctu-ous concoction of saccharine keyboards and cloying percussion. "Grapevine/Introspective" (1996) followed suit with the kind of instru-mental melodrama that would make Sasha or Brian Transeau look like a stoic. Highlighting the non-Doc Scott side of the Midlands drum 'n' bass sound, Mitton-Wade compiled the **Transcentral Connection** (1996) album as part of Moving Shadow's regional compila-tion series.

With Mike Hall and Sophie Parks, Mitton-Wade formed Guardians of Dalliance. Their singles, "Laid Up/Laid Off" (1996) and "The Look/Reflex" (1997), tried to toughen up their sound with a hint of tech-menace, but the shallow positivity and relentless agreeability of

"Beneath Sunrise/New Swing/Solitaire" (1998) showed their true colours.

⊙ **"Northern Lights"**   Moving Shadow, 1995

A rare ambient drum 'n' bass track that uses the genre conventions to heighten emotional tension rather than convince you of its intelligence, this doesn't immediately congeal or waft away (available on **A History of Hardcore**).

Fabio

Although he hasn't set foot inside a studio for nearly a decade, Fabio has done as much as anyone in shaping Britain's break-beat sound. Playing the good cop to Grooverider's synth-squalling bad cop, Fabio is the scene's other godfather who was a patron to breakbeat's more progressive leanings while Grooverider was giving his imprimatur to the rumblings from its dark side. Along with Grooverider, Fabio has become drum 'n' bass' leading taste-maker and, while he doesn't seem to have the king-making abilities of his partner, he has consistently set the agenda towards a more "musical" drum 'n' bass.

Fabio's DJing career started at Brixton's Phase 1 FM pirate station where he played rare groove and hip-hop. As Chicago House made its first in-roads on the British club scene, Fabio and Grooverider became the residents at a tiny club in Brixton called Mendozas which, under their tenure, became *the* after-hours club in London. Already, the rough vs. smooth dialectic that characterised their partnership was taking shape as Fabio was championing the deeper sounds of

Mr. Fingers while Grooverider was banging the wigged-out Acid tracks of Sleazy D and Tyree.

It was Rage at London's Heaven, though, that created Fabio's reputation as the prime mover of drum 'n' bass. According to the accepted mythology, Rage, which ran from 1990 until the end of 1993, was where the breakbeats of hardcore Techno broke away from mainstream Techno and House and developed into Jungle and drum 'n' bass. Of course, the breakbeat sound was developing elsewhere, but Fabio can take credit for the first public airing of Joey Beltram's "Energy Flash" whose edgy whomp made dance music faster and darker than ever before. With Fabio and Grooverider playing records from labels like Reinforced and Production House while nearly everyone else was waxing lyrical about the inanities of Progressive House, Rage was also a Hardcore stalwart during the media's campaign against rave.

A year after Rage ended, Fabio started Speed at London's Mars Bar with LTJ Bukem. A reaction against the bad bwoy vibes ruling the breakbeat scene, Speed was where Jungle's unruly ghettocentric mentality was gentrified into the upwardly mobile, streamlined sound of drum 'n' bass. With the rare groove credentials of Fabio and Bukem, Speed was where the soothing textures of jazz-fusion entered the breakbeat matrix and artists like Alex Reece, PFM and Wax Doctor made their names. With the success of the Speed sound, Fabio started his Creative Source label in 1995. With releases from Carlito, Intense, Neil Trix and Hidden Agenda, Creative Source established itself as Good Looking's main rival in the Ambient/Jazzstep sweepstakes.

Drum 'n' bass had now fully entered the dance mainstream: former House and jazz bores were now firmly on the breakbeat bandwagon, it could be heard on car adverts and Fabio was a BBC Radio

One DJ. Alongside Grooverider, Fabio hosted the One in the Jungle show which further cemented his position as the don of drum 'n' bass. In 1998, after two years of Techstep bluster and coffee-table tedium, Fabio started Swerve as an antidote to drum 'n' bass' doldrums. Playing a style he apparently called "liquid funk", Fabio latched on to the emerging fad of updating blaxploitation chase themes with breakbeats as the way to inject some excitement back into drum 'n' bass. Championing records like Shy FX's "Bambaata" and Adam F's "Brand New Funk", he might very well have succeeded.

◉ Various Artists – Promised Land Volume 2   Higher Limits, 1996

Paired with MC Cleveland Watkiss, Fabio mixes his way through jazzy records by the likes of Adam F and Carlito.

Mickey Finn

U nintentionally taking his name from a slang term for an alcoholic beverage that's been spiked with drugs, Mickey Finn (né Michael Hearne) started adulterating House music's pristine blueprint with a raver's sensibility in 1988 when he began DJing at his sister's club in south London. Moving away from the soothing Balearic bliss that predominated in clubland, Finn was one of the pioneering exponents of the breakbeat sound and ushered in the Hardcore era with his appearances at raves like Biology and Genesis.

While his enduring influence will be as a DJ, as a producer in his own right Finn has created some of the most abiding tunes in the breakbeat continuum. Using the alias Bitin' Back (also the name of his record store in Gravesend), Finn extensively sampled the intro of *The Six Million Dollar Man* for his exhilarating "She's Breaking Up" (1991) which was released on Tim Taylor's American Focus label. Forming Urban Shakedown with long-time collaborator Aphrodite and Claudio Guissani in 1992, Finn was responsible for one of Hardcore's eternal classics, "Some Justice". Based around a deceptively simple oscillating keyboard riff and a breakbeat swiped from an old Run DMC record, "Some Justice" exploded into the British Top 20 on the back of a sample of CeCe Rogers' "Someday" that warped his vocals until they sounded like the benediction of a helium angel.

Far less heavenly was the bass cauldron of a club called AWOL where Finn was a resident DJ alongside Randall, Kenny Ken, Dr. S Gachet and Darren Jay. Beginning in 1992 at north London's Paradise Club, AWOL (A Way of Life) was a pressure chamber of dense, low-end frequencies punctuated with the stench of lighter fluid and piercing cacophony of air horns that replaced Rage as the unofficial headquarters of Junglism. It was here that Finn became one of the patron saints of jump-up with his sets of militantly minimal, hip-hop-sampling tracks with ricocheting breakbeats.

In between weekends spent criss-crossing the country to fulfil his DJing commitments, Finn re-emerged as Urban Takeover with Aphrodite in 1997 with the irrepressibly funky "Bad Ass!" The New Birth-sampling track was released on their own Urban Takeover label which has since introduced the world to new talent like Natural Born Chillers and Mulder. With their remix of the Jungle Brothers' "Jungle Brother" (1997) reaching the British charts in 1998, Aphrodite and Mickey Finn deservedly became two of drum 'n' bass' highest-profile names.

⊙ Various Artists – Dreamscape Volume 2   ESP, 1998

This three-disc mix compilation that also features Top Buzz and DJ Vibes displays Mickey Finn in top jump-up form with help from MC GQ.

⊙ The Takeover Bid   Mixmag, 1998

A double-CD mix compilation that has Aphrodite ripping it up on one CD, while Mickey Finn gets loose with a disc of two-step beats and shows that even Techstep can be funky in the right hands.

Flynn & Flora

P robably the most unsung of all the exponents of "the Bristol sound", Flynn & Flora have been one of the few production teams to fully incorporate a rare groove/fusion sensibility into drum 'n' bass without sacrificing its primary rhythmic motivations. Their relatively low profile is perhaps surprising given that Flynn was a member of the group that first heralded the arrival of Bristol swing, the Fresh Four. Along with his brother DJ Krust, DJ Suv and Judge, Flynn hit the British Top 10 with a Smith & Mighty-produced cover of Rose Royce's "Wishing on a Star" in 1989.

With the rest of the group, Flynn quickly disappeared from the public eye after too much record company pressure and, along with his brother, got involved in the West Country's breakbeat Hardcore scene. A partnership with Flora developed and the duo produced the atmospheric classic "Dream of You" in 1993. In tandem with the early records of Krust and Roni Size, "Dream of You" helped usher in the vogue for the jazzy, sensual and celestial. What "Dream of You" didn't do, however, was make the bottom end as smooth as its melodic touches. Understanding that it was the tension between the rough and smooth that made this kind of Jungle so effective, Flynn & Flora continued to lace their scatter-shot breakbeats with rhapsodic pianos and choruses of "oohs" and "ahhs" on "Jungle Love" and "Flowers" (both 1994).

Both sumptuous and wistful, "Dream of You Remix/Silk Cut" (1995) continued to explore the emotive possibilities of the breakbeat blueprint and heralded their debut album as one of the genre's most impressionistic. **Native Drums** (1996) was a rare combination of both hip-hop-flavoured militancy and pastoral melodicism that managed not to dilute either extreme by occupying a watered-down middle ground. Recognising that the urban-underbelly power fantasy and the urge to escape the city's pollution are the flipsides of the same coin, Flynn & Flora orchestrated a union of low-end boombastics and rain-forest mirages and harp reveries. Krust's remix of "Bass Speaker" (1996) shattered this harmony with a vicious, distended piece of dark hip-hop-influenced Jungle that was as hollow and airless as an empty gun chamber.

The **New Road** EP (1997) reinstated the balance between jazz eddies and bass storms, while "Sunrise" from the **Versatility** compilation (1997) introduced a crackling static feel to their previously organic productions. However, with "Pimp" (1997) and the **Seek & Destroy** EP (1998), Flynn & Flora backed away from the edgier sound and lost their way in drum 'n' bass' matrix of funkless rigidity.

⊙ Native Drums   Independent Dealers, 1996

One of the best single-artist Jungle albums because it integrates the rough and smooth and doesn't just throw in different elements haphazardly for the sake of variation.

Flytronix

As one half of Hyper-on Experience, Danny Demierre has played a significant role in shaping the trajectory of breakbeat music. Moving from the sampladelic exuberance of early Hardcore through the pharmaceutical fallout of Darkcore to the classicism of Jazzstep, Demierre has helped breakbeat science develop from a pre-cocious necessity-is-the-mother-of-invention spirit to a complacent stage of posturing maturity.

Demierre's first solo release as Flytronix was "Ricochet/Shine a Rewind" (1995) which began to show the growing influence of London jazz impresario Giles Peterson. Engineering work for Foul Play and Peshay followed as Flytronix honed his studio chops to the point of dullness and moved further and further away from the delirium of Hyper-on E. The Tom Browne-sampling "Rare Tear/Ready to Flow" (1996) followed with ultra-smooth Acid Jazz grooves that made Alexander O'Neal seem like Swamp Dogg.

Working with school chum and one half of E-Z Rollers Jay Hurren as JMJ & Flytronix, he released "In Too Deep/Delusions" (1996). Practically nothing but a succession of viscous synth pads, "In Too Deep" was so unctuous it would have given vibes maestro Roy Ayers pause. More jazzy spinelessness followed in the form of "The Rhode Tune/To Ya!" (1997) which took the smoove intro of Kool & the Gang's "Summer Madness" and mixed it with quasi-empyrean synth chimes so that it congealed into a glutinous ooze.

The unsurprising appearance of a double bass marked one of the worst-titled records ever – "Contemporary Acousticz Jam" (1998) – which was released in advance of his debut album, **Archive** (1998). Yet more evidence that drum 'n' bass took itself far too seriously, **Archive** was a double CD that tried to span drum 'n' bass, hip-hop and Down Tempo with mixed results at best. The drum 'n' bass tracks were fine if you like your Jean-Michel Jarre with limp breaks, but the hip-hop was half-baked at best and the desire to create "music that went somewhere" was about as exciting as the filler on a Seal album.

⊙ **"The Rhode Tune"**   Moving Shadow, 1997

If you've been studying Joe Zawinul licks at the Berkeley School of Music, you'll like this ode to the Fender Rhodes.

Force & Styles

Getting together in 1991 in their hometown of Clacton, Force (aka Darren Mew) and Styles (aka Paul Hobbs) have gone on to produce some of Happy Hardcore's most delirious records. Carnival rides of whirling keyboards, stomping drum beats and helium divas, Force & Styles' tracks are relentlessly upful as they impel you to enjoy the funhouse atmospherics.

Despite hooking up at the dawn of Hardcore, the duo would have to wait until Happy Hardcore fully broke away from the Jungle to make their mark on the scene. Tracks like "Wonderland" (1995) and "Harmony" (1996) both featured the almighty breakdowns and addictively saccharine keyboard hooks so beloved by the Happy community and marked them out as rising stars. "Funfair" (1996) was unadulterated rollercoaster exhilaration, while "Your Love (Get Down)" (1996) had the kind of enormous breakdowns that Sasha would approve of.

"Simply Electric" (1996), released on their own UK Dance label, had a piano riff that sounded like a Mike Post TV theme tune before the synth stabs and bouncing drums entered. Hooking up with the United Dance organisation for their debut album, **All Over the UK** (1996), Force & Styles made one of the genre's most energetic tunes on UD's theme song, "United in Dance" (1997). In addition to nearly making the pop charts with "Paradise and Dreams" (1997), Force & Styles were also part of 1997's biggest anthem, the classic screamer "On Top" (1997) by A Sense of Summer.

"Shining Down" (1997), "Feeling Fine" (1998) and "Apollo 13" (1998) continued their rave dominance, but their biggest track was "Heart of Gold". Although it had been around on dubplate for almost a year, "Heart of Gold" didn't get officially released until 1998 when it hit #51 on the British charts. More elegiac than their usual tracks, "Heart of Gold" featured vocalist Kelly Llorenna and updated the kind of heroic heartbreak that was the preserve of Hi-NRG and Latin Freestyle for the Ecstasy generation.

⊙ **A Sense of Summer – "On Top (Remix)"**   Universal Records, 1997

A screamer in the finest tradition of Manix and Vibes & Wishdokta, "On Top" is diva bliss at its most intense.

Foul Play

Criminally ignored in the media stampede to anoint Goldie and LTJ Bukem as the figureheads of drum 'n' bass, Foul Play are certainly among the genre's finest producers and have been responsible for just as many landmark records as any of their more illustrious peers. Initially a trio consisting of Steve Bradshaw, John Morrow and Steve Gurley, Foul Play burst onto the Hardcore scene in 1992 with their **Volume 1** and **Volume** 2 EPs which they released on their own Oblivion label. With "Dubbing U" and the distinctly jazzy beat and ragga oscillator bass riff of "Survival", **Volume 2** was one of the most original Hardcore 12"s of the time and attracted the attention of Moving Shadow.

After the Ecstasy overload melancholy of "Drowning in Her" (1993), released as 4 Horsemen of the Apocalypse for Darren Jay's Tone Def label, Foul Play released another MDMA-fallout tone poem in the form of the dizzying Janet Jackson samples of "Finest Illusion/Screwface" (1993) on Moving Shadow subsidiary Section 5. Foul Play's masterpiece, though, was the **Volume 3** EP (1993) which along with Goldie's "Angel" heralded the end of Darkcore. The EP's centrepiece was "Open Your Mind" which, in its subsequent remixed form, morphed the breathy, unctuous mannerisms of vapid '80s street soul into bliss incarnate – it sounded almost exactly like the feeling you get when they crack your back after a Turkish bath.

Probably drum 'n' bass' finest remixers, Foul Play were responsible for definitive remixes of Nookie's "Sound of Music" (1993) – which transformed an anthem into a rugged, craggy drumscape – and Hyperon Experience's "Lords of the Null Lines" (1993). Their best mix, though, was their sublime VIP mix of Omni Trio's "Renegade Snares" (1994) which took the disembodied soul vocal exhortations, Michael Nyman glacial piano riff and almost melodramatic synth bassline and wove them into a breakbeat symphony that was anchored by the cascading snares that provided the song's hook.

Volume 4 (1994) followed with the plangent synth washes and Mary J. Blige samples of "Being With You" and the collaboration with vocalist Denise Gordon, "Music Is the Key". After this release, Steve

Gurley left the group to produce his own tracks as Rogue Unit for
Labello Blanco. Foul Play's "Stepper/Total Control" (1995) was their
first record as a duo and displayed a more minimal feel, particularly
with the Chinese-water-torture percussion of "Stepper". Their debut
album, **Suspected** (1995), was largely a collection of remixes of tracks
like "Open Your Mind" and "Being With You", but new material like
"Ignorance" introduced the talents of Adam F to the drum 'n' bass
world.

After the lacklustre "Vice/Karma" (1996), Bradshaw and Morrow
started the Panik label, but it never really got off the ground due to
the tragic death of Steve Bradshaw in 1997. With Neil Shepherd,
Morrow re-emerged in 1998 as Foul Play Productions with "Synthetic Bitch/Golden Gate" – a brilliant rapprochement between contemporary dystopian visions and a time when the "Think" break wasn't
such anathema to drum 'n' bass producers.

⊙ **Suspected**   Moving Shadow, 1995

Covering the entire emotional spectrum, this album proves that drum 'n'
bass is anything but one-dimensional.

4 Hero

Dego McFarlane and Mark Clair's (aka Mark Mac) legendary
eclecticism goes back to the days when there were no divi-
sions between Techno and House and breakbeat. With their Reinforced label, the duo pioneered the fusion of Joey Beltram's
"Mentasm" synth stab with breakbeats to create Darkcore. As
Manix, Mac has created classic rave screamers. As Tek 9, McFar-

lane pioneered gangsta Jungle and Down Tempo beat collage. As Nu Era and Jacob's Optical Stairway, the two created some of the best non-Detroit Detroit Techno. As Tom & Jerry, they created a compelling combination of jazz textures and roughneck beats. And, as 4 Hero, they have charted the growth of drum 'n' bass from speed-freak thrills to upwardly mobile quest for respectability. In other words, the history of 4 Hero (and their associated aliases) is the history of drum 'n' bass.

McFarlane and Mac (along with Ian Bardouille and Gus Lawrence) started Reinforced in 1989 in an attic in Dollis Hill, London. Responding to the sub-bass whomp of LFO and the breakbeat House of Shut Up and Dance, the duo released their first EP, **Combat Dance**, in 1990. It would be their next release, however, that would mark them out as breakbeat's most pioneering producers. Like Sleazy D's Acid House classic "I've Lost Control", "Mr Kirk's Nightmare" (1990) was about the link between dancing and chaos, specifically pharmacological chaos. The intro ("Mr Kirk, do you have a son, Robert, aged 17?" "Yes." "I'm sorry, Mr Kirk, you better come to the station house, your son is dead." "Dead? How?" "He died of an overdose") replayed the tabloid press's moral panic about escalating use of Ecstasy, but it was the rhythm that gave the track its force. Sampled from the Isley Brothers' "Get Into Something", the "Give the drummer some" chant running through the track seemed like it was inviting ravers to dance to their own destruction.

Their debut album, **In Rough Territory**, and the **Headhunters** EP (both 1991) were similarly delirious, but the sleeve of **Headhunters**, which depicted the deformed bodies of 4 Hero, suggested that the producers knew that something was going horribly wrong in the laboratory. The **Where's the Boy** EP (1992) put sounds to the rash of Ecstasy deaths during that year: "Burning" and "Cooking Up Ya Brain" were intense collages of feverish synths and hyper-speed breakbeats. With gushing diva vocals and upful piano riffs, Manix's "Feels Real Good" and "Head in the Clouds" (both 1992) were the flipside of **Where's the Boy** – they were so relentlessly ecstatic that the feeling became unsustainable, they were so happy they were dark.

The irony of all this was that McFarlane and Mac both abstained from drugs, which was probably why they moved so far away from rave culture with their next releases and why their panic songs always felt like sick jokes.

4 Hero's **Journey From the Light** and **Golden Age** EPs (both 1993) retreated from the annihilating momentum of their previous releases into a morbid shell of gruesome synth stabs and abrasive textures. Tek 9's "Slow Down" (1993) and "Just Can't Keep My Cool" (1994) reacted by appropriating the cocooning warmth of jazz-fusion and Detroit Techno. McFarlane's awesome "A London Sumtin'" (1994), which was released under the Code 071 moniker, fled from the excesses of rave by adopting a gangster swagger, while Tom & Jerry's "Maximum Style" (1994) combined criminal-mindedness with disco strings, ragga-chat, fusion flutes and triggered snares.

The fullest expression, though, of their attempt to escape the spectre of rave culture and both the physical ghettoes and the ghettoes of the mind was **Parallel Universe** (1994). Recorded using a museum's worth of vintage synths and keyboards, **Parallel Universe** referenced the '70s astral jazz of Herbie Hancock and Pharoah Sanders which imagined outer space as offering transcendence from the material reality of the inner city. The truly amazing production took off from where their collection of warm Techno, **Deepest Shade of Techno** (1994), left off with igneous globules of bass and the biggest synth washes this side of a Tangerine Dream record. The best tracks ("Wrinkles in Time", "Terraforming", "Follow Your Heart") were as futuristic as they made out they were, while the "jazzy" (even though the other tracks had more to do with jazz because of their approach to rhythm) tracks were saved by their connection to something other than pastiche.

Tek 9's **It's Not What You Think It Is** (1996) was mostly Blue Noted Down Tempo beats that oozed "sophistication", but early versions included a second disc that collected Tek 9's seminal Junglist tracks recorded from 1991 to 1995. **Jacob's Optical Stairway** (1996) was a fusion of Techno and drum 'n' bass that erred a bit on the lyrical side, while Nu Era's **Beyond Gravity** (1995) eschewed breakbeats altogether.

4 Hero's **Two Pages** (1998) was hailed as their magnum opus, but the melodrama and saccharine vibes of the first disc were too unctuous even for Jazz FM. The second disc, however, was like the best parts of **Parallel Universe,** where they created a new sound to go along with their visions of the future and didn't just borrow someone else's. Remixes of Two Pages material (1999), unfortunately, kept the schizophrenia intact and didn't really play around with the concept.

⊙ **In Rough Territory**   Reinforced, 1991

Next to impossible to find now, but it remains an essential document of early Hardcore.

◉ **Parallel Universe**   Reinforced, 1995

Along with A Guy Called Gerald's **28 Gun Bad Boy** and **Black Secret Technology**, this remains the best single-artist album drum 'n' bass has produced.

Gabba

While Britain combined droning synth stabs with accelerating breakbeats in the aftermath of Joey Beltram's "Energy Flash" and "Mentasm", the Netherlands went on a Techno chainsaw massacre. Combining the Black Sabbath dynamics of "Mentasm" with the even more metallic stabs and beats of Mescalinum United's "We Have Arrived", Dutch DJ Paul Elstak created the lowlands form of Hardcore known as Gabba with his track as the Euromasters, "Amsterdam Waar Lech Dat Dan?" ("Amsterdam Where the Fuck Is That?") (1991). Taking a Yiddish slang term that had developed into a derogatory term for a hooligan and using brutal drum-machine beats pushing past the 200 bpm mark and trashy horror movie samples, Rotterdam's Gabba artists represented a working-class uprising against Amsterdam's cosmopolitanism.

Taking its name from an old video game, Maurice Steenbergen's Rotterdam Termination Source defined the sound of Gabba's beats with "Poing" (1992), while label-mate Sperminator defined its attitude with "No Women Allowed" (1992). While "Poing" was a hit throughout Europe, The Euromasters' "Alles Naar De Kl—te" (1992) was a screaming track full of ruthless synth stabs and heart-attack beats. Patrick Van Kerckhoven's Ruffneck label wired up Gabba to hip-hop with tracks like Wedlock's "Bass For Yer Face" (1993).

Amsterdam eventually got into the act with Mokum Records and Vitamin's "The Point/Cosmic Trash" (1993). Chosen Few's "Freedom" (1993) continued Gabba's strange alliance with hip-hop, sounding like a union between Public Enemy and Black Sabbath. Mokum's most controversial release was probably Annhilator's "I'll Show You My Gun/Psychotic/Into the Wildstyle" (1994). The work of Scottish producer Scott Brown, "I'll Show You My Gun", as well as the tracks on his own Dwarf label, drove a rift into the scene by slowing the bpms way down and lightening things up.

On the other hand, there was Australia's Nasenbluten and their Bloody Fist label. With records like the **500/600/1200 EP** (1994) and the awesome "Intellectual Killer" (1996), which had a sample that went something like "Open up the devil's head and hang him from my testicles", Nasenbluten and Bloody Fist took Gabba into previously unimagined extremes. Their "Blows T' the Nose" (1995) on Industrial Strength, sampled Public Enemy on its way to becoming the genre's most invigorating record. A close second might be the Dogge Team's "We Came to Hool" (1995) on the PCP-related Kotzaak label which sampled The Monkees.

○ **Various Artists – Hardcore Terror:**
The Dutch Masters Volume 1   Rumour, 1995

An excellent compilation that features most of Gabba's early classics.

Dr. S. Gachet

With a decade and a half behind the wheels of steel, Dr. S. Gachet is one of drum 'n' bass' elder statesmen. Following a similar path to DJ/producers like Grooverider and Jumping Jack Frost, Gachet started out spinning jazz-funk and rare groove and followed the trend towards Acid House and then on to breakbeat. As one of the residents at legendary Jungle club AWOL along with Mickey Finn,

Randall, Kenny Ken and Darren Jay, Gachet helped promulgate the hardstepping hip-hop vibe of rollers' music against the encroaching tedium of "intelligent" Jungle.

In 1995 he started his Audiomaze label with his bad bwoy elegy "Remember the Roller" (1995). Based around a wailing diva and a bass drop that had the emotional weight of a Detroit synth wash, "Remember the Roller" proved that you could be just as expressive with rhythmic elements as you could with keyboards. His "The Dreamer" (1995) for Labello Blanco off-shoot Urban Gorilla also showed the "intelligent" wing a thing or two about what was truly important in a production. Building a dense rhythm track and a shattering bassline into crescendo after crescendo, Gachet gave an audio lecture on creating and releasing tension – something almost totally absent from drum 'n' bass since the rise of the jazz influence.

Unfortunately, his "Forbidden Agenda" (1996) single forsook the rhythmic impetus in favour of the refinement and sophistication of the drum 'n' bass mainstream. The title of the flip of his oily single "The Message" (1997) seemed to suggest an ambivalence towards drum 'n' bass' mainstream sound. With its pseudo-celestial synth pads and tepid beats, however, "Half-Hearted Monty Business" didn't seem to rediscover the excitement of the rave or jump-up. "It's All Gone Sideways" (1997) was slightly better, but its flip, "Night Owl", was the same old schlocky jazz you could hear during a drive-time jazz radio show. The synth sweeps continued apace on Sub Sequence's thoroughly ephemeral "Drum in Space/Upsta" (1998). With Gachet's recent drum 'n' bass-by-numbers, it should have come as no surprise that he turned to Speed Garage on "Understand Me" (1998).

⊙ **"Remember the Roller"**   Audiomaze, 1995

Proving that you could be intelligent and complex as well as funky, this is Gachet's finest moment.

Goldie

I f there is one person who represents drum 'n' bass for the mainstream media it is Goldie. With natural charisma and a larger-than-life personality, Goldie is one of the few producers, in a scene that once thrived on its anonymity, who is able to fit into the music industry's established promotional machine. While his stardom may be not unconnected with his willingness to play the celebrity game, the roots of his reputation lie in the ground-breaking Darkcore tracks that he produced in the early '90s, which created the foundation for Jungle's above-ground cross-over.

Born in Walsall in 1966 to a Scottish mother and an absentee Jamaican father, Goldie was raised under sometimes brutal conditions in numerous foster families. After being seduced by hip-hop culture, he moved in 1986 to Miami, where he set up a shop selling the engraved gold teeth from which his *nom de disque* is derived. Goldie then moved back to England, where he fell in with the Reinforced Records crew, for whom he did both design and A&R work. After a 12" as Ajax Project, Goldie released the completely blissed-out "Menace" (1991) using his Rufige Kru alias – "rufige" being his term for the nth-generation samples that he used to give his tracks a dirty, rough edge. This sound was writ large on **Dark Rider** (1992), an EP characterised by its skittish drums and relentlessly staccato synth stabs which created a tension that was miles away from the giddy energy of most Hardcore of the time.

Now recording as Metalheadz, Goldie released what may be the scene's most pivotal track, "Terminator" (1992). Lifting the buzz-saw synth riff from Joey Beltram's "Mentasm" and pitch-shifting the drums so that they stayed in tempo, but got progressively faster, "Terminator" became the ultimate darkside track by mutating breakbeats into something that sounded as out of control and messed up as the ominous synths and freak-out spoken-word samples that characterised Darkcore.

But just as he epitomised the dark sound, Goldie put down the foundation of its demise with the extraordinary "Angel" (1993). A fusion of blistering breakbeats, "Mentasm"-style synth drones, samples from Brian Eno and David Byrne's **My Life in the Bush of Ghosts** and unctous jazz-lite vocals from Diane Charlemagne, "Angel" was one of the few tracks pushing Hardcore in a more musical direction that didn't forget what made the music so exciting in the first place. Unfortunately, by using the timestretching technique that he pioneered on "Terminator" to keep Charlemagne's voice from veering into helium territory, he also enabled other jazz-fusion-obsessed producers to become as smarmy as their idols.

Goldie's fusion fetish continued to pay dividends, however, with the outrageously over-the-top, but somehow rather good, twenty-minute-plus magnum opus about the nature of time and ghetto living, "Timeless" (1994). A beat suite that incorporated the urge to release the pressure of "Inner City Life", the breakbeat dub of "Jah", a passage of massed strings and a reprise of "Inner City Life", "Timeless" was the brutal urban experience in (not so) miniature. According to Goldie, it was also the ultimate statement of drum 'n' bass's technical sophistication and breakbeat manipulation.

"Timeless" was the title track of Goldie's 1995 debut album. Recorded with engineers like Rob Playford, Dillinja and 4 Hero's Dego McFarlane, **Timeless** was almost universally hailed as a masterpiece upon release. More realistically, it was half mind-boggling ("Timeless" and "This Is a Bad") and half the sort of mawkish fusion ooze inhabited by the likes of The Yellowjackets and Spyro Gyra ("Sea of Tears"

and "Adrift"). **Timeless** marked drum 'n' bass' shift from the populist get-out-of-your-head energy of Hardcore to the elitist "progressivism" of what Simon Reynolds labelled Artcore.

With the release of **Timeless** Goldie became Jungle's unofficial figurehead. His new club, Metalheadz Sunday Sessions at London's Blue Note, replaced LTJ Bukem's Speed as *the* place to be seen and to hear the cutting edge. His newly formed Metalheadz label pushed his cyber-skeleton with headphones logo even further into the public consciousness. By the time of his high-profile relationship with Björk, Goldie had reached media saturation.

The inevitable over-heated reaction to too much press was turned into an album even more overblown than **Timeless**. With one or two exceptions, **Saturnz Return** (1998) was everything bad about **Time-less** magnified twenty times: there were tracks with David Bowie and Noel Gallagher, more ghastly over-ripe fusion moves and an hour-long orchestral piece called "Mother". His former partner, Rob Playford, once said that he hoped that Jungle would become progressive rock for the 21st century. **Saturnz Return** made his wish come true a little early. A pared-down remix album, **Ring of Saturn** (1999), helped slightly, but the damage had already been done.

⊙ Timeless   London,1995

Although it could have easily been pared down to a single-disc album and it helped enshrine drum 'n' bass' cult of the engineer, the technical sophistication is aligned to music that admits that there's a world outside of the studio.

Grooverider

I n Junglist folklore no one occupies a more central role than Grooverider (he refuses to divulge his real name), the man nearly everyone calls "the godfather". Almost universally revered by the drum 'n' bass community because of his commitment to the music since the early days of rave, Grooverider has parlayed this affection into a position of unparalleled power within the scene. As drum 'n' bass' main taste-maker and most in-demand DJ, Grooverider has the ability to make or break artists: Goldie, Photek, Optical, Matrix, John B and Boymerang have all benefited from the Rider's conferral. While those outside of his coterie have, perhaps unfairly, suggested that he lives up to his nickname and runs his domain like the Mafia, it is certain nonetheless that where Grooverider goes, the rest of the scene soon follows.

Grooverider's path to becoming the king of the Jungle began at a tiny, dingy after-hours club in Brixton called Mendoza's in 1987. Teamed with fellow Choice FM pirate DJ Fabio, Rider played early Acid House 12"s to a small crowd of committed club cognoscenti who would stumble down to south London after Shoom closed. By 1989 the buzz surrounding Fabio and Grooverider had grown to such an extent that they were offered a backroom slot at Heaven – one of London's biggest clubs.

In classic clubland style, they were so successful that, in 1990, they took over Heaven's main room for their now-legendary Rage night. According to the accepted mythology, Rage, which ran until 1993, was where the breakbeats of hardcore Techno broke away from mainstream Techno and House and developed into Jungle and drum 'n' bass. What-ever the veracity of this particular creation tale, we can be sure that Fabio played the jazz-tinged straight-man to Grooverider's battering bar-rage of darkside beats, thus setting in motion drum 'n' bass' rough vs. smooth dialectic. Whether it was the actual DJing skills and musical taste of Fabio and Grooverider that made Rage what it was or just the copious amount of drugs consumed by the clubgoers, the almost mysti-cal aura surrounding Rage ensured Grooverider's enduring prominence.

Despite his peerless reputation, Grooverider's first tracks were released almost anonymously (under the psuedonym Codename John) on his then-unpublicised Prototype label in 1994. He dubbed the roughneck style he championed in his DJ sets – typified by tracks like his own "Kindred" (1994) – Hardstep, and his two **Hardstep Selection** (1994, 1995) compilations, featuring tracks by Dillinja, J. Majik and DJ SS, were definitive overviews of the mean and moody sound that char-acterised drum 'n' bass before its mainstream acceptance.

Goldie repaid his enormous debt to Grooverider, who was largely responsible for the success of "Terminator" in 1992, by inviting him to be the resident at the influential Metalheadz Sunday Sessions club. Goldie's Metalheadz label also released Grooverider's fearsome, sirens-at-the-gates-of-hell track "The Warning" in 1997. This sound of technology gone horribly wrong was writ large on Grooverider's **The Prototype Years** (1997) compilation. As it introduced drum 'n' bass to the skewed visions of producers like Optical, Matrix and John B, **The Prototype Years** enshrined the sound of malfunctioning machines and obsessive-compulsive drum loops as the new wave of drum 'n' bass.

With nearly everyone jumping on the bandwagon and recycling the same two or three skronk riffs, it all got a bit too much for even a noise addict like Grooverider, who admitted, "Everyone's doing the

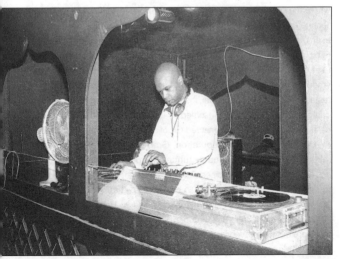

noisy stuff now. It all gets a bit confusing after a while." **Mysteries of Funk** (1998) responded by incorporating some of old sparring partner Fabio's jazzisms into his usual matrix of dystopian synths and basslines that make you want to hide in the corner. While the intimidation of old was present on tracks like "Where's Jack the Ripper", the double bass riff of "On the Double" and the "Rainbows of Colour" suggested that Grooverider's strand of drum 'n' bass might have found a way out of the dead end of technological extremism that it had been stuck in for two years.

⊙ Grooverider's Hardstep Selection Volume 2 Kickin',1995

Featuring Grooverider's VIP mix of his own "Kindred", Dillinja's "Angels Fell", Splash's "Babylon" and Roni Size's "Jazz Thing", this is an excellent mix of dancefloor classics from 1994–95 that has a seething hip-hop-derived menace.

⊙ Mysteries of Funk Sony/Higher Ground,1998

Not as unremittingly scary as his **The Prototype Years** compilation, Grooverider's debut album shows that there's a place for melody, hooks and nuance in even the hardest drum 'n' bass.

James Hardway

Also known as former Andrew Weatherall and Psychic TV collaborator Dave Harrow, James Hardway attempted another reprise of the myths of the cool jazz outlaw riding atop the new sound of the underground. His debut, the **Cool Jazz Mother Fucker** EP (1996) had some nice Middle Eastern samples in among the jazz slurs and brittle breakbeats. His debut album, **Deeper, Wider, Smoother**

Shit (1996), worked along similar lines with horn samples, flanged keyboards and a general air of goateed beatnik attitude.

"Illustrated Man" (1997) followed suit with a plaintive flute and Spanish guitar intro that gave way to wind chimes and way too fluid breakbeats. With a band consisting of Theo Gordon on brass, Miles Ofuso Danso on bass and Simon Smith on drums, Hardway tried to make those "drum 'n' bass is the new jazz" metaphors flesh with live performances. His second album, **Welcome to the Neon Lounge** (1998), meanwhile, changed his persona from a cigarette-smoking jazzbo in a black and white photo to a cocktail-sipping man of leisure wearing loud suits in pre-family destination Las Vegas. As Magnetic, Harrow recorded his efforts to make drum 'n' bass on the fly during long road trips on the **A La Magnetica** album (1998).

⊙ **Welcome to the Neon Lounge**	Recordings of Substance,1998

Although this jazz move was slicker than Gordon Gekko, it managed to never get smarmy.

Hidden Agenda

The sons of an ex-drummer, Geordie brothers Mark and Jason Gooding have been at the forefront of drum 'n' bass' jazz mood since their arrival on the scene in 1995. Working on the less stream-lined and more experimental end of the Jazzstep sound, Hidden Agenda have managed to purse fusion's smoothness into breakbeat science's prismatic angularity.

After Mark graduated from a music engineering course, the duo set up a home studio and sent DATs to Fabio who then passed them on to Goldie. Signed to Goldie's Metalheadz label, Hidden Agenda's debut was "Is It Love?/On The Roof/Flute Tune" (1995). Although made from very suspect base materials, "Is It Love?" and "Flute Tune" transcended their sources with clipped, stuttering beats and an approach to texture that turned the silky élan of the jazzy samples into a detached melancholy.

Their follow-up, "Pressin' On/Get Carter" (1996), opened with louche vibes and bass groove before being transformed into a track that grooved like someone juggling scissors by an incredible, slicing sample of New York disco dons D-Train and beats that fell like sheets of metal. With *X-Files* synth squiggles and blasts of howling metal wind, "Dispatch #1/Dispatch #2" (1996) introduced the kind of paranoia that Photek and Source Direct made their careers on into Hidden Agenda's increasingly precision-tooled jazz matrix. Their debut on Fabio's Creative Source label, "The Sun" (1997), featured a more typical shimmering, cascading, jazzy production and seemed to back away from the sharp corners that had characterised their previous work.

With its two-step beats and steely synth washes, "Channel/Channel Beyond/No Man's Land" (1998) had more of a tech sound, but was similarly sleek. A joint release with new producer Seven for Reinforced, "Transmission/Fish Eggs" (1998) was their best record yet. "Fish Eggs" teasingly situated attenuated handclaps in the densest, most highly detailed Junglist psychoscape ever produced and showed that some drum 'n' bass producers could wring emotion and tension out of the scene's preoccupation with technique and technology.

⊙ **"Fish Eggs"**   Reinforced,1998

An amazing record that, unlike nearly every other jazz-based drum 'n' bass record, took Miles Davis as its model, rather than The Yellowjackets.

Hixxy & Sharkey

ailing from Portsmouth, Hixxy & Sharkey are perhaps the biggest names in English Happy Hardcore. With their five **Bonkers** compilations on React, they have accumulated over 300,000 record sales and the genre's biggest mainstream success, while Hixxy's Essential Platinum label is one of Hardcore's two or three most important.

Taken under the wing of fellow south coaster DJ Ramos (whose tracks with Supreme, "Crowd Control" and "Sunshine", are some of the scene's defining anthems), Ian Hicks began DJing at the age of fifteen and swiftly became one of rave's major players. Similarly, Jonathan Kneath started MCing at raves when he was fifteen and soon became the leading MC on the Happy Hardcore circuit, later turning to DJing and producing. It wasn't until 1995, though, that the duo would rise to the force that they currently are.

"Toytown" (1995) was, for better or worse, the biggest Happy Hardcore track of the last half-decade. A cheery rumpus of rinky-dink keyboard riffs, bouncy kick drums and quasi-Junglist snare rolls, "Toytown" was a rapprochement with the juvenilia of early Hardcore tracks like The Prodigy's "Charly" and The Smart-E's "Sesame's Treat". Of course, the mainstream dance press saw it as proof of the genre's terminal cheesiness, but "Toytown"'s sugar-coating, in the right atmosphere and right frame of mind, pretty irresistible and its hooks were undeniable.

After the romper-room delirium of "Toytown", however, both Hixxy and Sharkey took big left turns towards more "serious" music. Sharkey's "Revolution" and the Depeche Mode-sampling "E-Nuff" (both 1997) were huge, melodramatic, acidic, Trance-influenced tracks that weren't exactly dark, but didn't need pacifiers either. Hixxy, on the other hand, started his Legendary label to enable him to dabble in pumping, Euro-style House tracks.

Influenced by the "Nu Energy" of clubs like Trade and DTPM, Sharkey pushed the limits of "Trancecore" on his debut album, **Hard Life** (1998). With detours aplenty from the standard Hardcore blueprint, **Hard Life** tracks like "The Awakening" and "Forever Flying" were more than just rushing keyboards, spring-loaded drums and ascendant diva vocals that signalled Happy Hardcore's "maturity".

⊙ **"Toytown"**   Essential Platinum, 1995

The epitome of Happy Hardcore's trampolining drum beats and impossibly up keyboard lines, "Toytown" was one of the scene's most influential and popular tracks.

DJ Hype

Much is made of breakbeat's inclusiveness – that your colour doesn't matter as long as you worship at Jungle's temple of boom. With a series of implausibly funky tracks and a DJing style that owes more to hip-hop than perhaps any other Junglist, DJ Hype, a white guy from London's East End, epitomises drum 'n' bass' colour blindness.

Hype started out DJing in the early '80s on a sound system he set up with PJ and Smiley, who would eventually become Shut Up and Dance. In 1989, Hype (under the name Doctor K) won the European DMC mixing championships and his hip-hop-honed turntable skills have paid handsome dividends in his career as a breakbeat DJ. Along with Danny Breaks, Hype created part of early Hardcore's exhilaration by bringing scratching into the music – an awesome feat at 150-plus bpm. When Hype landed a job at London pirate station Fantasy FM in

1989, he would layer House music over hip-hop beats played at 45 rpm in order to get a presciently breakbeat feel.

Through his connections with Fantasy and SUAD, Hype became the in-house producer and A&R man at Kickin' Records. As The Scientist, Hype recorded some of rave's first forays into breakbeat and darkness (albeit with an almost camp pomposity) with "The Bee" and "The Exorcist" (1990) and "The Kick Squad" (1991). During this time, he was also building a reputation as the most formidable DJ on the scene and was voted Fantasy's best DJ.

His first track as DJ Hype, "Shot in the Dark (Gunshot Mix)/I Can't Understand It (Scratch The Fuck Out Of The Beginning Mix)" (1993), was released on Suburban Base and served as a blueprint for Hype's future excursions into lightning-speed hip-hop mutations. The remixes were accompanied by the mind-boggling "Weird Energy" which was a stunning combination of wind chimes, Mentasm synths and a hyper-speed cut-up of The 45 King's "The 900 Number".

As great as his early tracks were, they were nothing compared to "Rrrroll da Beats" (1994). Just as Jungle was being divided by the "intelligent" movement, "Rrrroll da Beats" proved that Jungle's *raison d'etre*, breakbeat science, was more exciting, more challenging and more intelligent than any smarmy Fender Rhodes lick. Not only did it have a stunning variation on the "Think" beat and a bassline that would come to define the jump-up and Hardstep sub-genres, it had actual hooks courtesy of MC GQ whose refrains "Absolutely 'T' for tremendous" and "Wheel up, come again, please, please, please" echoed around London for a year after its release.

1994 also saw the formation of Hype's Ganja label, which was inaugurated by the release of the dancefloor anthem "Computerised Cops". Released under the moniker Dope Style, "You Must Think First" (1994) was little more than a kung-fu flick sample and a video

game effect on top of an oscillating bassline and rolling, tumbling breakbeat that epitomised Hype's production style. Ganja would continue to release floor-filling rinse-outs like "Mash Up da Place" and "Pum Pum Must Smoke Ganja" (both 1995), but its biggest success would be DJ Zinc's "Super Sharp Shooter" (1996).

The Malcolm X-sampling "We Must Unite" (1996) displayed Hype's extraordinary low-end sensibilities with a rubbery, almost sing-song bassline that was murderous on the dancefloor. "We Must Unite" was featured along with tracks by Pascal and Zinc on the enormously successful **Still Smokin'** (1996) compilation which was the genesis of their True Playaz label and collaborations as the Ganja Kru. Hype's best, certainly most devastating, moment, though, might be his semi-legal mix of "Ready or Not" (1996) which redefined "tearing". When the True Playaz posse shifted their focus away from the dancefloor as on the **Real Vibes** collection (1998), however, their sense of dynamics got lost in the effort to make an album that worked as well at home as it did in the club.

◉ **United Dance Presents**
The Designer Collection   United Dance,1996

It has what could be the worst graphics on an album since Whitesnake's
early albums and doesn't feature any Hype tracks, but Hype's mix is as
stirring as Jungle gets.

Hyper-On Experience/E-Z Rollers/JMJ & Richie

Early breakbeat Hardcore was nothing but a great carnival ride on
synths, samplers and almost out-of-control drum machines. Few
tracks expressed this rushing sensation better than Hyper-on Experience's "Assention (to the Ninth Level)" (1992) which was like hotwiring
Malcolm McLaren's "Buffalo Gals" and doing donuts in an empty car
park. Early Hardcore was too much of a good thing, however, and the
giddy thrills of tracks like "Assention" soon burned out.

Sampling both Kym Mazelle ("There's a void where there should be
ecstasy") and *Predator 2* ("Fucking voodoo magic"), Hyper-on Experience's "Lords of the Null Lines" (1993) was perhaps the ultimate Darkcore
tune. While the Kym Mazelle sample expressed the hollow come-down after
too much Ecstasy, it unfortunately also seemed to express drum 'n' bass'
lack of direction after it lost its initial *raison d'etre*. Paralleling drum 'n' bass'
often fruitless search for a new paradigm, Hyper-on E's Alex Banks and
Danny "Flytronix" Demierre quickly moved away from the skittering energy
of "Lords of the Null Lines", the Carl Stalling-like excitement of "Thunder
Grip" and the frenzy of "Imajicka" (all 1993) towards the embalmed classi-

cism of Bukem-style jazz fetishism.

Banks and Demierre hailed from Beccles, Suffolk, which was also the home of PFM and JMJ (aka Jay Hurren). While Hyper-on Experience were recording their fol-

low-up to "Lords of the Null Lines", "Disturbance" (1994), Hurren, along with Andrew Riches as JMJ & Richie, released "Case Closed/Hall of Mirrors" (1993). In 1994, as E-Z Rollers, Banks and Hurren released "Believe/Rolled Into One" which remains one of the few celestial drum 'n' bass 12"s to retain the polyrhythmic excitement of breakbeat Hardcore and established E-Z Rollers as one of the premier production duos in this awkward sub-genre.

Despite the "Amen" break of JMJ & Richie's "Free La Funk/Universal Horn" (1995) and the rolling drums of JMJ & Flytronix's "In Too Deep" (1996), though, things got progressively more glutinous and less exuberant. E-Z Rollers' debut album, **Dimensions of Sound** (1996), had completely abolished any sense of gurning exhilaration or dumb thrills in favour of the "sophistication" of George Benson and Vangelis. Compiled by Hurren and Banks, the Suffolk compilation, **Storm From the East** (1996), featured more of the same emollient grooves and aquatic atmospheres. The one exception was E-Z Rollers' "Walk This Land" which appended a reggae horn burst to a liquid bassline to create a track that actually moved and didn't seek to replicate the vapour of the clouds.

Unfortunately, their next single, "Retro" (1997), was mired in hopelessly clichéd Fender Rhodes licks, a non-existent rhythmic sensibility and one of the worst samples ever. Their second album, **Weekend World** (1998), followed suit with congealed keyboards, soothing vibes and simplistic hooks that showed just how creatively bankrupt jazzy drum 'n' bass was. Hopefully, their new label, Intercom, will be able to inject a woefully tired scene with some new ideas. If their remixes of "Walk This Land" (1999), which was propelled to prominence by its appearance on the soundtrack of *Lock, Stock and Two Smoking Barrels*, are anything to go by, it should succeed admirably.

⊙**Hyper-on Experience Lords of the Null Lines/Thunder Grip/Imajicka/Time Stretch** Moving Shadow, 1993

A true Hardcore classic, the excitement generated by this EP is light years away from the drab celestial musings that this duo would soon be responsible for.

⊙**E-Z Rollers Believe/Rolled Into One** Moving Shadow, 1994

Easily one of the best singles to emerge from the jazzcore scene, this is the E-Z Rollers' finest moment by some distance.

Ibiza Records

ormed by Paul Chambers in 1991, Ibiza Records was one of the most important of the early breakbeat labels, if only for the name it bestowed on the scene: "Junglizm". Roaring out of east London with little regard for legal niceties like cleared samples or mainstream propriety, Ibiza released a series of white labels and legitimate records that were all DIY energy and populist electricity.

The label's first release was the **Happy Hour** EP (1991) which picked up on an idea from Shut Up and Dance and sampled Rik Mayall exclaiming, "Five pounds to get into my own bedroom?!?" Noise Factory (aka James from the Kemet Crew) followed with the febrile "Set Me Free/Bring Forward the Noise" (1992) and the frenetic ragga cut-up "Warning" (1992). Bad Girl's "Bad Girl" (1992) was little more than a speeded-up sample of a dreadlocks singing a paean to a deep dub bassline.

In association with pirate station Kool FM, Ibiza started the Jungle Fever and Jungle Splash clubs, the soundtrack of which was captured on **Junglism Volume One** (1994). A collection of tracks that cared little for technological innovation or polish, **Junglism Volume One** got over entirely on its infectious enthusiasm. Nigel Wonder's "Maggie" recklessly sampled John Barry's James Bond theme, while Merleen Allen's "Birds" was actually a Junglist cover of The Carpenters' "Close to You". With their breakneck snare patterns, gun shots and ragga samples, however, Ibiza's style was quickly left for dead by a drum 'n' bass scene hellbent on running away from anything that might make it popular.

⊙ **Various Artists Junglism Volume One**   21st Century Opera, 1994

Although their early records were probably better, they are also impossible to find and this collection is to Jungle what The Kingsmen or Sam the Sham & the Pharaohs were to '60s rock 'n' roll.

Da Intalex

Although the production team of Marcus Kaye and Mark McKinley have been linked with the "intelligent" Jungle scene, it's their beats and bass that you notice and not the neon textures. In a way not dissimilar from their fellow Mancunian A Guy Called Gerald, Da Intalex, at their best, manage to incorporate "musicality" into their music without forsaking the rhythmic impetus that is drum 'n' bass' *raison d'etre*.

Kaye and McKinley first attracted attention with "What Ya Gonna Do" (1994) which was released on L Double's Flex Records. Combining the Detroit synth washes and coffee-table chimes of Bukem-style drum 'n' bass with hardsteppers' breaks and torpedoing bass subs, "What Ya Gonna Do" represented the best of both of drum 'n' bass' competing schools. The duo spread their catholic gospel further by hosting Kiss FM's Jungle show in Manchester and by running the Jungle counter at Manchester's premier record store, Eastern Bloc.

Following a similar blueprint to "What Ya Gonna Do", "I Like It" (1995) welded the tasteful vocalese of a soul diva and Derrick May synth patterns with a tearing "Amen" break and the periodic stabs of a seemingly random bassline. The devastating bottom-end antics of "Mercy" (1995) followed "I Like It" as a dancefloor standard during the latter half of 1995 and proved that Da Intalex were defiantly unintelligent.

As The X, McKinley indulged his roughneck side with Hardstepping tracks like "Boomin' in Ya Jeep" and "New Dawn" (both 1995). With its almost morose vocals and distinctly subdued feel, the VIP Mix of "New Dawn" (1996) sounded like Hardstepin dub. "Turn Da Lites Down" (1996) chopped up the "Apache" break and oozed jazziness until McKinley tore things apart with a series of severe bass modulations which rubbed against the track's smoothness. Jumping on the Wu-Tang bandwagon, McKinley sampled Hong Kong chop-sockies on top of flailing breaks and dextrous bass manipulation on "Shaolin Style" (1996), which showed that even the slightest low-end tweaks could yield tumultuous results on the dancefloor.

⊙ **Da Intalex "I Like It"**   Intalex, 1995

Probably the finest rapprochement of jazzy drum 'n' bass and
roughneck Jungle ever produced. Available on the **One in the Jungle**
and **DJ Box 2** compilations.

J. Majik

Yet another one of drum 'n' bass' seemingly endless list of childhood prodigies, Jamie Spratling is further proof of rock-crit
Lester Bangs' belief that attitude is everything in popular music. Fed
on a diet of Miles Davis and Buddy Rich by his parents, Spratling
melded these formative influences with the Hardcore of his very early
adolescence. DJing by the time he was 15, Spratling produced one of
numerous breakbeat tracks titled "Six Million Ways to Die" (1993) as
Dextrous at the age of 16.

"Six Million Ways to Die" was picked up by Lemon D's Planet
Earth label and the next two Dextrous tracks were engineered by him
and Dillinja. "Six Million Ways to Die" also attracted the attention of
Goldie, who invited Spratling to record for Metalheadz. By this time he
had become aware of the existence of DJ Dextrous, and so
Spratling's Metalheadz debut was released under the name of J.
Majik. "Your Sound" (1995) was an eye-opening combination of
melancholy synth washes and rough-as-can-be "Amen" and
"Apache" breaks that seemed to encompass drum 'n' bass' aggression and its detachment from the outside world.

In 1995 J. Majik formed his Infrared label, whose debut single,
"Lush Life", was overgrown with melodic synth pads and string sam-

ples. His second record for Metalheadz, "Jim Kutta/Needle Point Majik" (1995), made dark, unsettling music out of the same material and aligned his output with similar tracks by artists like Source Direct and Photek even if they weren't as clinical. Displaying a keen sense of dynamics, "Arabian Nights" (1996) was centred around a break that went on longer than it should have which gave the track a disturbing, disruptive quality.

Tracks like "Apache" and "In the Shadow/Digital Readout" (both 1996), which was released under his Inner Visions moniker for Reinforced, were bleak dubscapes that Lee Perry might have made if his Black Ark Studio was in a mausoleum in Finland. Innervisions'

"Inside Yourself/Static Link" (1996) was another astonishingly forbidding track with a painfully brittle drum sound and a near-death bassline.

"Mermaids" (1996), a downbeat track released on Mo' Wax, marked a change in mood and a shift towards a more viscous production style. The transition from nightmare to reverie was made complete on the gurgling "Repertoire" (1997), his fourth single for Metalheadz. His debut album, **Slow Motion** (1997), had a couple of harder tracks, but the romantic visions of "Chakra" and "Kindred Spirit" predominated and foreshadowed the breezy, babbling-brook drum 'n' bass of "Rotation" and "Atlas Colours" (both 1998). "Freefall" (1998) continued his descent into watercolour drum 'n' bass, while its b-side, "Transmission", had the sinister edge he was best at.

⊙ **Slow Motion**   Infrared ,1997

Mixing light and dark with aplomb, this debut album managed to avoid the "home-listening" trap that ensnared so many drum 'n' bass albums.

John B

I n the person of John B, a former genetics and cell biology student at Durham University, drum 'n' bass finally had a producer who could actually live up to its claims of being breakbeat science. Far outside the standard b-boy to rave to Jungle route of the majority of drum 'n' bass producers, John B cites industrial noiseniks Throbbing Gristle, Moog pioneer Walter/Wendy Carlos and Karlheinz Stockhausen, the godfather of electronic music, as formative influences.

John B was still at university when his first release, "The Busker" (1996), came out on Shoebox under his real name, John Williams. Signing with DJ SS's New Identity label, John B made his name with the punishing rhythms and bruising, distorted bassline of "Sight Beyond" (1996). "Fermat's Theorem" (1997) followed in the same vein and caught the ears of Grooverider, who released another track of gruesome extremism, "Secrets" (1997), on his Prototype label.

An appearance on SS's **United Colours of Drum & Bass** (1997) as IC1, "Green", predated his first single on SS's main label, Formation. "Slamfunk/Undertow" (1997) was marked by tidal, acid basslines, moonstomp beats and blasts of white noise. His debut album, **Visions** (1997), was a sprawling double CD divided into an "Organic" half and a "Synthetic" half. Disc one, "Organic", had unspeakably naff titles like "Sax Therapy" and "Jazz Sessions Vols. 1 & 2" and the insipid flute and sax to match. The "Synthetic" disc, on the other hand, felt like German Trance with a bottom end designed by the Baader-Meinhoff Gang.

The two-step-beats-meets-computer-pulsing formula continued on "Star Burst" and "Travelogue/Pressure" (both 1998). "Hi Band/Crystal Wind" (1998), released as Vortex featuring John B, cemented his sound as that of a mad scientist caught in the belly of a whale. His contribution to the Country series, "Viva/Olé" (1998), released as Mexico, broadened his sound with Latin percussion and flanged horns.

○ Visions   New Identity, 1997

Half watery jazz posturing, half sinewaves and oscillations, this album is the epitome of the style that journalist Simon Reynolds has dubbed "Neurofunk".

Jonny L

Howard Jones is hardly the most inspiring of influences, yet his name always comes up when breakbeat survivor Jonny L talks about his musical past. Then again, given his haircut and the sheen of his synths, maybe the Howard Jones link isn't so surprising.

Jonny L first attracted attention in 1992 with the hands-in-the-air Hardcore anthem "Hurt You So". "Ansaphone" (1993) followed in a similar style, but as clubbers and producers distanced themselves from rave's exuberance, this and subsequent releases like "Ooh I Like

It" (1993) and "Transonic" (1994) couldn't make the transition well enough and fell on deaf ears.

Unlike many rave casualties, Jonny L re-emerged in 1995 with the trebly "I Won't Let U Go" and the more melodic "I'm Leaving" which was a favourite of Bukem and Fabio at their Speed club. The Larry Heard-wannabe part of his personality came through in "This Time" (1996), particularly with Detroit Techno demigod Carl Craig's Deep House remixes. His obsession with depth and warmth continued with "Underwater Communication" and the **Two Of Us** EP (both 1996).

Jonny L's debut album, **Sawtooth** (1997), however, marked a change in direction. With an overall effect akin to someone banging a baseball bat against a dutch oven for eight minutes, "Piper" was a hard two-stepper that in many people's minds was the drum 'n' bass track of the year, proving just how far the scene had disassociated itself from the rhythmic invention of old. Only slightly less metallic were "Moving Thru the Air" (which became just as clanging in the hands of Optical on his remix) and "Wish U Had Something" which had a secondary drum break ticking away in the background to make things a bit less monotonous.

The **Magnetic** (1998) album followed swiftly and continued in the same brutalist style. Tracks like "Intasound" and "Viper" were all short-circuiting synths and buzzing, high-voltage-wires-in-water basslines. "Accelerate" (with Lady Miss Kier of Deee-Lite fame) and "20 Degrees" (with MC Silvah Bullet) attempted to broaden the sonic palette, but the textures were just too viscid and the rhythms too overbearing to let any air in.

⊙ Sawtooth   XL,1997

Featuring "Piper", the track which defined two-step drum 'n' bass, this album pounds you into submission.

Juice/
Splash Records

One of Jungle's finest steppers' labels, Juice Records was formed in east London by school chums Daz Ellis, Darren Hickey and Jeff Hickey in 1995. The Hickeys had already left their mark on the breakbeat scene with a series of singles on their own Rise label, while Ellis had run his own pirate radio station and started Splash Records a year earlier with his own release as Undercover Agent, "Barracuda/Rougher Part 3".

Juice's first release was Undercover Agent's massive "Oh Gosh" (not to be confused with the 23 other drum 'n' bass tracks that share its title) which rode an enormous bassline straight to the middle of every Junglist dancefloor in Britain. As Daz on Splash, Ellis had another dancefloor hit with the hard drums and pro-cannabis sample of "Identity" (1995). Ellis would really make his name, though, with a release for Deejay Records as Splash, "Babylon" (1995). With Space Age electronic sounds, an "Amen" break cut with stuttering snares, roots reggae samples and Cerberus barking while guarding the gates of Hell, "Babylon" became an instant classic of militant drum 'n' bass.

Undercover Agent With the Kriminal World's "World Mash Up" (1995) was the echo-chambered follow-up to "Babylon" and was released on Suburban Base. Ellis and Darren Hickey released the "Amen" burners "Baad Boy Sound/Inspiration" and "Brothers and Sisters/Assembly Line" (both 1995) as M.T.S. More of Daz Ellis' butt-shaking bottom end followed in the form of Undercover Agent's Masters at Work-sampling "Bass Kick" (1996) and "Dangerous/Dream" (1996).

Ellis was not the only Juice artist capable of working up a frenzy on the dancefloor, though. Embee's bass bombing "Is It Good Enough For Ya" (1996) was one of jump-up Jungle's more effective and creative re-interpretations of gangsta hip-hop's booming low-end frequencies, while Majistrate's "Under Attack" (1997) and his earlier "Pressurous" (1995) single for Splash retained the labels' rolling blueprints to perfection.

Even as drum 'n' bass dismissed breakbeats in favour of rigid two-step beats, Juice and Splash stayed true to the cause of dubwise basslines and stepping beats with records like Embee's "Get Funky in the Place", Undercover Agent's "Five Tones", M.T.S.'s "Vengeance/The Instigator" and Majistrate's "Let It Off" (all 1997). M.T.S.'s "Hard Disk" (1997) broadened their sound with the introduction of old-school Belgian Hardcore terror riffs on top of the usual frantic rolling beats. With vicious mixes of "Hard Disk", "Babylon" and "Oh Gosh" by DJ Zinc, Daz and Swift respectively, the remix EP, **Way of Life** (1998), was a manifesto for the old virtues of crashing beats and rumbling b-lines. Further affirmation of the eternal bad bwoy principles could be found on the excellent **Splash Collective** EPs, the best of which was Volume 3 (1998) which featured furious "Amen" breaks and deadly bass tones.

Undercover Agent's "Crazy Shit/Everytin's Ready" (1999), however, appended his traditional hip-hop samples to a rigid beat and a squelching bassline which proved that the two-step victory over polyrhythm was nearly complete.

◉ Various Artists Way of Life   Juice,1998

With killer remixes of classics like "Oh Gosh", "Babylon" and "Hard Disk", this six-track EP proved that drum 'n' bass could still rock bells despite the cyborg temper tantrums of Techstep.

Jumping Jack Frost/ V Records

O ne of the mainstays of drum 'n' bass, Jumping Jack Frost has had a huge influence on the music, but with little of the fanfare that other pioneers attract. He got his start by playing rare groove tracks on Brixton's pirate station, Passion FM, and he soon became one of the first south London pirate DJs to play Acid House. He progressed to playing major events like Sunrise and Energy and soon became one of the most popular breakbeat DJs on the scene.

A collaboration with DJ SS, "Pornography" (1993), was his first track. Sampling Ecstasy, Passion & Pain's disco classic, "Touch and Go" on top of a cheap and cheerful keyboard riff and James Brown's "Funky Drummer" beat, "Pornography" was a brilliant example of Hardcore's promiscuity.

As Hardcore was splintering into Jungle, drum 'n' bass and Happy Hardcore, Frost hooked up with old friend Bryan Gee and formed V Records in 1993. The label's first release was an EP by two unknowns from Bristol calling themselves The Deceivers. The **Fatal Dose** EP (1993) marked the arrival of Roni Size and DJ Krust on the scene and the West Country duo would herald V's position of pre-eminence with Size's "It's a Jazz Thing" and Krust's "Jazz Note" (both 1994).

Kicking off V's Philly Blunt imprint, Frost produced one of the definitive Jungle tracks with "The Burial" (1994) released under his Leviticus guise. Riding the "Think" beat, Frost looped the same sample of Foxy's "Mademoiselle" that Roni Size used on "Music Box" and punctuated it with a killer ragga sample and some diva vocals courtesy of his sister Yolanda. Philly Blunt represented the more roughneck side of V's jazzy

cool, and Size (as Firefox) followed the boss' example with the eternal floor-filler "Warning" (1994) and the mind-boggling rhythm manipulation of "Bonanza Kid" (1995).

V, meanwhile, continued to define cutting-edge drum 'n' bass with records like Krust's militantly minimal "Set Speed" (1995) and the post-industrial holocaust of his "Warhead" (1997) and Ed Rush & Optical's "Funktion/Naked Lunch" (1998). Despite some weak beats, the **V Classic** compilation (1997) made clear the label's claims to greatness with tracks from Size, Krust, Dillinja, Lemon D and Ray Keith. **Planet V** (1999) was the follow-up and featured Frost's (aka The Punisher) wicked "Resident Evil".

V also provided a platform for other Bristol artists like DJ Die and DJ Suv. The two collaborated on "Play It For Me" and "Get on Down/Out of Sight" (both 1996) and "War and Peace" (1997) which was featured on **V Classic**. As a solo artist, Die released the dark stepper "Reincarnations" (1996), on Full Cycle, as well as "Something Special" (1997) and the techy "Clear Skyz/Reminisce"(1998) for V.

Meanwhile, Suv's **V Beat** EP (1998) was a classic mish-mash of voices from the lunatic fringe, "Ride Your Pony" gun shots, all sorts of bass gurgles, urban jungle coos and caws on top of a toe-tapping riddim which had the bong-hot massive screaming for rewinds.

⊙**Leviticus "The Burial"**   Philly Blunt, 1994

One of the undisputed classics of the genre, "The Burial" encapsulates nearly everything worth remembering from the last three decades of black music.

Ray Keith

Like nearly all of his fellow original Junglists, Ray Keith started DJing in his teens playing soul, hip-hop and rare groove. Following the Acid House explosion to the capital, Keith landed a gig at the Crazy Club at The Astoria, started working at City Sounds and Blackmarket Records and has been involved with the inner machinations of the breakbeat scene ever since.

The first track to get him noticed was an unsolicited mix of Orbital's "Chime" (1990) which became a Grooverider staple and was eventually released by Orbital's label ffrr as an official mix. A series of remixes including his definitive rework of Subnation's panic song classic "Scottie" (1993) and re-interpretations of Shades of Rhythm's "Sweet Sensations" and "Peace Sign" (both 1993) for Labello Blanco followed, but his major breakthrough as a producer was "Terrorist" (1994) which he released in collaboration with engineer Gavin Cheung (aka Nookie) on Moving Shadow as Renegade. Opening with elegiac piano chords,

"Terrorist" quickly became a cauldron of dense bass effects and an "Amen" break. It was the secondary breaks that ran in tandem with the main "Amen" break that really set "Terrorist" apart, though, by giving the track both added propulsion and added tension.

Renegade Terrorist Two's "Sing (Time)" (1995) filled out the low-end minimalism with guitar loops courtesy of Pink Floyd and vocal swatches, but the rupturing bass returned with the Nina Simone-sampling "Rinse/Yes Yes" (1995) on his new label Dred. The most dance-floor-friendly of his three labels, Dred was responsible for rolling anthems like Terrorist's "Amen" monster "Chopper" (1996) and Aven's "Woo Tang" (1997) as well as the Techstep in dub sound of Dark Soldier's "Dark Soldier" (1997).

The real technoid fury was reserved for his Penny Black imprint, however. Releases like Twisted Anger's "Society" and "Techno Funk" (both 1997) explored the most nihilistic parameters of Reese bass and rhythmic white noise. The **Breakage Volume 1** compilation (1997) collected only the most virulent strain of the Techstep bug where so many of its contemporaries seemed to be merely the placebo.

While Keith released a couple of EPs on his ambient label, UFO, his heart didn't really seem to be in it. Instead, Keith learned how to engineer and loaned his crash-test beats and concussive basslines to labels like V ("Do It/The Reckoning (Remix)") and Emotif (the collaboration with Elementz of Noise, "Neon/D4 Toxic Waste") (both 1998).

⊙**Various Artists Classified**   Dred,1997

A fine collection of Techstep textures combined with jump-up dynamics.

❶**Various Artists Breakage Volume 1**   Penny Black,1997

The world's first postage stamp may not be the most potent symbol of snarling, metallic drum 'n' bass, but this compilation of Penny Black material will satisfy any low-end extremist.

Kemet Crew

U nlike pop Egyptologists like Earth, Wind & Fire, Jungle's premier champions of black culture the Kemet Crew didn't peddle fey spirituality and brotherhood bromides or parade around in silly costumes. Instead, Nation of Islam disciples James and Mark X wore sensible black turtlenecks and let the breakbeats speak for themselves as both a connection to a centuries-old historical legacy and a unifying force that transcended the boundaries of race and class.

Their Third Party/Kemet label was started in 1992 by James after working for Paul Chambers' Ibiza label. He continued using his Noise Factory moniker for Third Party releases like "Set Me Free/The Fire/Skin Teeth" (1992) which combined primitive collage techniques with roots reggae and Fleetwood Mac samples. The awesome "Breakage #4" was the featured cut on Noise Factory's edgy **The Capsule** EP (1993) which was one of the pivotal records in the transition between Hardcore and Jungle.

After getting turned away from one too many raves because of their colour, James and Mark named themselves after the proper name of ancient Egypt and marked the end of the utopian rave dream with Family of Intelligence's "Champion of Champions" (1994). Beginning with tense strings and woodblock percussion, "Champion of Champions" soon erupted into a brutal soundbwoy murder metaphor from a dancehall in Spanish Town that seemed aimed straight at the rave promoter's head. Not quite as uncompromising was the Brain Killers' "Screw Face" (1994) which started off with a werewolf howl before taming the "Amen" break with catchy secondary breaks that magnified Jungle's percussive aspect rather than its ferocity.

There were some soulful and jazzy moments on the Kemet Crew's **Champion Jungle Sound** album (1995), but it was mostly concerned with creating a militant, steppers' vibe. With tracks like "The Box Reopens" and help from one of the original bad bwoys Remarc, **Champion Jungle Sound** succeeded so well in creating a roughneck exhilaration that they even proclaimed, "Jungle, I run it." Unfortunately, they hadn't learned the lesson of General Levy's notorious "I run tings" boast and quickly disappeared from view, although the label made a strong comeback in 1998 with Lazarus' devastating jump-up track, "Strong".

◉ Champion Jungle Sound   Parousia,1995

The sound of Jungle militancy and one of the few successful single-artist records the genre has produced.

Kenny Ken

T he moral guardians who think that dance music is good for nothing but encouraging criminal behaviour should lend an ear to the tale of jump-up don Kenny Ken. After a youth spent in and out of jail, Kenny Ken turned to DJing and an apprenticeship with Dem 2 DJs as a way of going straight in 1988. A year later he had secured a prime slot on pirate station Centreforce, became a fixture on the rave scene and left prison behind for good.

In 1992, Ken was one of the residents at the Roast club, which, along with Rage, transmuted Hardcore into Jungle. A year later he was a resident at AWOL and became one of the architects of the jump-up sound with fellow AWOL DJs Randall, Mickey Finn, Dr. S

Gachet and Darren Jay. The "Amen" roughness, the echoes of reggae's famous "Stalag 17" and the ferocious sub-bass of DRS & Kenny
Ken's "Everyman" (1994) were aimed at directly at AWOL's dancefloor
and quickly became an anthem.

In 1996 he started his Mix 'n' Blen label with the debut release
by South Londoners G-Squad. "Coppershot/Bounce" was an enormous collision between the metallic keyboards and industrial bass of
Techstep and swingbeat samples from K7 and Zhané. A collaboration with teenaged Brightonian DJ Mace, "Reminiscence/Clap to
This" (1997), was a nice little roller with rather too obvious hip-hop
samples.

With G-Squad, Ken started the Cold Steel label in 1997 with the
acid tones and Reese bass of tracks like "High and Dry" and "Jo
Bad" (both 1997). He abandoned the technoid flirtations altogether
with the mashed-up "Amen" breaks of "So Much Trouble" (1997), a
collaboration with Cool Breeze on Labello Blanco. Ken's younger
brother (aka Stingray) tried to fuse the excitement of jump-up with
the nightmarish precision of Techstep on "Venom/Flight Control"
(1998), while Ken's own "Project One/Watertight" (1998) reconciled
his obvious passion for the hyped-up electricity of the hip-
hop/ragga-influenced style with the fact that the taste-makers left
that style for dead in their endless quest to purge the rave from its
bloodline.

⊙**DRS & Kenny Ken "Everyman"**   Rugged Vinyl,1994

A killer combination of "Amen" beats, rolling percussion, roots reggae
and rave electronics that lived up to the promise of Jungle's soundclash
dynamics.

◉**Various Artists Kenny Ken Presents Full Force**   Full Force,1998

One of the better commercially available testaments to Kenny Ken's
skills behind the wheels of steel.

Krome & Time

Five-year veterans on the reggae sound system scene by the time of their first record, DJ Krome & Mr. Time produced some of the most electrifying singles of early breakbeat Hardcore. Their debut single was "This Sound Is For The Underground/Manic Stampede" (1992) for Suburban Base which was a thrill ride on their sound system chops that became even more invigorating with DJ Hype's "Sandringham Road Mix" of "Manic Stampede" and its catalytic sample of Roxanne Shanté.

Their sophomore effort, "The Slammer/Into the Night" (1993), was even better. The enormous breakdown of "The Slammer" was built around a sample of disco vocalist Nona Hendryx that was morphed until she lost all of her toughness and became a warbling songbird singing an ode to ecstatic freefall: "The dance that we're dancing, now who's in control". The equally excellent "Virtual Reality" (1993) followed on the **Sub Plates Volume 2** compilation and confirmed their reputation as some of Hardcore's best producers.

In 1994 they started their own Tearin' Vinyl label and hit immediately with the all-time classic "License". Rolling through three different breaks and using samples of Buju Banton and one from one of their own sound system tapes, "License" was all about tearing the rave to shreds. "Ganja Man" (1995) carried Hardcore's tradition of gratuitous drug references into the Jungle as well as its polyrhythmic exuberance to produce another "Amen" classic. More bad bwoy bizness came in the form of the gangsta anthem "Studio One Lik" (1995).

With the release of "Mad Funk" (1995), Krome & Time moved away from their ragga roots and towards a more pronounced hip-hop feel. "Cyber Funkin'" and "The Hood" (both 1996) continued this pattern as

Krome & Time, like most of their fellow Junglists, moved away from not only the sound, but the whole aesthetic, that had made them so exciting in the first place. "Nonstop Rocking" (1997) was close to living up to its title and Tearin' Vinyl releases like DJ Ash's "Applause for the Cause" (1997) followed the leaders.

⊙ **"The Slammer"**   Suburban Base, 1993

It's not as paranoid as some of the darkside records from the same period, but "The Slammer" is just as remarkable in its equation of thrills and chills.

DJ Krust

While Roni Size tends to accumulate most of the column inches in the dance mags, his long-time collaborator and partner in Reprazent, DJ Krust, is every bit the innovator that his more illustrious colleague is. Moving in tandem with Size, Krust has been responsible for bringing a more minimal sound to drum 'n' bass at the same time as unintentionally helping to instigate the "intelligent" movement with his rare groove sensibility.

Krust was one of the first representatives of "the Bristol sound" to taste commercial success. As a member of the Fresh Four (along with his brother Flynn – of Flynn & Flora – DJ Suv and Judge), Krust hit the British Top Ten with a Smith & Mighty-produced cover of Rose Royce's "Wishing on a Star" (1989). Despite crazy money being thrown at them, the group quickly disappeared from the public eye and Krust soon began frequenting the West Country's extensive free party scene where he was turned on to Hardcore and met Size.

Soon afterwards, the two set up Where's The Party Records (which became Full Cycle) and hooked up with Bryan Gee's and Jumping Jack Frost's V Records. V's first release was Size and Krust's **The Fatal Dose** EP (1993), which they released as The Deceivers. The one or two melodic samples in Krust's otherwise furiously percussive "Jazz Note" (1994) were mis-heard as the clarion call for a new age of traditional musicality in breakbeat music. Krust continued his manic syncopation and deep bass exploration with tracks like "Quiz Show", "Jazz Note II" and "Set Speed" (all 1994), which expounded on and expanded hip-hop's sampladelic low-end theories.

Krust saved his most viscerally exciting dialogues with hip-hop for his rinsing outings on Dope Dragon and Philly Blunt. His recordings with Size (as Gang Related and Mask) like **The Terrordome** EP, "Oh My Gosh!" (both 1994), "Ready Or Not", **Reasons For Living** EP (both 1995), "Concentration", "Dictation" and "One Time/Tear It Up" (all 1996) were stripped down to the bare essentials of detonating bass bombs and thrilling breakbeats, with nary a Fender Rhodes sample in sight. His outings on Philly Blunt as Glamour Gold (again usually with Roni Size, who recorded as Firefox) were similarly hardstepping tracks that either tore the listener to shreds with flying drum shrapnel (1996's "Check Da Skills" and "You Can Run") or glided along with the smooth élan of Snoop Doggy Dogg's low rider (1996's "Gangsta"). Following a similar pattern, his astounding remix of Flynn & Flora's "Bass Speaker" (1996) kicked holes in speakers just like its Rakim sample suggested it would.

Krust's music became even more apocalyptic with his remix of his own "Maintain", "Soul in Motion", "Warhead" and the **Genetic Manipulation** EP (all 1997). All glowering basslines and rigid drums caught in a swamp of metal shavings, these tracks were Krust's take on the Techstep sound and showed that he was equally adept at the soulful and the post-human. The **Rearrange It** EP (1998) attempted to blend this sound with the lush life sound of Size's Reprazent project on which Krust contributed strings and atmospheres. On the **True Stories** EP (1998), Krust was trying to introduce a sense of mystery and suspense that was sorely missing from the two-strep onslaught. With a tune circulating on dubplate that samples *The A-Team*, Krust's future plans seem to be assured of coming together.

⊙ Genetic Manipulation EP   Full Cycle, 1997

Four tracks of gruesome robo-funk that proved Techstep was here to stay.

⊙ Various Artists Wayz of the Dragon   Dope Dragon, 1998

This essential compilation of hip-hop sampling hardsteppers features several Krust cuts recorded under his Gang Related alias.

L Double/Flex Records

Perhaps more than anyone, Yorkshire's finest Junglist, L Double, can say he was there from the very beginning. Influenced by hip-hop DJs like Cash Money and Aladdin, the reggae sound systems of Bradford and Huddersfield and the industrial tradition of Sheffield, he became a member of the seminal bleep and bass trio Unique 3 at the age of 17 in 1988.

Comprised of nothing but a drum machine loop, a glacial motif played on a tinny synth and knock-your-wind-out sub-bass, "The Theme" (1989) was one of the pivotal tracks in the creation of an original strain of British rave music outside of the parameters laid down by the House and Techno synods in Chicago and Detroit. The chart-bothering follow-up, "Weight for the Bass" (1989), was similarly minimal with a cheesy piano vamp providing the only camouflage for the brutally sparse bottom end. Although their singles and album, **Jus Unique** (1990), laid down the foundations for what would become Hardcore, Unique 3 were dumped from their label (Virgin) just as rave culture was producing a succession of Top 20 singles.

After a couple of low-key years where he would cut up Shabba Ranks records over accelerated breakbeats at parties around Leeds, L Double re-emerged in 1994 as the main man behind Flex Records. The label's first release was Da Intalex's awesome fusion of deep, deep bass, steppers' beats and diva vocals, "What Ya Gonna Do". The remixes featured tearing reworks by Nasty Jungle (L Double and Deadly D) who have also famously remixed 4 Hero's "Universal Love" (1995). Other outside projects for L Double have included the snapping snare workout of "Da Base II Dark" (1994) recorded as Asylum for Metalheadz and outings as Low Key Movements for Reinforced.

Yet another L Double alias is The Dubster which saw the release of the swaggering, b-boy braggadocio of "Retreat" (1994). L Double's "Little Rollers Volume 1" (1995) kept the cardiac drums and bass bombs of "Retreat", but fleshed out the bottom end with vocal samples out of a Jamaican dancehall. The gangsta lean continued on his huge collaboration with Shy FX, "The Shit" (1995) which was a torrent of percussion sounds and bass effects. "Break It Down" and "The Rider" (both 1996) kept L Double pressure sealed in his bass cauldron, while Sappo's "Oh Gosh" (1996) brought Flex into contact with the acid droid sound of Techstep.

While keeping the rolling drums, the Flex sound has become progressively more metallic with records like Neo's "Provider/Zone" and Keen's "Theory/Return" (both 1997). Imprints like Rinse Out and Rollers have kept the hip-hop vibes alive, however, with dancefloor anthems like Sappo's "Ding Dong Bass" (1996) and Darkman's "Let's Roll" (1997).

⊙ **L Double "Little Rollers Volume 1"**   Flex,1995

With his roots in hip-hop, L Double is a master of the breakbeat and this might be his most pulsating track. Featured on **SOUR's Journeys Into Jungle** (1995) compilation.

Labello Blanco

R un by Andy Swallow and Jimmy Jungle, Labello Blanco was one of the first labels to develop a ragga-breakbeat style and can thus lay a claim to be one of the first strictly Junglist labels. Strictly Rockers (aka Danny Coffey of Endemic Void) set samples of toasting dancehall DJs to speeded-up breakbeats on records like "Strictly Rocking" (1991), the **Murder** EP (1992) and "Lightning and Thunder" (1993), while Bug Kann & the Plastic Jam's "Made in 2 Minutes" (1992) and "9 MM" (1994) did the same with hip-hop samples. Unlike the predominant rave style of The Prodigy or SL2, however, the synth riffs and piano samples were downplayed or done away with altogether to produce a more strictly rhythmic, less euphoric music.

Smokey Joe's **Bad Boy** EP (1993) followed suit with an explicitly funky, rather than ravey, feel as did his awesome "Special Request" (1994). 88.3 Featuring Lisa May (aka Aphrodite and Mickey Finn), meanwhile, took Jungle out of the hands of the bad men and ragga roughnecks with their stirring cover of Rose Royce's "Wishing on a Star" (1994). Badman's "War in '94" (1994), however, restored business as usual with a stepper's version of the famous horn sample from Lafayette Afro-Rock Band's "Darkest Light" used by Public Enemy and growling ragga-chat. Following a similar formula, Prizna Featuring the Demolition Man's "Fire" (1994) became the label's biggest hit by making the lower reaches of the Top 40 on the strength of hyper-kinetic MCing and a no-nonsense bassline.

Prizna soon formed their own Kickin' Underground Sound label and released more rootsical tracks like "10,000 Babylong" (1995) and "River Nile" (1996). Labello Blanco, meanwhile, released "Rogue Unit Jam" (1995) by former Foul Play member Steve Gurley and "Gladi-wax" (1995) by Dr. S Gachet. While Labello's Urban Gorilla imprint has released tracks by Ray Keith and Nookie, the label has been over-shadowed since drum 'n' bass started to take the break out of break-beat and releases like Rogue Unit's "Jazz Steppin'/Secret Motion" (1998) and remixes of Subnation's immortal panic song "Scottie" (1998) have been fairly uneventful.

⦿ Various Artists Jungle Massive 3   Labello Blanco,1995

An excellent compilation of some of 1994's biggest tracks like Krome & Time's "Ganja Man" and Prizna's "Fire".

Lemon D

Taking his *nom de disque* from the French newspaper *Le Monde*, the artist formerly known as Kevin King has consistently taken the drum 'n' bass path less followed. One of breakbeat's leading eclectics, Lemon D is one of the rare producers capable of creating both blinding rinse-outs and delicate Garage-influenced numbers without opting for a mealy-mouthed middle ground.

Getting into rave at the turn of the '90s, Lemon D started his own Planet Earth label in 1993. Releases like the **Pursuit of Vision** and **Toxic Rhythms** EPs showed that Lemon D was capable of balancing nose-bleed Techno and breakbeats with finesse. "Down With the Lights/Step 1-2 1-2" (1994) released on Hardleaders under his Souljah moniker was all kamikaze bass swoops and hell-for-leather drums. His breakthrough, though, was the "Feel It/Don't Make Me Wait/Bad Man" 12" (1995) on Conqueror which made Jungle's snare detonations the sound of James

Brown with ants in his pants. The follow-up, the **Jah Love** EP (1995), displayed his broad sound palette with an integration of Deep House and drum 'n' bass on "Manhattan Melody" (if only Alex Reece were this good).

Jah Love pricked up Goldie's ears and he released the lazy insouciance of "Urban Style Music/This Is LA" (1995) on his Metalheadz label. More airy jazziance continued on "I Can't Stop/Change" (1996) for the V label, while "The Going Gets Tough/Subphonic" (1996) on Grooverider's Prototype label gave vent to his dark side. The real aggression, though, was reserved for his output on the Valve and Pain labels that he formed with long-time friend Dillinja. "12.01" (1997) featured clanging drums and fearsome acid synth drones, while "One Out of Many" (1997) trapped his jazzy sensibilities in a airless mountain cave without any natural light. More brutality, albeit with a gangsta lean and a pimp stroll, appeared on his debut album, Souljah's **Urbanology** (1997).

◉ Souljah Urbanology   Hard Leaders,1997

There's some stylistic variation, but mostly this album is a rough ride across an uncompromising drumscape.

Lenny Dee/
Industrial Strength

Not to be confused with his namesake, the Canadian king of easy listening, Hardcore's Lenny Dee is New York's king of queasy listening. From the same working-class Brooklyn neighbourhoods that spawned the uncompromising Techno of Joey Beltram and Frankie Bones, Lenny Dee has molded Hardcore into a muscular, often brutal form of dance music that conflates flesh, machine and militarism. If this sounds a lot like Heavy Metal, the coincidence is entirely intentional: like Beltram, Dee was a Black Sabbath fiend before discovering the synthesizer and he has since remixed New York thrash band Corrosion of Conformity.

When Dee and Beltram did discover the synthesizer, they started off making Electro and Freestyle tracks and then became two of the mainstays at legendary New York House label NuGroove. Working with Victor Simonelli as Critical Rhythm, Dee helped establish the jazzy synth pad sound that became synonymous with NuGroove. Working with Frankie Bones, Dee released the enormous "Just as I Got You" (1990) as Looney Tunes for XL Records and the influential **Looney Tunes Volume 1** (1991) album.

Tiring of formulaic House, Dee formed Industrial Strength Records in 1992 initially to release the awesome "We Have Arrived" by Frankfurt's Mescalinum United. Dee's own "Blood of an English Muffin" (1992) reduced Techno to pounding kick drums and the mutant bass drones of the Roland Juno synthesizer and helped kick-start the Dutch Gabba scene. Dee continued making Hardcore that took the term literally on tracks like DJ Skinhead's "Extreme Terror" (1994) which took a wild keyboard riff and a buzzing synth drone for a death ride on poinging beats.

In collaboration with Australia's Bloody Fist label, Industrial Strength released Nasenbluten's (German for nosebleed) frighteningly intense **100% No Soul Guaranteed** (1995) double album whose "Blows T' the Nose" surrounded Chuck D in a whiteout of synth *Sturm und Drang*, chest-caving low-end terror riffs and hyper-speed James Brown breakbeats that made Jungle sound like Debussy. The combination of hip-hop samples and Oi! stomp continued on Delta 9's **Disco Inferno** and **Doomzday Celebration** (both 1996) EPs which savaged American TV evangelists along with the band's synths.

Industrial Strength's sub-label Ruff Beats was home to more hip-hop savagery in the form of Lenny Dee's **Spontaneous Combustion** EP (1996) and DJ Demigod's **D-Day** and **OG Live** EPs (both 1997). DJ Narcotic vs. UVC's "Step Into the Pit" and DJ Freak's "I Will Fight" (both 1998) brought Speedcore's crypto-fascist infatuation with machinery and weaponry to the fore, while the sample of Jack Nicholson playing American labour leader Jimmy Hoffa on Lenny Dee's "Scratch Junkies" (1998) was an explicit nod to the unarticulated class consciousness that underpinned self-consciously prole scenes like Hardcore and speed metal.

> ◉ **Various Artists Industrial F**kin'**
> **Strength Volumes 1 and 2**   Industrial Strength, 1997, 1998
>
> Two excellent collections of jack-hammer drums, oscillators and basslines with some witty samples thrown in for good measure.

LTJ Bukem

E ven the hardest and most uncompromising of tough-guy Jungle dons owes a debt of gratitude to the laid-back vibes and soothing mysticsm of LTJ Bukem. While Bukem may be the godfather of such mellow sub-genres as Jazzstep, "artcore" and "intelligent Jungle", he was also responsible for bringing the archetypal tearing drum break – the "Amen" break – into drum 'n' bass, thus launching hundreds of mean and moody bad-bwoy tracks.

LTJ Bukem was born Danny Williamson in Croydon and raised in Watford where classical piano lessons and his teacher's Lonnie Liston Smith records gave him his enduring love for the sound of the Fender Rhodes keyboard, samples of which have graced almost all of his records from "Demon's Theme" (1991) to the **Mystical Realms** EP (1998). When he wasn't memorising Tchaikovsky arpeggios, Williamson was watching *Hawaii Five-O*, whose catch-phrase – "Book 'em Danno" – gave him half of his *nom de disque* (the rest is a perversion of the Italian for "the DJ".

After DJing in local sound systems and then graduating to large-scale raves like Raindance in Essex, Bukem released his debut single, "Logical Progression", on Vinyl Mania in 1990, which previewed his

patented mixture of Gilles Peterson-style rare groove ambience with Hardcore's hyper-speed drums. The next year "Demon's Theme" appeared on his own label, Good Looking, and permanently altered the face of breakbeat music with the juxtaposition of a propulsive rhythm with the gelatinous sound of the Rhodes. The warm keyboard and string sounds of 1992's "Atlantis (I Need You)" and 1993's "Music" were similarly against the flow of the prevailing trend for huge, almost siren-like keyboard riffs and marked the beginning of Jungle/Hardcore's transition to the more "sophisticated" music of drum 'n' bass.

The lush string arrangement and oozing synth pads of "Music" were layered on top of what has now become the quintessential breakbeat. Taken from a hopelessly obscure gospel instrumental – The Winstons' "Amen Brother" – that was also used by Mantronix on his 1988 hip-hop cut-up "King of the Beats", the "Amen" break provided a startling counterpoint to Bukem's jazzy textures. This combination of jazz-fusion instrumentation and breakbeat innovation continued on his 1995 single, "Horizons". Using a James Brown drum break first used by Wax Doctor on "Kid Caprice" that has since become *the* break to use on more atmospheric drum 'n' bass tracks, Bukem fleshed out his Lonnie Liston Smith and Roy Ayers soundbites with a sample of the writer Maya Angelou.

Bukem firmly established himself as the main mover of jazzy drum 'n' bass when he started the now legendary Speed Club with Fabio at the Mars Bar in London in late 1994. With Bukem playing sets that verged on total Ambience and Fabio playing tracks infested with the Rhodes and clavinet samples that would become the hallmarks of Jazz-step, Speed became the headquarters for a mini-scene fed up with the heavy vibes of Darkside and ragga-chat and launched the major-label trajectory of artists like Photek, Source Direct and Alex Reece.

While Bukem's own output has been relatively small (aside from two tracks on his two **Earth** compilations, the fine, if a bit clinical, **Mystical Realms** EP [1998] was his first release since "Horizons"), his Good Looking/Looking Good labels have continued to release scene-defining records by the likes of Aquarius (aka Photek), PFM, Blame and Peshay. Heavily featuring tracks from his two labels (including "Demon's Theme" and "Music"), his **Logical Progression (1996)** compilation was a commercial and critical blockbuster that neatly delineated the parameters of aquatint drum 'n' bass and confirmed Bukem's position as one of drum 'n' bass' most influential personalities.

⊙ Logical Progression Volume 1   Good Looking/London, 1996

Although it doesn't include the oceanic "Atlantis (I Need You)", this is the place to find the best of Bukem's output ("Demon's Theme", "Music" and "Horizons") with the added bonus of essential tracks by Aquarius, Chameleon and PFM.

Marvellous Cain

While everyone around him was going "intelligent" and sampling lame jazz-fusion records, Marvellous Marvin Cain was partying like it was 1993 and sampling ragga's don gorgons. Marvellous Cain took the jump-up scene by storm in 1995 with his debut single "Hitman" on IQ Records. With a complete disregard for fashion, Cain sampled Cutty Ranks' enormous dancehall hit "Limb By Limb" on top of blistering "Amen" drums and ballistic bass to produce the year's biggest dancefloor anthem.

Cain continued to mash up the dance with "Dub Plate Style/Jump Up" (1995) for Suburban Base. Following the same path of using ragga's soundboy murder metaphors to provide a contact high of rhetorical violence for the thrill-seekers, "Dub Plate Style" was almost as visceral as "Hitman" and almost as big. Following a re-issue of "Hitman" with the original version of "Limb By Limb" and mixes from DJ SS, his debut album, **Gun Talk** (1996), featured exclusive vocals from stars of the Jamaican dancehall like Cutty Ranks, Frankie Paul and Daddy Freddy. With its rude bwoy discourse and sound system noises, **Gun Talk** brought the Yard to London and echoed Kingston's obsession with the bass as the sound of menace and dread.

Cain started his Runninz label in 1996 with the fairly facile "Hi Chapparal" which sampled the theme from the old Western TV series. Far better was his collaboration with Bizzy B on his new label Macca, "Everyday Junglist" (1996), which began with the groove from Stetsasonic's "Talkin' All That Jazz" before collapsing into a sparse, bleak drumscape with only a torpedoing bassline as ornamentation. Libra's "Nu Musik" (1996) was similarly minimal and hollow-sounding – the drums and the bass never really got going and felt as if its life-force was drained away.

Cain continued to distance himself from the crowd-pleasing jump-up style with the blizzard of analogue sound effects on Notorious' "Action/Hard Drive" (1997). The **Full Velocity EP** (1997) showcased the same muddy dynamics of "Nu Musik" and "Everyday Junglist", but with some acidic squelch running underneath for good measure.

⊙ **"Hitman"** IQ, 1995

Cutty Ranks' "Limb By Limb" was pretty brutal in its original form based on ragga's ever-popular "Pepper Seed" riddim, but with flailing "Amen" snares it was as awesomely visceral as any record ever made.

Matrix

Since the apotheosis of Alex Reece's "Pulp Fiction" in 1995, drum 'n' bass has slowly but surely backed away from the bionic-funky-drummer sound of its mainstream cross-over towards the rigid rhythms of the two-step stomp. In the hands of producers like Matrix, drum 'n' bass' breakbeat science has been replaced by the sound of engineers splitting hairs in the pursuit of sonic perfection.

The brother of the similarly hyped Optical, Matrix (aka Jamie Quinn) was first turned on to dance music through the Spiral Tribe whom he followed around the country as if they were the Grateful Dead. Matrix claims that his hero is Miles Davis, but any traces of jazz-funk in his music have been processed and re-processed until the music is so thick with swampy, fetid basslines and pristine, digital clockwork beats that it resembles the Terminator with a head cold.

The birth of the gruel was "Area 39" (1996), a punishing 12" released on DJ SS's Formation records. More No U Turn-style sketches of pain followed on Formation's more experimental sub-label, New Identity. "Seabreeze/The Message '96" (1996) had absolutely nothing to do with balmy tradewinds or Grandmaster Flash, while the surfaces of "Junk/Fluid Motion" (1997) were so sterile that you could've performed an operation on them.

"The Vandal" (1997), a collaboration with Moving Shadow's Dom, had chugging, winded beats and stiff bass jabs that hit like a tired Jack Johnson. Another soundclash, this time with his brother, was "Data Life/Crossfire" (1998), which featured smooth strings gliding on top of an over-programmed rhythm. With celestial synths and a bassline more enveloping than it was bludgeoning, "Mute" (1997), which first appeared on Grooverider's **Prototype Years** compilation, was the closest Matrix would ever get to grooving in a silent way. A remix of "Mute" appeared the following year and was backed up by the crashing beats of "Convoy" as if to prove that he hadn't gone soft.

Matrix launched his Metro label with his own "Double Vision/Sedation" (1997). Marking the total victory of purist Techno's aesthetic of abstraction over the visceral excitement of rave, "Double Vision/Sedation" was all swollen electronics and distended basslines put together with an inordinate attention to detail. Metro has gone on to release tracks by Optical and Ed Rush which were models of precision, but rarely were they big fun.

⊙ **"Mute"**   Prototype, 1997

Available on the **Prototype Years** compilation, this represents either the zenith or the nadir of drum 'n' bass' cult of technique, depending on your point of view.

M Beat

No one has paid the price for Jungle's success more than producer M Beat. The creator of some excellent ragga-flavoured Jungle tunes in 1993 and 1994, he quickly became the scapegoat for Jungle's overground explosion, was shunned by the scene's main players and has since vanished from the scene.

First hitting with the massive "Rumble" (1993) for Renk Records, M Beat peppered his ragga samples with high-speed scratches and catchy piano riffs. Dancing its way into a Kingston dancehall with a sample of Buju Banton, "Boo-yacka" shouts and video game sound effects and then out to a rave in Essex, "Rumble" epitomised early Jungle's delight in the sound-for-sound's-sake play of textures and noises. "Shuffle" (1993) followed in similar fashion with a ragga DJ chatting on top of a hyper-speed "Think" break which mutated into a tearing "Amen" break and the helium squeals of disfigured divas and MCs. "Sweet Love" (1993), meanwhile, sampled smooth R&B singer Anita Baker's song of the same name.

Riding an exhortation swiped from a Terror Fabulous record, "Surrender" (1994) showed the durability of M Beat's formula and its success on the dancefloor. "Style" (1994) was more of the same, but crucially it never nodded towards the rave – it focused almost exclusively on the ragga chanting and the "Under Me Sleng Teng" bassline.

"Incredible" (1994), however, was the tune that M Beat will forever be identified with. With infectious vocals by ragga DJ General Levy, "Incredible" became Jungle's first and only Top 10 single. Soon enough, the dancehall don who had probably never been within ten miles of a rave claimed that he was "runnin' Jungle". The inevitable backlash was swift in coming. Seeking to protect their little slice of Thatcherite enterprise culture against the major labels' corporate raiders, a group of top Jungle producers calling themselves The Committee boycotted "Incredible" and DJs who played the track out. The ploy was ruthlessly effective: General Levy had issued a grovelling apology, M Beat was *persona non grata* and mainstream media attention suddenly focused on the "artier" end of Jungle.

⊙ **"Rumble"**   Renk,1993

It may be a bit sloppy, but it's also one of the most exciting and funky of all of the ragga Jungle tracks. (Available on **Drum & Bass Selection 1**.)

MCs

L ike the other crucial musical development of the last thirty years – dub's use of the mixing board as an instrument – the art of MCing can trace its roots back to the Jamaican sound system culture of the late '60s/early '70s. Originally men like Count Machuki and Sir Lord Comic who would get on the mic at ska dances in the late '50s to shout song introductions or interject catch-phrases at just the right time, the "deejay" truly came into his own with U-Roy's "Wake the Town" in 1970. Instead of using catch-phrases, U-Roy chatted a long series of street-jive non-sequiturs over the top of popular records

which sent the dancehalls and Jamaican charts into a tizzy and fomented a musical revolution.

Like their Jamaican forebears, drum 'n' bass MCs are there to create intensity, to get the crowd "hyped up". Where their American cousins have become the stars of the show, Junglist MCs are still very much second fiddle to the DJ and the majority of their exhortations are to "big up the DJ" and to heighten the sensation of the music: "Oh my goosshhh", "Locked upon a roll".

The early rave MCs, however, had seemingly more connections with East End wideboys than old Kingstonians. But as Hardcore started flirting with the Jungle, the rude bwoy patois and phrasing of the dancehall dons became intermeshed with the E'd-up excitement and language of the ravers. Pirate radio MCs like Kool FM's MC Det and MCs like Moose and Navigator pioneered this syncretic style, while Don FM and No U-Turn MC Ryme Tyme stole tricks from human-beatboxing hip-hop MCs.

Although ragga MCs like General Levy and UK Apachi stole the thunder from the Junglist MCs by taking it into the charts, the greatest of all the tracks to feature an MC was DJ Hype's collaboration with GQ, "Rrrroll Da Beats" (1994). Inventing one of Jungle's great catchphrases, "Wheel up and come again, please, please, please/Absolutely 'T' for tremendous", GQ translated the coded chatter of the clubspace to vinyl and created one of Jungle's few true hooks without diluting the pure sensation of beats, textures and words that is Jungle's essence. GQ has gone on to work with other producers like Kenny Ken, L Double and Tek 9 and provided killer MCing for Mickey Finn on his **Dreamscape Vol. 2** (1997) mix.

With backing tracks from Elementz of Noize, L Double and T. Power, MC Det's **Out of Det** (1996) was the first album by an MC. Swaggering tracks like "Stick Up" and "Can't Sample Det" turned the gospel hosannahs of the original "Amen Brother" into the fervent, escapist release of gangsta chat. While MCing definitely worked best in a jump-up and Hardstep context, MCs like Conrad developed a style that flowed with the sophisticated élan of LTJ Bukem's jazz vibes, while MC Fats soothed the roughneck music he usually worked with by crooning like ragga star Pliers alongside his more Chaka Demus-like toasts. Det and Ryme Tyme explored other routes out of the narrow confines of Junglist MCing by working with Downbeat weirdos Red Snapper and by moving into production respectively.

⊙MC Det Out of Det   SOUR,1996

Featuring one of Jungle's great criminally minded tracks, "Stick Up", this is a fine album which showed how crucial MCing was to creating Junglistic excitement.

⊙Various Artists AWOL   Live Ministry of Sound,1995

A live album from the legendary Jungle club that captures the live Jungle experience featuring excellent MCing from GQ and Fearless, not to mention a chorus of air horns and whistles.

Metalheadz

F ormed in 1994 to release the VIP mix of Doc Scott's Darkcore classic "Here Comes the Drumz", Goldie's Metalheadz has since become, unsurprisingly, the most visible label in drum 'n' bass. Fortunately, this is the result not just of Goldie's high media profile, but also of the quality of the "21st century urban breakbeat music" the label releases as well.

After the auspicious beginnings of the debut which included Goldie's VIP mix of his Grooverider tribute, "Riders Ghost", on the flip, Metalheadz continued to innovate (for better or for worse) with Alex Reece's breakthrough 12", "Fresh Jive/Basic Principles" (1994). The ultra-crisp drum sound and production of "Basic Principles" would continue with the release of Reece's enormously influential "Pulp Fiction" which changed the face of drum 'n' bass by downplaying the role of splintering breaks.

Almost as break-free as Reece's tracks were the live-sounding drums of Peshay's "Psychosis" (1994) and Doc Scott's Speed anthem, "Far Away" (1994). Alex Reece's partner in crime, Wax Doctor, introduced the James Brown-derived "Kid Caprice" drums on, naturally enough, "Kid Caprice" (1995), which have since become the standard break of Ambient drum 'n' bass.

On the harder and darker front, Dillinja wreaked havoc with his **The Angels Fell** EP (1994), which is one of Hardstep's masterpieces, and J. Majik's "Your Sound" made you grab onto your seat and say, "Amen" as it went on a joyride on the wheels of steel through classic breakbeat territory. Lemon D's "Urban Style Music" (1995) echoed Dillinja's "Angels Fell" with its dark and brooding atmosphere and rough drums.

Metalheadz also brought the rigorous production styles of Photek, Source Direct and Hidden Agenda to a larger audience. Photek's stunning **Natural Born Killas** EP (1995) showed off his technical wizardry with the water-dropping-on-a-trash-can beats of "Consciousness" and his facility with Down Tempo beats on "Into the 90s". Hidden Agenda's "Is It Love?" and "Pressin' On" (both 1995) proved that you could be jazzy and funky at the same time, while Source Direct's antiseptic "A Made Up Sound" (1995) showed that there were more obsessive-compulsive producers than Photek.

After a slow start, the label grabbed 1996 by the short and curlies with Adam F's remarkable study of urban paranoia and existential dread, "Metropolis". It was followed by Ed Rush's equally dark and foreboding **Skylab** EP which was more clinical than his previous releases and foreshadowed the two-step beat that would take over in the following year with the success of such releases as Optical's "To Shape the Future" and Grooverider's windswept "The Warning" (1997).

⊙ Various Artists Platinum Breakz   Metalheadz,1996

With several epochal tracks, this compilation collects records that, for better or worse, changed the course of drum 'n' bass.

⊙ Various Artists Platinum Breakz II   Metalheadz,1997

Although it's not quite as ground-breaking as the first instalment, it does have Adam F's fabulous "Metropolis".

More Rockers/ Smith & Mighty

Along with Massive Attack, Smith & Mighty helped define the dark insouciance of what came to be known as "the Bristol sound" in the late '80s. Producers Rob Smith and Ray Mighty perfected the blend of rare groove, hip-hop, reggae, ganja, dread, Bacharach and bass that would become the sound of Britain, not just Bristol, in the '90s.

Heralding Bristol's emergence from its cardigan-indie shroud, Smith & Mighty produced Massive Attack's first single, a melancholy cover of Chaka Khan's "Any Love" (1988), as well as The Fresh Four's chart-bound cover of Rose Royce's "Wishing on a Star" (1989). Under their own name, Smith & Mighty released the languorous, off-kilter and bass-heavy covers of the Burt Bacharach and Hal David standards "Walk on By" and "Anyone Who Had a Heart" (both 1989), which made them the focus of the music industry's hype machine. Eventually signing to ffrr/London, Smith & Mighty had a fractious relationship with the label and almost disappeared from sight. Although they were involved with London for five years, only one EP, the excellent, proto-Junglist **Stepper's Delight** (1992), ever appeared under their own name and only one album, "Any Love" vocalist Carlton's **The Call Is Strong** (1991), featured their production skills.

Disillusioned, Smith lay low until hooking up with sometime Massive Attack collaborator Peter Rose to form More Rockers. Their first single, "The Rain" (1994), came out on their own More Rockers label and featured what would become their signature blend of dub stylings with Junglist tempos. Their debut album, **Dub Plate Selection Volume 1** (1995), continued this pattern with rootical Jungle that could have come from a nyabinghi session in Ocho Rios. Meanwhile, liberated from London, Smith & Mighty finally released their debut album, **Bass Is Maternal** (1995), on More Rockers to a rather lukewarm reception.

Expanding their sound, More Rockers released the digi-dub of Bristol sound system Henry & Louis on the **Rudiments** (1996) album and collaborated with LA producer The Angel and keyboardist Brian Auger on Jaz Klash's "Intrigue" (1996). More Rockers' own "1,2,3 Break/Dis That One" (1996) was a harder, more minimal brand of Hardstep Junglism than they had previously released and took them out of the reggae-influenced ghetto that they had been stuck in.

Featuring their own Bacharach covers and DJ Krust's brilliant remix of Flynn & Flora's "Bass Speaker", Smith & Mighty's contribution to the **DJ Kicks** series (1998) was a stunning overview of the history of the Bristol sound since 1988. More Rockers' **Selection 2** (1999) was another vital mash-up of reggae vocals, tearing drum breaks and Diana Ross references.

⊙ **More Rockers Dub Plate Selection Volume 1**   More Rockers,1995

Existing in the shadow of Bristol's drum 'n' bass big boys, More Rockers have pursued a visceral blend of reggae influences and rhythmic militarism.

Moving Shadow

Unquestionably one of the three most important Hardcore/Jungle/drum 'n' bass labels, Moving Shadow was founded by Rob Playford in Stevenage, Hertfordshire in 1990. Sold by Playford out of the back of his car, the label's first releases like Earth Leakage Trip's "No Idea", DVuS's "The Last E" and Kaotic Chemistry's "Five in One Night" and "Space Cakes" were characterised by the incredibly cheap-sounding keyboards and gratuitous drug references that were the hallmark of all early British rave tracks.

The first Moving Shadow masterpiece was 2 Bad Mice's remix of Blame's "Music Takes You", "2 Bad Mice Take You" (1992), which orchestrated a sample of Loleatta Holloway on laughing gas, huge keyboard vamps and scratching at 140 bpm into an epic of blissed-out momentum. 2 Bad Mice was one of Playford's numerous aliases (which also included Cosmo & Dibs, a duo with Steve Thrower, and Kaotic Chemistry, with Sean O'Keefe and Simon Colebrooke) and the label boss (along with O'Keefe) was responsible for the label's next big success – 2 Bad Mice's **Hold It Down** EP (1992) which included the title track, "Bombscare" and "Waremouse". These tracks went even further than "2 Bad Mice Take You" in their explorations of high-speed scratchadelia and the limits of oscillating synth riffs.

Moving Shadow continued to define the sound of Hardcore with Kaotic Chemistry's "Drum Trip II" (1992) and Hyper-on Experience's **Keep It In the Family EP** (1992) which included the amazing "Assention", a track that sounded like the World Famous Supreme Team caught in a William Friedkin car chase sequence. The label's finest explorations of super-sonic hip-hop, however, were DJ Trax's (Rob Playford and Devro Davies) cut-up of Masta Ace, Grandmaster Flash

and skanking guitar, "We Rock the Most" (1992), and Mixrace's utterly preposterous "Mixrace Outta Hand" (1993).

As Darkcore took over the dancefloors, Moving Shadow kept pace with 2 Bad Mice's "Mass Confusion" (1993) and Hyper-on Experience's gothic "Lords of the Null Lines" (1993). But just as the dark sound was reaching its creative climax, Moving Shadow laid the foundations of the "artcore" of the years to come with Foul Play's gorgeous and pin-sharp "Open Your Mind (Foul Play Remix)" (1993) and Omni Trio's "Mystic Stepper" and "Renegade Snares" (both 1993). Deep Blue's (Sean O'Keefe) "Helicopter Tune" (1994) sped up a conga sample until it sounded like the spinning chopper blades suggested by the title.

With groups like Aqua Sky, E-Z Rollers, JMJ & Richie, Moving Shadow helped popularise the Fender Rhodes samples and streamlined breaks that constituted the Jazzstep style. The release of Dom & Roland's "The Planets/Dynamics" (1996) ushered in the clinical production values of the Techstep/two-step brigade, which by the time of Moving Shadow's hundredth release, Rob & Goldie's "The Shadow"/Dom & Rob's "Distorted Dreams" (1997), had been confirmed as *the* sound of drum 'n' bass. Moving Shadow continued to push this robo-funk with releases from artists like Technical Itch and the Tooting-based duo Calyx.

After some unpleasant internal wranglings, most of the label's staff left to form the Partisan label, which released quality tracks by the likes of Neil Trix, Q Project, Foul Play Productions and Tertius (aka Endemic Void) in 1998.

⊙ Various Artists A History of Hardcore:
Moving Shadow & Suburban Base Joint,1995

Not quite definitive, but as good an overview of two of the best labels involved in breakbeat music as you're likely to find.

Jamie Myerson

The journey that drum 'n' bass has taken from gloriously sloppy Hardcore delirium to hospital-standard sterility is epitomised by the apotheosis of Jamie Myerson. Obsessed with the sheen of '80s pop music, Myerson has plumbed the depths of assembly-line pop perfection and his clinically soulful and stereotypically pretty records have been held up as models of "class" and "quality" by his fellow producers. Whether anyone but these producers and technically minded critics actually listens to his aquatint noodlings is another question entirely.

Discovered by 4 Hero when Dego was passed a tape while DJing in Philadelphia, the New Order fan from suburban New Jersey was still in high school when he was anointed as "the first American Junglist". His debut was "Find Yourself" on the **Enforcers 6** compilation (1994). Owing a large debt to Techno producer Carl Craig, "Find Yourself" was one long synth sweep riding a wave of cascading drums that heralded the emergence of Ambient Jungle. Anchored on a remix of "Find Yourself", his follow-up, the **Matter of Trust** EP (1994), worked along similar lines, but the post-coital nostalgia of "Words Between Us" had the garish blue-lit quality of a bad movie and foreshadowed drum 'n' bass' headlong dive into gushing eddies of melodrama.

Credited to JLM Productions, Myerson's next release, "Missing From the Picture/No Appreciation" (1995), completely abandoned any sense of the polyrhythmic logic that was Jungle's gift to the world in favour of the lukewarm classicism of melodies and song structure. "Autumn/I Hear You" (1996) was the closest he or any Junglist had yet come to the watered-down jazz of Shakatak, but was, of course, held up as an example of drum 'n' bass' progression towards "musicality".

After a couple of lacklustre releases on New York's Sm:)e label, Myerson released his debut album on Josh Wink's Ovum label. **The Listening Project** (1998) was everything his production style had always threatened: smarmy keyboards, flamenco guitar passages and fey spirituality. Production credits for the next Kenny G album can't be far away.

⊙ **"Find Yourself"**   Reinforced, 1994

Available on the **Enforcers 6** EP, this was a visionary combination of Techno textures and Jungle's rhythm engine before the cult of technique took hold.

No U-Turn

P robably the most influential drum 'n' bass label of the last half of the '90s, No U-Turn defined the gruesome fusion of flesh and machine that characterised the music after its mainstream cross-over. Sounding like an armament factory churning out tanks and ICBMs to an "Amen" beat, No U-Turn records were as dark and intense as the blackest black metal, but without the cartoonish demeanour.

No U-Turn's main man was producer/engineer Nico Sykes. A studio engineer who was turned on to Hardcore by neighbour Ed Rush, Nico started the label out of his cramped loft studio and would have a hand as producer or engineer in every one of the label's releases. Working with Ed Rush, he engineered the rough basslines on the No U-Turn posse's calling card, "Bludclot Artattack" (1993). Even though the Darkcore tracks were trying to distance themselves from rave as much as possible, they still had the same dynamics, the same manic energy; "Bludclot Artattack", on the other hand, was a vortex of torpor.

Nico started No U-Turn's sister label, Saigon, in 1994, which would soon introduce Dom & Roland to the drum 'n' bass world. It was the buzzing intensity of Ed Rush's "Guncheck/Force Is Electric" (1995), though, that truly announced No U-Turn as a force on the scene. Nico and Ed Rush both worked on Trace's landmark remix of T.Power's "Mutant Jazz" which heralded the arrival of the distorted Reese bassline.

Nico and crew disfigured the bass even further on tracks like Ed Rush's "What's Up" (1996), Trace's "Amtrack/Squadron" (1996) and Spidernet's "The Sleeper/Awake" (1996). Ed Rush's "Sector 3/Comatone" (1996) was a sci-fi death shuffle that had all the energy of a Temazepam casualty trudging through mud. **Torque** (1997) compiled the terrible trio's viciously viscous output along with material from new collaborator Fierce.

Trace & Nico's "Cells" (1997) continued to dredge the dark side with pummelling basslines and ferocious rhythms, but by this time the No U-Turn sound had been superseded by the corpse-dragging beat of the two-step acid wash of producers like Optical and Matrix.

Incoming (1998) was a compilation of the lesser-known artists that had released material on Saigon and showed that there were only so many permutations of the Reese bass.

⊙ Various Artists Torque   No U-Turn,1997

Still able to strike fear into the hearts of able-bodied men, this compilation of prime No U-Turn material is a bottom-heavy journey to the dark side.

Nookie/Cloud 9

Beginning his production career with a remix of ragga don Ninja-man's "Zig It Up" (1989), Gavin Cheung has gone on to pro-duce some of the most electric Hardcore and most mellow drum 'n' bass around. With releases on Moving Shadow and Reinforced as well as engineering work for Ray Keith, Cheung has worked with some of the genre's biggest names but has remained well outside of the limelight.

He started producing rave tracks in 1990, but his profile soared with "You Got Me Burnin'" (1992), released on Moving Shadow under his Cloud 9 alias. An awesome mix of a diva giving it some, a future-gothic synth wash, the "Funky Drummer" and the synth effect from the soundtrack to the classic kung-fu flick *Five Fingers of Death*, "You Got Me Burnin'" made Ecstasy-induced heat stroke sound as exciting as hot flashes. Nookie's **The Return of Nookie** EP (1992) on Reinforced confirmed Cheung's growing reputation with the breakbeat melancholy of "Gonna Be Alright" and "Shining in Da Darkness".

The grand synth washes continued on Cloud 9's "Mr. Logic/The Dreamer" (1993), while Nookie's "Give a Little Love" (1993) was a delirious piano stormer fuelled by a motivational Lisa Stansfield sample. "Only You/Celebrate Life" (1994) blended ethereal textures with booming bass and heralded Nookie as one of the prime movers of the cyberdelic soul movement within drum 'n' bass.

Cheung's deft touch with gossamer jazz continued on Nookie's floating "A Piano, a Drum and a Bass" (1995) and the plaintive Rhodes licks and cooing vocals of Cloud 9's "Jazzmin/Snow" (1995). Taking its title from his Hardcore anthem of the same name, Nookie's debut album, **The Sound of Music** (1995), was this hazy, 4am bliss writ large. Cloud 9's "Ultimate Seduction" and Nookie's "Pot Belly/The Blues" (both 1996) were both perfect disco hangover tracks with their flickering neon glow and back-in-the-mix detachment. Cloud 9 brought this sensibility to bear on the Techstep formula with the drifting metallic Ambience of "The Twist/See" on Ray Keith's Penny Black label.

⊙ **Nookie "Give a Little Love"**   Reinforced,1993

Classic Hardcore piano screamer whose breakneck pace prevented it from becoming mere hands-in-the-air fodder.

Omni Trio

W hile melody and drum 'n' bass almost always make awkward bedfellows, Omni Trio's early records successfully merged

the two by recognising that in breakbeat Hardcore the drums often *were* the melody. Building on a history of involvement in Britain's early '80s industrial-funk scene and a love of Krautrock bands like Can and Neu!, Rob Haigh, the reclusive producer behind Omni Trio, updated the rhythmic play that characterised his influences for the post-rave Hardcore scene and created an intense emotional aspect to his music without ever degenerating into schmaltz.

Haigh's first forays into the funk mutations that have characterised his career took place in the early '80s with his avant-funk group The Truth Club who were allies of industrial funkateers like Cabaret Voltaire and 23 Skidoo. As a solo artist Haigh released **Notes**

From Underground (1983) which was a collection of dark Ambient sound tapestries that recalled the gothic swathes of groups like Controlled Bleeding.

Haigh then dropped out of music for several years until he discovered the bleep music being released on Warp Records in the late '80s and opened up a record store in Hertfordshire. Haigh's first breakbeat track was "Feel Good" which he released on his own Candidate label in 1993. The cavernous sub-bass and *Exorcist*-style keyboards piqued the interest of the Moving Shadow label, who then released the **Volume 2** EP (1993) which contained Haigh's remix of "Feel Good", "Mystic Stepper (Feel Good)" and "Stronger". **Volume 2** was marked by its wavering between bliss and sorrow: the diva purring "feel good" while the drums shake uncontrollably and the piano hits mournful notes like it was scoring the funeral scene of a Michael Mann movie.

This conflation of ecstasy and come-down marked all of Haigh's next records, especially the eternal "Renegade Snares" (1994), which was released on the **Volume 3** EP. All four versions of "Renegade Snares" are classics of breakbeat manipulation, but the most startling is Foul Play's VIP Mix which took the disembodied soul vocal exhortations, Michael Nyman glacial piano riff and almost melodramatic synth bassline and wove them into a breakbeat symphony that was anchored by the cascading snares that provide the song's hook. "Rollin' Heights" from **Volume 4** (1994) was a union of roughneck beats with what would soon be called "intelligent" textures with its heart-tugging strings and gushing vocal sample on top of a tearing "Amen" break.

The First Choice-sampling "Soul Promenade" and the emotionally draining "Thru the Vibe" from **Volume 5** (1994) appeared along with tracks from his previous EPs on **Volume 1: The Deepest Cut** (1995), which still remains one of the best full-length statements by a drum 'n' bass artist. "Nu Birth of Cool" which followed towards the end of 1995 marked a shift in Omni Trio's sound. The soaring chords and tough beats were replaced by a more streamlined feel that sounded more like House than it did like Jungle. Haigh's love of Michael Nyman's treacly piano arpeggios was displayed on his contribution to **Lo Recordings Volume 1: Extreme Possibilities** (1995), which had no beats at all.

Haigh has said that he thought that his tracks worked because of their "haunted feel". He made this idea explicit with the title of his second album, **Haunted Science** (1996). The album, however, suffered from the rigid drums of tracks like "Trippin' on Broken Beats" (whose beats didn't really break) and the aquatint production of "Astral Phase" and "Who Are You". "Twin Town Karaoke" (1997), which was backed by a VIP mix of "Trippin' on Broken Beats", and "Sanctuary" (1997), both from **Skeleton Keys** (1997), continued in the same style and similarly failed to catch fire.

O Volume 1: The Deepest Cut   Moving Shadow, 1995

With tracks like "Renegade Snares" (Foul Play's VIP mix), "Rollin' Heights" and "Living for the Future", this is easily one of the two or three best single-artist albums to come out of drum 'n' bass.

Optical

From seemingly out of nowhere, Optical suddenly became the producer to watch on the drum 'n' bass scene in 1997 and 1998. Anointed by Grooverider as his engineer of choice, Optical was suddenly an inescapable presence in the dance press and everything he released was heaped with praise as the cutting edge of technological advancement.

Optical's legendary facility and stamina with the machinery of drum 'n' bass was developed when he was still known as Matt Quinn and was working as a studio engineer. He gained notoriety in the Jungle community for engineering Leviticus' "The Burial" (1994) and has since worked on Goldie's **Saturnz Return** album (1998) as well as Grooverider's **Mysteries of Funk** (1998). Along with his brother Matrix, Optical has pioneered drum 'n' bass' obsession with precision and he claims to spend weeks on end perfecting his beats.

While he was still a jobbing engineer, Optical started two labels, Genetic Stress and Blame Technology, which sounded as if he was fending off criticism before the fact. Optical started to get noticed for his production skills with records on Prototype, but it was "To Shape the Future" (1997), a grinding bass-tech monster with whip-crack beats, on Metalheadz and "Quadrant 6", a collaboration with Dom on Moving Shadow that truly made his name. "Bounce/The End" (1998) came out on Doc Scott's 31 Records and continued to set the scene alight with its body-blow two-step and dyspeptic bassline.

With jittery, skitting, skidding 808 beats and fast synth wooshes, "Moving 808's/High Tek Dreams" (1998) sounded a bit like the Trans-Europe Express breaking up on re-entry, while Fortran's (Optical, Ed Rush and Fierce) "Search/The End Pt. 2" (1998) wailed the body electric. Optical & Ed Rush's "Funktion/Naked Lunch" (1998) showed that they understood building tension – a quality that was in mind-bogglingly short supply in drum 'n' bass at the time. What was dangling on the end of the fork of "Naked Lunch" was well-formed, jazz-tinged drum 'n' bass in which the appallingly thin drum sound that was so voguish actually made sense.

Ed Rush and Optical started their Virus label with "Medicine/Punch Bag" (1998) which replayed the familiar pattern of machine juggernauts recreating the over-the-top sound effects from '70s kung-fu flicks. The bass sludge and dry ice synths continued on the duo's "Lifespan/Crisis" and "Zardoz/Satellites" (both 1998). **Wormhole** (1998) was the culmination of the duo's partnership and stretched their doom and gloom over an album's worth of paranoid urban underbelly soundscapes, microchip jazz-fusion and distended bass manipulation.

◉ Ed Rush & Optical Wormhole   Virus,1998

Although the sampler stopped sounding as fascinating as it had in 1994–'95, Ed Rush and Optical used their Akais the way Slayer and Black Flag used their guitars.

Origin Unknown

Beginning in 1991, the partnership of Essex lads Andy C and Ant Miles has consistently been one of the most fertile patches in drum 'n' bass. A combination of youthful vigour (Andy C was 16 when the duo started making tracks) and technical know-how (Ant Miles used to engineer for The KLF), the duo has turned out ground-

breaking tracks with a regularity that ranks them among the Jungle elite, even if they don't get the media exposure they deserve.

Within earshot of the pirate station Centreforce, Andy C and Ant Miles started their Ram and Liftin' Spirits labels in their home town of Hornchurch, Essex, in 1992, but they wouldn't really make a name for themselves until the following year when they released one of drum 'n' bass' undisputed classics, "Valley of the Shadows" (1993), as Origin Unknown. Also known as "31 Seconds" or "Long, Dark Tunnel" because of the track's spoken word samples, "Valley of the Shadows" brought the idea of dancing on the edge of apocalypse to its limit. Not as furious as darkside contemporaries like Doc Scott's "Here Comes the Drumz" or as gothic as something like Boogie Times Tribe's "Dark Stranger", "Valley of the Shadows" didn't clobber you on the head with its sinister vibe. Instead, it insinuated itself while you were grooving to its understated "Think" beat and slightly askew funk feel and the chiming synth lines gave the track an astral aura that blended perfectly with the sample about a near-death experience.

"Beyond Bass" (1993), which they released as Desired State, was edgier, with its chattering voices, half-speed drum loop in the background and the roughneck who came up and announced "Annihilating" halfway through the track. Built around a break that sounded more like Indonesian gamelan than a bionic James Brown and a sample from *Predator* ("the jungle just came alive and took him"), their track with Shimon, "Predator" (1994), was an awesome slice of dystopian urban dread.

Andy C's collaboration with jump-up don Randall, "Sound Control" (1994), was a stunning example of breakbeat mutation. With multiple drum loops, a disorienting backwards piano sample and steely percussion, "Sound Control" created a sci-fi feel where so much drum 'n' bass was "futurist" merely through reference. Origin Unknown's moonwalking "Truly One", Desired State's "Here and Now" and Andy C's "Roll On" (all 1995) all fused Hardstep sub-bass and rolling breaks

with flowing loops of metallic melody which gave the tracks a dreamy, other-worldly quality.

Ant Miles collaborated with DJ Rhythm as Higher Sense, whose 1994 debut, "Cold Fresh Air", helped inaugurate the era of obsessive craftsmanship with its meticulous breaks.

While all of Miles's tracks were well crafted, it was the high-definition production values of tracks like "People of the Universe" (1995), "Metallic FX" and "Out There" (both 1996) that highlighted the precision involved.

Origin Unknown's massive remix of Busta Rhymes' "Woo-Hah" (1996) brought them some long-overdue acclaim from outside the scene and their first album, **The Speed of Sound** (1996), built on that momentum. More of a label overview than a single-artist album, it still showed Andy C and Ant Miles to be among drum 'n' bass' most innovative producers. **Sound In Motion** (1998) followed up **The Speed of Sound**'s success with a potent combination of jump-up dynamics and Techstep sound sculptures.

Moving Fusion's "Turbulence" and Ram Trilogy's (Andy C, Miles and Sh??) self-titled album (both 1998) pushed drum'n'bass even further into the dark heart of the producer's machines with a claustrophobic sci-fi feel.

⊙ **The Speed of Sound**   Ram,1996

Proving that dancefloor-friendly tracks can be just as "progressive" as any other kind of drum 'n' bass, **The Speed of Sound** includes such essential tracks as "Roll On", "Truly One" and the classic "Valley of the Shadows".

Panacea

D rum 'n' bass might have emerged out of a scene hooked on euphoria and empathy, but its base materials – high-speed drum shrapnel, noises from shoot-'em-up video games and bass bombs – are easily mutated into sonic armature. In the hands of Panacea, a Heavy Metal and Test Dept. fan from Germany, drum 'n' bass is an act of symbolic violence against a rigidly conservative, stultifying culture.

Born into a musical family in 1977, Mathis Mootz spent his formative years in a German boys' choir and learning classical piano. He rebelled against this upbringing by turning on to the industrial sounds of groups like Front 242 and the "non-music" of early rave. Inspired by the Techstep of Ed Rush and DJ Trace, Mootz adopted the Panacea moniker and recorded "Tron" (1996) which was soon released by Force Inc. subsidiary Chrome Records. Where Techstep sang the cyborg electric, "Tron" was that same cyborg writhing in an iron maiden. "Stormbringer" and "The Day After" (both 1996) followed with similarly punishing future-gothic takes on drum 'n' bass.

All of these appeared on his debut album, **Low Profile Darkness** (1997), which remains one of the most uncompromising statements of synth turbulence, rhythmic aggression and general crash-test aesthetics ever recorded. Undoubtedly influenced by the breakbeat extremism of fellow Germans Alec Empire and the PCP label, Panacea brought white noise (static, drones, system dirt and sirens) into the Techstep matrix. Most Techstep was clinical and precise – a music of control; Panacea's version was brutal, chaotic and very exhilarating.

However, Panacea has since backed away from such "revolutionary noise" as he terms it. As Bad Street Boy, he released the Electro-fetishising **Ladykiller** EP (1998) for Jammin' Unit's Pharma label, while he has released a 7" of Speedcore Techno as Kate Mosh on Loop. Panacea's second album, **Twisted Designz** (1998), brought his vision of drum 'n' bass closer to the world of Heavy Metal with a dystopic sci-fi concept, medieval imagery and titles like "Lightbringer" and "Unglory". The album also approached metal in its rhythmic torpor;

where **Low Profile Darkness** had beats that ricocheted across the soundfield, **Twisted Designz** was mired in a two-step swamp. However, his remix of Alien Hunt for the German drum 'n' bass label Don Q showed that Panacea was still capable of forcing his audience to stare down the barrel of a gun.

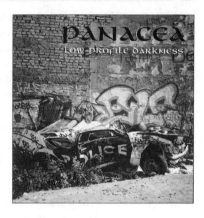

⊙ **Low Profile Darkness**   Chrome, 1997

What early Hardcore would have sounded like in a Hammer horror film, **Low Profile Darkness** is sonic violence at its most exhilarating, exciting and euphoric.

Paradox

One of the more versatile producers on the scene, Dev Pandya has been producing tracks since the earliest days of Hardcore. As part of Mixrace, he was responsible for some of Moving Shadow's most vital Hardcore like "The Future Is Before Your Eyes/Too Bad For Ya" (1991) and the hyper-kinetic "Mixrace Outta Hand" (1993).

As Alaska, he was responsible, with partner Nucleus, for celestial tracks like "The Nautilus" and "Project Two/Persistence of Vision" (both 1996) for Good Looking sub-labels Nexus and 720 Degrees, as well as material on the Timeless and Vibez labels. Alaska's "Vortex" (1997) on Renegade, however, had a distinctly harder tech edge.

It was as Paradox, however, that he would gain the most recognition. "New Statement" (1996) didn't exactly live up to its title with its concussive "Amen" break, but it was effective nonetheless. "A Certain Sound/Deep Sleep" (1996) on Renegade Hardware followed with another walloping "Amen" and sinister strings. Teaming up with Noise, Paradox released the explosive, FX-laden "A Time Existence" and "Transmograpfication/Sudden Impact" (both 1997) for weirdbeat label Ninebar. Paradox's "Cuba/Scanners" (1997) was his debut for Reinforced and managed to combine the jazzy flavours of his outings as Alaska with the more tech-noirish elements of his Paradox persona.

More releases for Reinforced followed with the claustrophobic atmosphere of "This Side of Forever/Decompositions" and the dense percussion/bass interaction of "Dioxide 170873/Give the Drummer Some" (both 1998). Teaming up with DMR, Paradox released the paranoiac "Abstraction/Krystaline" (1998) for Certificate 18, while on his own he unleashed the crashing "Pandemonium/Coaxial" (1998) for Italian drum 'n' bass label Sonica. Noise & Paradox's debut album, **Transmograpfication** (1998), was another very effective blend of jazziness and post-industrial apocalypse.

◉ Transmograpfication   Ninebar, 1998

Probably because his idea of jazz had more to do with the fission of Miles Davis than the fusion of Lonnie Liston Smith, Paradox was able to blend harps and strings into the clinical drum 'n' bass labs of Source Direct and Optical.

Pascal

Drum 'n' bass may very well be Britain's first indigenous form of dance music, but it wouldn't exist without hip-hop, which is as American as apple pie. Early hip-hop DJs excavated the breakbeat from the musical landfill of the '70s, thus creating the foundation for Hardcore and Jungle. Almost as important, though, was hip-hop's obsession with criminality which, via sampling, has given Thatcher's children the tools to express the black hole that exists in (the lack of) British society.

One of Jungle's original ballistic b-boys, Pascal abandoned hip-hop for rave in 1992 when he started to make breakbeat Hardcore tracks as Bad Influence. Teaming up with Sponge, Pascal started Face Records and released the classic "Johnny" (1992) as Johnny Jungle. One of the first "panic songs", "Johnny" looped horror movie screams and "help me" quivers around a skidding breakbeat and a John Carpenter-style eerie synth motif to create a musical analogue of both the Ecstasy come-down and the growing sense of lawlessness and fear in this once "green and pleasant land". "Johnny" was so successful that it has been remixed fifteen times, the best of which was probably Origin Unknown's mix of "Johnny '94".

Still using the Johnny Jungle moniker, Pascal recorded "Flammable/Devoted Drummer" (1993) and the exceedingly roughneck "Killa Sound" (1995) for Suburban Base. After parting with Sponge, Pascal set up Frontline Records in 1994 and hit immediately with Rude Bwoy Monty's "Out in the Streets/Jungle Man". The label really hit its stride, though, in 1995 with a string of remarkable singles: P-Funk's (Pascal) "P-Funk Era", HMP's "Runnin's", Rude Bwoy Monty's "Summer Sumting/Warp 9 Mr. Zulu" and Dope Skillz's (aka DJ Zinc) "6 Million Ways". The undeniable "P-Funk Era" and the moody "Runnin's" were both "Amen" burners constructed around killer hooks, while "Warp 9 Mr. Zulu" mutated from chiming slide guitars into ridiculously overmodulated basslines. Best of all, though, was "6 Million Ways" which welded together East coast (Wu Tang Clan samples) and West Coast (G-Funk keyboards) hip-hop with a sing-song bassline and a rolling "Amen" break.

The hip-hop antics continued unabated with Pascal and Bigga World's A Tribe Called Quest-sampling "Oh My God" and Pascal's "Reality" (both 1996). Rude Bwoy Monty's Junglist reworking of "Gonna Fly Now" from *Rocky* anchored the collaborative compilation with DJ Hype's Ganja Records, **Still Smokin'** (1996). Since then, however, Pascal's brand of floor-filling jump-up has been largely ignored in favour of the post-industrial doom and gloom of the Techsteppers, and "Amen"-damaging tracks like Pascal & Phantasy's "Terradaktil" (1996) and Aura's "Slow Down/Escape" (1998) have been sidelined as critics rush to embrace the latest technological nuance from Optical or Matrix.

⊙ Various Artists Still Smokin'   G-Line Records, 1996

It might not feature either Pascal or Hype's best tracks, but it is a fairly consistent romp through the "Amen" and overmodulated bass territory that they have chartered.

Peshay

O ne of the crusaders for bringing "musicality" into drum 'n' bass, Paul Pesce is a Lonnie Liston Smith fanatic who has flirted with House and jazz in order to tame the frenetic breakbeats of Jungle. With his latest work, he has gone one step further and attempted to ditch the sampler altogether.

Things used to be very different, though. Peshay's first records, like the **2 Dope** EP (1993), were released on the king of sampling Bizzy B's Brain label at the dawn of Hardcore. Hooking up with Reinforced, he released the **Protege** EP (1993) which was a masterpiece of chiming tones that epitomised the label's obsession with futurism and science fiction. The celestial ambience continued on the collaboration with LTJ Bukem, "19.5" (1994), his scatting first release for Goldie's Metalheadz label, "Psychosis/Represent" (1994), and the enveloping reverie of "World of Music" (1994).

"Futurama/Endless Thoughts" (1995) on Basement Records plucked his vision of drum 'n' bass from the firmament and plunged it in the depths of an aqueous fantasy world populated by Garage mermaids. Even more Garagey was the "Vocal Tune/Piano Tune" (1995) 12" on Bukem's Good Looking label which liberally sampled Masters at Work vocalist India's incantations to the gods of *Santeria*.

It was for his jazz licks, though, that Peshay was revered on the scene. The "Predator/On the Nile" (1996) 12" on Metalheadz was filled with shuffling rhythms, string trills, wind chimes, flutes, double-bass and anodyne vibes samples. Remixes of DJ Shadow's "What Does Your Soul Look Like?" and Dark Star's "Graceadelica" (both 1998) featured more acoustic basslines and brass fills.

Part of 1998's sound of smooth rolling fusion tracks, "Miles From Home" (1998) was released on Mo' Wax to great acclaim. Combining an unsubtle Techstep two-step with an overload of Fender Rhodes licks and yet another double-bass riff, "Miles From Home" was a favourite of DJs like Fabio who were pushing drum 'n' bass ever further away from its sampladelic roots. Fabio returned the favour by releasing Peshay's own remix of "Heaven" (1999) on his Creative Source label. Peshay's 1999 album for Mo' Wax ditched the Akai altogether in favour of a thirty-piece orchestra and live vocals from former Soul II Soul singer Caron Wheeler.

⊙ **Protege EP**	Reinforced, 1993

An early Ambient Jungle high-water mark featuring such journeys into cyborg dreamland as "Dreams" and "On the Firm".

PFM

Although they both suffer from similar delusions of grandeur, the Junglist PFM should not be confused with the Italian prog rock band Premiata Forneria Marconi. In drum 'n' bass the initials PFM stand for Progressive Future Music and Mike Bolton and Jamie Saker's vision of advancement doesn't stray too far from LTJ Bukem's party line: they replace Hardcore's visceral excitement with Deep House's aspirational sophistication.

The duo's debut single, "Wash Over Me/Love & Happiness" (1995), was released on Bukem's Good Looking label and quickly became a Speed favourite with its warm synth eddies and lapping bass pulse. "One and Only/Dreams" (1995) followed shortly thereafter on Looking Good and became one of Ambient Jungle's definitive moments. "Dreams" was a gentle, new age roller in typical Bukem fashion, while "One and Only" could have been a Larry Heard postcoital lament if it wasn't for the breakbeats.

"One and Only", drum 'n' bass' first love song, hinted that they had vaguely interesting ideas and "The Western Tune" (1995) proved this by attempting to translate Ennio Morricone's spaghetti Western stock phrases to breakbeat music. Unfortunately, the execution didn't live up to the concept and "The Western Tune" drowned in melodramatic synth washes and the cod-emotionalism that even a soundtrack hack like Danny Elfman would be afraid to touch. The flipside, "Hypnotising", was similarly narcotising and had the temerity to present one of dance music's biggest clichés (the "music's hypnotising" sample from Raw Silk's "Do It to the Music") as "progressive future music".

"For All of Us/Mystics" (1996) was another oleaginous 12" that oozed with treacly flute fills, Manheim Steamroller atmospheres and tasteful chords to excite the jazz bores. Bolton and Saker haven't been heard from much since they parted company with Good Looking in 1996 – perhaps the carnage wrought by Techstep scared these softies away.

⊙**"One and Only"**   Looking Good,1995

Also available on **Logical Progression Volume 1**, "One and Only" was not only PFM's best moment, but perhaps the genre's best as well.

Photek

The music of Hertfordshire's Rupert Parkes should be everything that's wrong with the "intelligent" strain of drum 'n' bass: jazz-fusion as the model of the union of "complexity" and groove, "concept" records and a pseudo-scientific approach to beat construction. However, Parkes' music rises above its base materials by virtue of his belief in the emotion of the drum and a sense of texture and tension that is more developed than almost anyone else's in drum 'n' bass.

Straying slightly from the standard progression, Parkes was a hip-hop fiend who listened to Gilles Peterson's rare groove/jazz-funk radio show and went to raves like Telepathy before buying his first sampler in 1991. While a teenager living in Ipswich, Parkes released a couple of breakbeat tracks under the name Origination with Rob from Motive One. His first solo releases for Ipswich's Certificate 18 label, Synthetics' "Four Track" and Studio Pressure's "Jump" (both 1992), featured the liquid flow that would become one of the features of his productions and quickly became favourites of LTJ Bukem.

Bukem's Good Looking/Looking Good labels released Parkes' first forays into aquatint territory, "Dolphin Tune" (1994), "Waveforms" and "Bringing Me Down" (both 1995), under his Aquarius moniker. He didn't drift completely into new age aromatherapeutics, however, as the Black Dog-esque minimalism of Studio Pressure's "Relics" (1994) showed. Seemingly naming himself after a British distributor of photo-electric equipment, Parkes' most famous pseudonym, Photek, was both a *nom de disque* and the name of his label. On the two **Form & Function EPs** (both 1994), Photek introduced his trademark Chinese gong drum sound which was the result of taking tiny fragments of percussion samples and painstakingly re-arranging and re-sampling them. Inspired by the martial arts TV series of the same name, "The Water Margin" (1995) connected Photek's sound with its inspiration – a process which was continued on "The Seven Samurai" (1995) and later on "Ni Ten Ichi Ryu (Two Swords Technique)" (1997).

His debut release for Goldie's Metalheadz label, the **Natural Born Killaz EP** (1995), was notable for the beat wizardry of the *X Files*-sampling "Consciousness" and for "Into the 90s" (a reference to the bpms, not the decade), his Down Tempo interpretation of the "Sneaking in the

Back" beat that was also used by Massive Attack. One of the few aquatint Jungle tracks to transcend the smarm of its source material, the final release on the Photek label, "UFO/Rings Around Saturn" (1996), was based around a Fender Rhodes sample from Pharoah Sanders' "Astral Travelling", which accounted for the track's other name, "Pharoah".

1996 also bore the first fruits of Photek's deal with Virgin and their Science imprint, **The Hidden Camera** EP. Making his beats even more metallic and the atmospheres sinister, **The Hidden Camera** was a neurotic commentary on the full arrival of the security state in Britain and his best release to date. After the very promising "Ni Ten Ichi Ryu", his debut

album, **Modus Operandi** (1997) was a big disappointment. Perhaps suffering from too much time spent deconstructing and recomposing breaks, **Modus Operandi** felt flat and almost narcotised, as if the computer screen had sapped his energy and stolen his scientific method. Unleashing a new alias, Parkes' Special Forces project for his own Photek label continued his penchant for clinical beat manipulation, albeit with more of a booming bottom end than usual.

○ Form & Function   Science, 1998

Despite the title, this is a fine collection of the six 12"s that Photek released on his eponymous label and probably the best single volume of his work. The remixes are a bit annoying, however.

Prisoners of Technology

From time immemorial, music has always been ruined when musicians have tried to impress other musicians. Ignoring their fans, musicians get in a tizzy about virtuosity, whether it's playing a Bach arpeggio at light speed or the latest filter tweak on their Aphex Aural

Exciter, and forget about the vast majority of people in the world who couldn't care less about technique and are only interested in the results. Drum 'n' bass' cult of the engineer has meant that producers have ignored the dancefloor in favour of wowing other producers. Along with Aphrodite's Urban Takeover posse, Essex's Prisoners of Technology are just about the only die-hards left who care about dancefloor impact.

First gaining attention with "Technology" (1997) on their own Fresh Kutt label, TMS1, K Dub and DJ Magic turned the acid bassline of the time into a jump-up component of epic proportions. "Delikutt Beats/What Does It Mean" (1997) followed step for step, while "Break-dance/Boogie" (1997) added some old-school samples to the formula. "One-Two/So Damn Tuff" (1998) had their biggest, most outrageously flatulent bassline yet and yet more old-school hip-hop samples.

The filtered bassline on Prisoners of Technology's "Crazzy/Cold Blooded (Pay Up Mix)" managed to even out-quake Aphrodite and Mickey Finn – the undisputed masters of sphincter loosening. Their biggest track, though, was undoubtedly their remix of the Beastie Boys' "Intergalactic" (1998) which sped up the beat from Rush's "Tom Sawyer" as a backdrop to its absurdly funky tear-out. Another enormous remix followed in the form of their reworking of Buddha Monk's "Gots Like Comin' Thru" (1998), while their own "Mother F#ckin' Real/The Flavour '98" kicked rude bwoy ballistics with fairly predictable but effective hip-hop samples. "Doomsday Boy/Unknown" (1998) followed with more ridiculously huge breakdowns, while the BASS 1999 EP (1999) fuel-injected "Delikutt Beats" with even more of a low-end boost.

○ **Beastie Boys "Intergalactic"**
(Prisoners of Technology/TMS1 Remix)   Grand Royal, 1998

Sure, they sound like Aphrodite, but unlike all of drum 'n' bass' hallowed producers who spent weeks on their beats, PoT's beats kicked ass and took names later.

The Prodigy

Quite simply, The Prodigy are breakbeat's biggest pop stars and the best example of how hip-hop got translated by British youth from "black America's CNN" into a music expressing nothing but sensation. Crucial to The Prodigy's success was the fact that, although the music was created entirely by Liam Howlett, The Prodigy was always presented as a band rather than a producer hidden behind his machinery.

Hailing from Braintree, Essex, Howlett was the archetypal British b-boy who got into hip-hop through breakdancing and "The Adventures of Grandmaster Flash on the Wheels of Steel". He eventually got involved in scratching and mixing and became the DJ for British hip-hop crew Cut to Kill. One of the crew's MCs gave Howlett his first Ecstasy tablet at a rave in Essex and he was immediately hooked on the experience and started DJing at raves soon afterwards. At one of his gigs in 1990 Howlett met Keith Flint and Leeroy Thornhill who were so impressed with his turntable skills and the demo tapes he played them that they decided to form a band with Flint and Thornhill as dancers. Their debut release, the **What Evil Lurks** EP (1991), included the excellent "Android", but it was their next release that would cause a storm in the British dance music community.

One of Hardcore's greatest singles, "Charly" (1991) hit #3 in the British charts on the strength of its sample of a cat meowing and a boy saying, "Charly says, 'Always tell your mummy before you go off somewhere'" which was taken from a public service announcement. The song started off the craze for "toytown Techno" and a deluge of songs with sweets-as-drugs metaphors followed in its wake: Smart E's "Sesame's Treet", Shaft's "Roobarb and Custard" and Urban Hype's "A

Trip to Trumpton". While "Charly" seemed to be about a drug-fuelled innocence, the songs that followed seemed like nothing but cheap and nasty cash-ins and the huge chart success of these records led *Mixmag* to run a cover with Howlett holding a gun to his head, accusing him of killing rave. "Charly"'s flip, the equally great "Your Love", was the epitome of early rave tunes with a soaring piano line, diva vocals that functioned as the mnemonic device and catalytic breakbeats. With "Charly" propelling the band towards stardom, they recruited MC Maxim to provide another visual focus for their soon-to-become legendary live shows.

"Everybody in the Place" (1992) did one better than "Charly" in the pop charts and even outdid it in exuberance with an incredible Woody-the-Woodpecker synth riff. "Fire" (1992) failed to reach a lofty chart position, but it did swipe the "I am the god of hellfire" beginning of The Crazy World of Arthur Brown's song of the same title. With samples of reggae crooner Max Romeo and Ultramagnetic MC's Kool Keith taking the track into a delirious state, "Out of Space" (1992) was (and remains) their best single yet. All of these singles would appear in one form or another on **Experience** (1992) which was one of the few (only?) Hardcore albums to justify its existence as an album and not just a collection of hits plus filler.

After remixes for the likes of Jesus Jones and Front 242 and a couple of low-key releases like "One Love (1993), The Prodigy returned with **Music For the Jilted Generation** (1994). One of the first dance records that seemed to challenge the government's crackdown on the rave scene, the album was enthusiastically received by the same mainstream music press that derided the band as know-nothing commercial ravers probably because the rock touches (like the collaboration with Pop Will Eat Itself, "Their Law") signified "artistry" and "intelligence". **Music For the Jilted Generation** was also the pop distillation of the previous year and a half's obsession with darkness: song titles like "Poison" and "Claustrophobic Sting", samples like "You're no good for me... don't need no one that's no good to me", melancholy piano lines and the acid sounds that dominated the record suggested that the uplifting energy of their earlier records had been replaced by paranoia.

With an arresting video that focused on the head-banging energy of Keith Flint, "Firestarter" (1996) became their first #1 and propelled the band to international stardom. Sampling The Breeders and Art of Noise, "Firestarter" was the best kind of ode to nihilism: one with a catchy beat. The riffing guitars of **Music For the Jilted Generation** and "Firestarter" appeared on nearly every track of **The Fat of the Land** (1997) which hit #1 in some twenty countries and suggested that, with its embrace of the instruments, sound and attention-getting antics (cf. the misogynistic Ultramagnetic MC sam-

MUSIC FOR THE JILTED GENERATION

ple and "scandalous" video of "Smack My Bitch Up") of rock, rave's maturity was now complete.

⊙ Experience
XL, 1992

Against a background of hopelessly dull progressive House compilations, the sheer buzzing energy of this album was a revelation and gave Britain's dance establishment the two-fingered salute.

⊙ **Music For the Jilted Generation**　　　　　　　　　XL,1994

Always beware albums that are praised by critics for being mature from bands who were previously derided for being air-heads. This may be an exception to the rule, but it's nowhere near as good as the first album.

Production House Records

B ased in Willesden, West London, the Production House record label was a collective of rave producers who couldn't get a foot in the door at any of the mainstream dance labels. Featuring artists and producers like Acen, Dyce, DMS, Jazz & the Brothers Grimm and Baby D, Production House epitomised Hardcore as the sound of E'd-up abandon and hyperactive thrills.

Production House started in 1991 and reinforced the sound of Hardcore as speeded-up breakbeats, gargantuan piano riffs and diva vocals with records like Baby D's "Daydreaming" and The House Crew's Todd Terry-sampling "We Are Hardcore". The House Crew's "Keep the Fire Burning", meanwhile, created Hardcore's enduring musical motto with its motivational hip-hop sample: "Cut the mid-range, drop the bass".

The label really found its feet in 1992, though, with a string of impossibly exciting and startlingly imaginative records. Acen's "Trip to the Moon" and "Trip II the Moon (Part 2, the Darkside)" sounded like Rakim, James Bond, Joey Beltram and a helium diva caught inside

Street Fighter II, while "Close Your Eyes" committed the ultimate rock heresy by transforming the "Lizard King" Jim Morrison into a puny 99-pound weakling with all the sex appeal of an old prune. Beseeching ravers to "Come and feel my energy", Baby D's "Let Me Be Your Fantasy" anthropomorphised Ecstasy into the emoting diva herself against an eerie background that felt both out of time and out of joy.

Best of all though was DMS's landmark of intensity, "Vengeance/Love Overdose (Remix)" (1992). Produced by Acen, Dyce and DMS, "Vengeance" remade the strutting boast of Run DMC's "King of Rock" as pure head-rush momentum, while "Love Overdose" signalled the inevitable outcome of pleasure worship and Ecstasy abuse. Based on the beat from Lyn Collins' "Think (About It)", the delirious rapture of The House Crew's "Euphoria (Nino's Dream)" (1993), however, showed that Production House still believed in the rave dream. But records like DJ Solo's "Darkage" (1993) and DMS & Boneman X's "Sweet Vibrations" (1994) pounded the exhilaration out of the gushing divas with ferocious "Amen" beats, skull-snapping snares and the rude bwoy vibes of the Jamaican dancehall.

As the heavy manners of Jungle allowed the cooler-than-thou dons of the dance scene to embrace Hardcore without losing face, the unabashed exuberance of labels like Production House went out of fashion. Loony records like Nino's "World Champion (I Feel So Real)" (1993), which bit *Fiddler on the Roof* and early '80s synth-pop, were as out of fashion as parachute trousers. Production House would have the last laugh, though. In 1994, "Let Me Be Your Fantasy" was re-released by London Records and with the backing of a major label's promotional machine, it was the #1 record in Britain for two weeks – a feat no po-faced drum 'n' basser has managed.

Baby D followed the re-release of "Fantasy" with a cover of NRG's The Korgis-sampling 1993 anthem, "I Need Your Loving" (1995). With its white-gloved ambience, their debut album, **Deliverance** (1996), was rave *qua* rave's last gasp as a pop force.

◉ Various Artists
The Best of Production House   Production House,1993

Containing most of Production House's finest moments, this is an essential document of breakbeat Hardcore.

DJ Pulse

There must be something in the water supply around High Wycombe. The suburban wasteland north of London is the home territory of Alex Reece, Wax Doctor, LTJ Bukem and DJ Pulse – the figureheads of the Jazzstep movement. Even though he runs the seminal Creative Wax label and is responsible for some indisputable classics of the jazzy genre, Pulse (aka Ashley Brown) is probably the least well known of the four.

Emerging in tandem with Sponge and Stretch as Dance Conspiracy on XL Records, Pulse was responsible for one of Hardcore's all-time greats, "Dub War" (1992). With a dull, low synth rumble, the same Lafayette Afro-Rock Band sample used by Public Enemy, some raggamuffin bizness and a shuffling break that almost doesn't work speeded up, "Dub War" wasn't quite as delirious as many of its contemporaries, but it seemed to have a kind of gravitas that few others had.

The group retreated under pressure from XL to produce a follow-up and Pulse formed Creative Wax with Wax Doctor and Jack Horner in 1993. Based around a jazzy diva cooing her way around an occasional darkside squall, the Bounty Killaz's (Stretch and Pulse) "Do It

Now" (1993) was the sound of sweetness and light escaping from the oppression of Belgian synth stabs. Releasing important tracks by Wax Doctor & Alex Reece like "Atlantic Drama" and "Taken Over" (both 1994), Creative Wax quickly established itself as one of the leading players on the "intelligent" scene. Pulse's "Stay Calm/So Fine" (1994) on Moving Shadow was another landmark of rich synths and deep textures that was even better in the hands of Foul Play on their remix.

Pulse's "True Romance" and "Dreams of You", released as The Rising Sons (both 1995), were drum 'n' bass oil slicks that oozed their way under your skin. Similarly oleaginous textures and suave synths could be found on "Let You In/Voyager" and DJ Pulse & the Jazz Cartel's "Let the Hustlers Play/Feeling Real" (1996) on Moving Shadow. The tension between the "Amen" shrapnel and the plasmatic synth gel that marked Pulse's earlier records had now disappeared completely in favour of a louche slackness on tracks like "U Down" (1996) and The Underwolves' "The Redeemer/The Crossing" (1997).

Freeform (aka Stretch) took this sound literally with the low-budget sleaze of the vocal sample on "Babies/Space" (1998). With less of a Teddy Pendergrass-like desire to rub you down with lotion, **Creative Wax: Nu Perspective** (1998) instead tried to sweet-talk you with its delusions of grandeur and progressivism. Despite its title, Justice's "Air Sign" alluded to the Electro groove of yore, but most of the tracks seemed to be made by producers who thought that tinkly keyboards and aquatic textures were the sound of the future and not the sound of a Tom Scott album circa 1978.

⊙ **Various Artists The Revolutionary Generation** Moving Shadow,1996

A collection of early Creative Wax material that set the whole Jazzstep thing in motion.

Q Project & Spinback

Forming Legend Records in 1991, Oxfordshire's Q Project & Spinback have been at the forefront of breakbeat music since the beginning. Their "Champion Sound" (1993) was a ground-breaking combination of ragga samples, rumbling breakbeats, dub bass and growling "Mentasm" stabs that bridged the dark side with the Jungle. The Cocoa Tea-sampling "Rikers Island" (1994) followed in a similar style.

As The Alliance, the duo released the Ambient Jungle classic "First Impressions" on Reinforced's **Enforcers 6** compilation (1994). "Airtight" (1995), released under their Funky Technicians moniker, moved the duo in a separate direction altogether with a sample of an old gospel singer reminiscing to a score of celestial synths and a lulling "Think" break. With similar Bukem-esque appeal, "Split Personality" (1996) on their new CIA label set caressing bass tones to gently rolling beats. "Algebra/Forcefield" (1997) was released on Bukem's Good Looking label as Total Science and put their sliding and gliding synths in a more technoid context. The tech-jazz continued on Q Project & Spinback's "Mars/Pleasure Principle" (1997) which featured impossibly deep synth pads and warm bass sounds, while Funky Technicians' "Planet Vibe" (1997) on Fabio's Creative Source label threw some vibes into the mix of enveloping synths.

With a bit more of a Techno influence and a hint of Photek-style paranoia, Total Science's "Espionage/Network" (1998) came out on Partisan and was co-produced by fellow Midlander Neil Trix. "Life Cycle/X-Raze/Break #2" (1998) followed on Passenger, only with more horror-flick dynamics and noises. Q Project's "Wake Up/Twist" (1998), however, restored the more accustomed astral travelling only to be out-snarled by Total Science's "Fifth Density/Radiu" (1998) which was characterised by its sinister strings and growling bass.

⊙ **"Champion Sound"**   Legend, 1993

An all-time rave anthem that sounds as good now as it did then. (Available on **United Dance Presents The Anthems '92–'97**.)

Randall

Getting his start in 1989–'90 at the pirate stations Rave FM and Centreforce, Randall quickly became one of Hardcore's most prominent DJs. With fellow Rave FM DJs Cool Hand Flex and Mike De Underground, Randall set up the DeUnderground label and record shop in the Forest Gate section of east London. In 1992, Randall became one of the residents at the legendary AWOL club in Islington where his "double impact" style of DJing (layering the drum tracks of two different records to create a percussion collision and maximum impact on the dancefloor) became the club's hallmark.

Randall's debut as a producer was "Da R" which appeared on Reinforced's **Enforcers 2** EP (1993). Hooking up with Andy C of Ram Records, the duo produced the awesome "Sound Control" (1994) which featured one of Jungle's greatest percussion tracks. With multiple drum loops, a disorienting backwards piano sample and steely percussion, "Sound Control" created a sci-fi feel where so much drum 'n' bass was "futurist" merely through reference.

After several years concentrating on DJing (which can be heard on mix compilations like AWOL, **Jungle Renegades** and **Dreamscape Vol. 1**), Randall returned to producing with "Flava's" (1996) on Reinforced's **Above the Law** album and "Hard Noize" with Tee Bone on the **Strictly Business** (1997) album. Randall started his Mac II label in 1998 with Randall & Flex's "Music Maker/Sahara Dawn" (1998), which featured surging breaks and acid-washed synths. Randall & A-Sides' "ID4/Mystical Merlin" (1998), meanwhile, tried to make a rolling break out of the two-step and succeeded with cavernous basslines and dubby effects.

⊙ **Randall & Andy C "Sound Control"**   Ram,1994

A mind-boggling example of low-end manipulation that was Jungle at its best.

DJ Rap

Amazingly for someone who sees DJing largely as the path to stardom, DJ Rap is unquestionably one of the fiercest, most ass-kicking drum 'n' bass DJs on the circuit. Then again, she was taught how to mix by one of the kings of jump-up, Cool Hand Flex, so her skills shouldn't come as too much of a surprise. As with most of the other big names of drum 'n' bass, however, trying to walk the fine line between staying true to a populist underground and fulfilling goals of cross-over success is becoming increasingly difficult for Rap.

The erstwhile Charissa Saveiro was born in Singapore and moved to England at the age of 12. A few years later, she ran away from home and was turned on to raving by the squatters she lived with. In 1990 she produced her first track, "Ambience – The Adored", which featured her own vocals and started DJing at venues like London's Astoria club and raves like Sunrise and Raindance.

"Divine Rhythms" (1993) furthered her reputation, but it was "Spiritual Aura" (1993) that made Rap's name. A collaboration with Aston under the *nom de disque* Engineers Without Fears, "Spiritual Aura" was one of the first Ambient Jungle tracks, but unlike the oceanic vibes of LTJ Bukem's "Music", "Spiritual Aura" seemed to spread out Hardcore's delirious bliss and make it more sensual. It may now sound like a precursor to one of Brian Transeau's overgrown epic House tracks, but at the time it heralded a new era.

Rap started her own Proper Talent label with the invigorating **Digable Bass** and **Total Tangent** EPs (both 1994). A big booyacka anthem that sampled Public Enemy's sirens, "Intelligent Woman" (1994) was Rap's first flirtation with quasi-feminist messages and succeeded admirably. After a disappointing mix album for the **Journeys By DJ** series, Rap released her debut album, **Intelligence** (1995), which was a compelling blend of wailing divas, female ragga toasting and Hardstepping beats that was let down only by the lame ballad at the end of the record.

Straight-ahead Ragga Jungle followed in the form of the floor-fillers "Roughest Gunark" (1995) and "Rumble" (1996). She started her Low Key imprint with more roughneck bizness courtesy of Special K & Rough Kut's scorched-earth "Give It to 'Em" (1996). Even more overdriven basslines and gangsta poses followed with Special K's "Knowledge/Pressure Roll", Rap's "Presenting the DJ" (1997) and the low-end boomer "NRG/Jacobi" (1998).

Her trademark rolling beats and bellowing basslines were nowhere to be found on her album for Sony off-shoot Higher Ground, however. There were some chugging two-steps on **Learning Curve** (1998), but it was largely a clumsy affair designed to show off Rap as a singer-songwriter complete with muddled pop arrangements and guitar doodling.

⊙ Intelligence   Proper Talent,1995

With the exception of the ballad, this album doesn't commit the usual
Junglist sin of tempering the Hardstep with Ambience in an effort to
conform to some ridiculous notion of an "album market".

Alex Reece

With the exception of LTJ Bukem and possibly Photek, no one
has done more to bring drum 'n' bass into a position of
"acceptability" than Alex Reece. His worshipping at the temple of
Chicago House and Detroit Techno led him to incorporate "jazzy"
chords and a streamlined groove into drum 'n' bass, thus allowing
taste-makers like Pete Tong and James Lavelle to get into drum 'n'
bass without sullying their hands with spotty ravers, unsophisticated
noises or crowd-pleasing breakbeats.

Reece discovered House music during Britain's 1988 Summer of
Love as a teenager in the London suburb of Ealing. The bare simplicity
of his collection of Trax and Nu Groove records and the lush musicality
of 808 State's "Pacific State" would eventually characterise his own
brand of drum 'n' bass. He started making brutal, industrial Techno
with his brother Oscar under the name of Exodus and, crucially, turned
down a deal from Gabba warlord Lenny Dee. Around this time he
became the house engineer for Basement Records, discovering breakbeats and meeting future partner Wax Doctor in the process. He was
first noticed on the drum 'n' bass scene for the Detroit-sounding synth
washes of his collaboration with Wax Doctor as Fallen Angel, "Hello

Lover" (1993). "Kudos" (1994) on Moving Shadow followed in a similar vein, but his breakthrough was "Basic Principles/Fresh Jive" (1994), his debut for Goldie's Metalheadz label. The jazzy, almost breakbeat-free sound of "Basic Principles" was a favourite of Fabio who was enraptured by its "classy" production.

Another Fabio fave was another collaboration with Wax Doctor, Unit 1's "Atlantic Drama" (1994), whose "Kid Caprice" drum break and Deep House vibes became the blueprint for "intelligent" Jungle. Jazz Juice's (with Wax Doctor yet again) "Detroit" (1995) was an explicit homage to Derrick May and Juan Atkins with "Strings of Life"-style chords cascading over gently rolling breaks. All of these records smoothed out Jungle's grape shot snares and gut-churning sub-bass, but the record that probably changed the direction of Jungle permanently was "Pulp Fiction" (1995). With an immense filtered bassline, a snippet of female vocals and hand-clapping drums that didn't break, the success of "Pulp Fiction" signalled the diminution of breakbeat science in Jungle and drum 'n' bass. Reece has said that he didn't want to make House tracks because they would sound imitative of the American masters, but with "Pulp Fiction" he remade drum 'n' bass in House's image.

His Top 30 debut for Island, "Feel the Sunshine" (1996), continued in this streamlined style, but with jazzier production and Björk-esque vocals. Further explorations of Fender Rhodes luxuriance and "quality" musicianship came with his Al's Records imprint which released "Touch Me/A Nu Era" and an EP of DJ Pulse material in 1996. "Feel the Sunshine", its flip, "Jazzmaster", and follow-up "Candles", were included along with a remade version of "Pulp Fiction" (called "Pulp Friction") on his debut album **So Far** (1996), whose fusion-esque textures and over-ripe sentimentality sounded like LTJ Bukem's wet dreams. With the exception of a reunion with Wax Doctor as Fallen Angels on the Loleatta Holloway sampling "Rapier/Biophonic" (1999),

Reece hasn't really been heard from since, but with the apotheosis of the Techstep two-step, the simplification of drum 'n' bass has carried on despite his absence.

◉ So Far Island,1996

If you like your drum 'n' bass with a hefty dose of "jazz" flavas, then this is for you.

⊙ "Pulp Fiction" Metalheadz,1995

A monumental release that changed the course of drum 'n' bass with its simple drum pattern and technoid bassline.

Reinforced Records

S tarted by fellow Strong Island pirate radio DJs Dego McFarlane, Mark Clair, Ian Bardouille and Gus Lawrence in 1989, Reinforced very quickly became the most important label in breakbeat music. Revolving around the core duo of McFarlane and Clair – who recorded as 4 Hero, Tek 9, Manix, Jacob's Optical Stairway and Nu Era – and artist/A&R man Goldie, the label pioneered the styles and techniques that would transform Hardcore into drum 'n' bass and as yet unnamed permutations on the basic formula of breakbeats and basslines.

Early 4 Hero releases like the **Combat Dance** EP (1990) were exercises in expanding the parameters of the Hip-House formula that combined hip-hop beats with House synthesisers and tempos. "Mr. Kirk's Nightmare" (1990) – an amazing mix of gallows humour, drug hysteria and joyous breakbeats – was the dawn of Hardcore and remains one of the decade's most exciting, inventive and devilish records. Centred on "Mr. Kirk's Nightmare", 4 Hero's debut album, **In Rough Territory** (1991), was pure energy constructed out of speeded-up samples and pitched-up breakbeats. The **Headhunters** EP (1991) suggested that rave's speed-freak producers were heading into a black hole of velocity where the mind and body would be mangled beyond all recognition.

Meanwhile, Clair's Manix project, with "Feel Real Good" and "Head in the Clouds" (both 1992), and Nookie, with "The Sound of Music" and "Shining in Da Darkness" (both 1992), explored the contours of bliss before the death drive first suggested by **Headhunters** hurtled out of control. Goldie's "Terminator" (1992) introduced pitch-shifting and an unholy mutation of Joey Beltram's "Mentasm" synth riff in what has become one of Hardcore's most pivotal records. Doc Scott's "Here Comes the Drumz" (1992), with its sample of Flavor Flav screaming "confusion!", was even more vicious and delirious. The darkness was less obvious on 4 Hero's "Cookin' Up Ya Brain" and Nebula II's "Explore H Core/Peace Maker" (both 1992), but the febrile quality of both was somehow even more sickening, even if "Peace Maker" was largely based on the theme to *Knight Rider*.

After pioneering the sound of the dark side, Reinforced inaugurated the appropriation of hip-hop's attitude as well as its sound with Code 071's (McFarlane) "A London Sumtin'" (1994) and Tek 9's "We Bring Anybody Down" (1994). Even more of a challenge to the Jungle community, however, was 4 Hero's **Parallel Universe** (1994) which followed Afronauts like Sun Ra, George Clinton, Dexter Wansell and Juan Atkins on a trip on the sweet chariot to create a new race on Mars. Imagining sounds from another galaxy, 4 Hero remade Jungle in the image of the Jupiter jazz of Detroit Techno futurists Underground Resistance and suggested that there was no hope left on Earth.

Why the slick fusion of the Mizell brothers was the pinnacle of futurism remains a question for the ages, but it certainly was the future sound of drum 'n' bass as **Enforcers Vols. 6 & 7** (1994) showed. Jamie Myerson's "Find Yourself" and Neil Trix's "Gestures Without Motion" were Ambient-breakbeat dreamscapes made of Techno pads and fusion textures, but without the millennialism of **Parallel Universe**. The **Intelligent Minds of Jungle (1995)** compilation showed the evolution of the jazz sound from the label's early days with tracks like Doc Scott's "Last Action Hero" progressing to JLM Productions' "Can't Understand".

While picking up new talent like J. Majik, Chris Energy and Arcon 2, Reinforced released their hundredth record in 1996 and celebrated with the **Above the Law – Enforcers** compilation which spanned all the styles of drum 'n' bass from the Hardstep of Tee Bone's "Sign of the Times" to the Zen-garden Ambience of Nookie's "The Eclipse". Despite showing signs of age, Reinforced continued to release ground-breaking records like the intense Miles Davis-esque psychoscapes of Nucleus & Paradox's "This Side of Forever/Decompositions" and Hidden Agenda's "Fish Eggs" (both 1998).

⊙ **Various Artists Definition of Hardcore**   Reinforced,1993

Living up to its title, this is the definitive compilation of the Darkcore sound that the label originated.

◉ **Various Artists Intelligent Minds of Jungle**   Reinforced,1995

One of the few compilations of "intelligent" Jungle that admits to the genre's roots in rave and Hardcore.

Remarc

O ne of the true "Amen" warriors, producer Remarc is one of the Junglist dancefloor's unsung heroes. The erstwhile Mark Forrester's productions are thrilling joyrides on the snares of death which epitomise Jungle's sole reason for being – release. Punctuating his grape shot drum breaks only with criminal-minded exhortations and sounds appropriated from ragga producers Steely & Clevie's laboratory, Remarc understands that the "Amen" break is every bit as eternal as the I-IV-V guitar progression and thus keeps the ornamentation to a minimum.

Remarc first attracted attention with "Ricky" (1994), a collaboration with Lewi Cifer on Dollar Records. A member of the panic-song sub-genre, "Ricky" sampled screams and dialogue from *Boyz in the Hood* and layered them with sheets of slicing, almost Wagnerian metallic synths and surging drum runs that made you feel as stable as jitter-bugging on ice. Far less uncomfortable were the rhythmic whiteouts of "Drum & Bass Wize" and "Sound Murderer" (both 1995). A sound-for-sound's-sake "Amen" burner that incorporated Ennio Morricone's whistle from *The Good, The Bad & The Ugly*, some disco strings and bad bwoy toasting, "Sound Murderer", in particular, was emblematic of Roland Barthes' concept of *jouissance*.

The textural ecstasy continued on the more diffuse, but equally anthemic "R.I.P." (1995) on Suburban Base. Another manic version of Jamaica's soundboy murder saga, "R.I.P." was less exciting than either "Drum & Bass Wize" or "Sound Murderer" because it wallowed in murky bass which gave the track's metaphorical violence a gritty, grimy, brutal context where the others still had a bit of the rave in them. Nonetheless, "R.I.P" was a firm favourite with the lighter fluid crowd.

Sampling Snoop Doggy Dogg and Gang Starr on top of a seriously flatulent synth bassline and ultra-funky breaks, "In Da Hood" (1996) more obviously courted the air-horn massive, especially with the killer Shy FX remix. "Single Finga Killa" (1996) was another overdriven bassline through the heart of hip-hop, while "You & Me" (1997) was a half-hearted attempt at creating a Junglist quiet storm. "2:01/Stick 'Em

Up" (1997) started off as a train-going-off-the-rails Techstep monstrosity, but it was just a ruse: the rolling breaks soon kicked in and showed how much more effective the chromium tornado of Techstep could be when the breakbeats actually broke instead of shuffling the two-step. Anyway, Remarc was always too funky to totally succumb to fashion.

⊙ **"R.I.P."**   Suburban Base,1995

With a muddy bassline and compressed dynamics, this felt closer in spirit to the grim social realism of Ken Loach than to the rave. (Available on **A History of Hardcore**.)

DJ Ron

E ast Ender DJ Ron is yet another seminal Jungle figure whose role has largely been obscured by the intense media spotlight focusing elsewhere. As the mainstay of Roast since 1991, Ron Samuels has presided over the shift from E'd-up Hardcore to chronic drum 'n' bass at one of Jungle's most influential clubs. With his taste for Quincy Jones, DJ Ron also precipitated drum 'n' bass' love affair with all things jazzy in his DJ sets and productions.

Legend has it that Ron was the first DJ to play Body Snatch's immortal "Euphony (Just 4U London)" (1992) which was the original "intelligent" track by virtue of its Sade-esque sax sample and synth washes. Ron's own material like "Crackman" (1994) and the nearly identical "Mo Musik" and "African Chant" (both 1994) set '70s soul-boy samples to an "Amen" background and, along with Roni Size's "Music Box" and "It's a Jazz Thing", laid the foundations for the hyper-soul sound that characterised Jungle's more adventurous records in 1994 and 1995.

It was "Canaan's Land" (1995), though, that really marked Ron as one of the prophets of Jazzstep. Originally released as an acetate in 1993 on his own London Some'ting label, "Canaan's Land" was presciently constructed of smooth vocal harmonising, lush keyboards and cushions of bass textures that taught producers like Hidden Agenda and Alex Reece a trick or two. More atmospherics followed with the drifting ambience of "Crackdown" (1995) and iridescent remixes of "Crackman" and "African Chant" (both 1996).

Signing with BMG's Parousia off-shoot, Ron released the **Quintessence** mini-album (1997). Featuring his remixes of both "Euphony" and "Canaan's Land", **Quintessence** saw Ron trying to reconcile his jazz tendencies with the prevailing trend towards angular beats and snarling basslines, with mixed results.

⊙ **"Canaan's Land"**   London Some'ting, 1995

Without gentrifying Jungle's bottom end, DJ Ron managed to make jazz signify something beyond superficial spirituality and upward mobility on this Jazzstep ancestor.

Roni Size/Reprazent

I n true Bristol fashion, Roni Size wonders aloud about the connection between the jazz-fusion of Lonnie Liston Smith and New York hip-hop, between the rhythmic repetition of the breakbeat and the galvanising catalysis of a well-aimed bass bomb. He is one of the few Jungle producers to combine the musical representation of the gangsta lifestyle (escape velocity breaks, foundation-shaking sub-bass, nasty MC samples) with the stuff real gangsters actually listen to (the soothing balm of the soft keyboards in jazz-fusion and '70s soul), creating a compelling take on the rough-smooth dialectic that has defined hip-hop since its inception.

His tracks started appearing to complete public indifference on Where's The Party, the label he set up with Chris Wharton, in 1991–92. The lack of attention was shocking considering one of these tracks was "Music Box" (a collaboration with DJ Die) which would take the Jungle community by storm when it was re-released in 1994. Unfortunately, people heard it as the clarion call for the jazzy era of drum 'n' bass, but it was really a

stunning example of breakbeat science's rehabilitation of hip-hop. Fender Rhodes licks and a nifty sample of Foxy's mellow '70s soul groover "Mademoiselle" colour a couple of breaks that run in tandem to each other, warped strings provide the bridge and a snippet of MC Lyte caught in a centrifuge gave the song its unforgettable vibe: "That dream is over".

In 1992, Size and constant collaborator DJ Krust hooked up with V Records which was run by Bryan Gee and Jumpin' Jack Frost. In 1994, V would release two tracks that, along with "Music Box", would establish Size as one of drum 'n' bass' leading figures. "Timestretch" was little more than a creepy crawly breakbeat, a shuddering bassline and a couple of samples every once in a while to add some texture, but its single-minded adherence to the percussive aspects of the drum and the bass reminded you why they called it that in the first place. Size and Die's follow-up to "Music Box", "It's a Jazz Thing", was similarly mis-heard as "intelligent" Jungle, but it was Jungle that you could only think about with your hips and feet as its mesmerising groove sucked you into its whirlpool of oceanic dub. V's subsidiary Philly Blunt released Size's showstopper "Warning" (1995) under the alias Firefox. Less minimal than his other records, "Warning" was based around the "Under Mi Sleng Teng" bassline and featured floor-filling samples of ragga chatter that made his gangsta leanings clear.

In 1993 Where's The Party became Full Cycle and sister label Dope Dragon. Full Cycle established itself immediately with "Music Box" and "11:55" (1995), another collaboration with Die. Sampling the original gangsta track, Lightning Rod's 1973 "Hustler's Convention", "11:55" was a brutal slice of percussion maximalism as urban tension. Dope Dragon showcased Size's most malevolent side. Under the pseudonym Mask, Size made the grape shot snares of the "Amen" break into an art form. With DJ Krust (who masqueraded as Gang Related), Size destroyed dancefloors with tracks like "Oh My Gosh!" (1994) and the Terrordome EP (1995). Their best Dope Dragon release, though, was the unbelievable "Tear It Up" (1996) which brought bass and break manipulation to the peak of gangsta escapism.

In 1996 Size formed the loose collective Reprazent with Krust, Die, DJ Suv and MC Dynamite. Guests from outside this core group like vocalist Onallee, bassist Si John and drummer Clive Deemer were added for the recording of the Mercury Prize-winning **New Forms** (1997) album. This union of live instruments and breakbeat science perhaps erred too much on the jazzy side, but the groove was present and correct on tracks like "Brown Paper Bag" and "Share the Fall". While the album itself might have been a tad over-rated, the group's live show was stunning and remains the only successful attempt to make drum 'n' bass work in a concert setting.

◉ Various Artists Music Box   Full Cycle,1995

A collection of some of Full Cycle's finest moments including "Music Box", "11:55" and Size and Die's "Breakbeat Era".

◉ New Forms   Talkin' Loud,1997

It might represent drum 'n' bass' mainstream acceptance, but it still has some very worthwhile moments, particularly "Brown Paper Bag".

Ruffneck Ting

Starting in Bristol in 1993, Ruffneck Ting is probably Britain's longest-running Junglist club. Launched by the Ledge crew with DJ Dazee as resident, Ruffneck Ting has since developed from a club to a record label with its own collective of producers and DJs who are effectively the Bristol Jungle scene's second string.

Occupying the shadow cast by Roni Size and his Full Cycle crew, Ruffneck Ting made their vinyl debut with the **Ledge Project** EP (1995) which was credited to Substance (a collective featuring Dazee and

Markee). Dazee's "Rude Girl" was one of those rare Jungle tunes that featured roughneck female vocals rather than a post-coital, gushing diva, while "Crazy Horse" was a roller with an affinity for the legendary Native American warrior. More jump-up business followed with "Damn Right" (1996) and "The Fly/Prisoner" (1996), both of which attained anthem status on more hip-hop-minded floors.

Following the fashion for two-step rhythms and distorted bass drops, Substance's "L.F. Ant/Think" (1997) had whooping synths atop a rigid, synthetic arrangement. Dazee's "Homeboyz (Remix)/Westside" (1997), meanwhile, was another jump-up tune made with air horns and rewinds in mind. With resident MC Jakes, Markee released "Street Life/No One Knows" (1998), while Ruffneck Ting's subsidiary label, Breakbeat Culture, released tracks like Felony's "Sound Chamber/Conflict" (1998), which was also included on their fine compilation, **Breakbeat Sampler Volume 1** (1998). Ruffneck Ting's **Spectrum** compilation (1998) collected the past few years' worth of jump-up floor-fillers along with more produced tracks by the likes of Technical Itch's Mark Caro.

○ Various Artists Spectrum   Ruffneck Ting, 1998

Aimed at the air-horn and lighter crowd, this compilation collected floor-burners like "L.F. Ant" and "Homeboyz".

Shut Up and Dance

I f one crew represented the original spirit of rave culture it was Stoke Newington's Shut Up and Dance. Before the dance scene became factionalised into hundreds of sub-genres, SUAD (both the group and the label) threw together House beats, Techno squiggles, hip-hop breakbeats, East End raps, ragga-chat and incredibly cheeky samples to create a unique sound that is the clear ancestor of drum 'n' bass.

Shut Up and Dance was the recording alias of Londoners PJ and Smiley who released their debut single, "5, 6, 7, 8", on their own GTI label in 1988. For the release of their follow-up single, the Suzanne Vega-sampling "£10 to Get In" (1989), they changed the name of the label to Shut Up and Dance as well. With samples of Raw Silk's "Do It to the Music" and Soulsonic Force's "Looking for the Perfect Beat", the flip, "Rap's My Occupation", was perhaps even more representative of their style. Both "£10 to Get In" and the remix, "£20 to Get In" with its very funny intro ("'I thought it was £10 to get in'; 'Nah, man, it's had a remix'"), were massive club hits and managed to make the lower reaches of the British Top 60. "Lamborghini/Change Soon Come" (1990) rode a scandalously large portion of Eurythmics' "Sweet Dreams (Are Made of This)" into the Top 50. While their obvious sampling is similar in its blatantly larcenous aspects to wack rappers like MC Hammer and Puff Daddy, PJ and Smiley performed their thievery with a knowing wink and cheerful grin that made it endearing and the breakbeat undertow made it evolutionary, if not revolutionary in the grand scheme of things.

The SUAD label really hit its stride with Ragga Twins' incredible "Spliffhead" (1990) which is proto-Jungle if anything is. With its irresistible "Ragga Twins dere 'bout" chant, "Spliffhead" and the follow-up, "Hooligan 69" (1990), made significant dents in the British Top 50. Even better was "Juggling/Wipe the Needle" (1990) which featured the Twins furiously boasting and toasting over a classic break, predating General Levy by some four years. Their **Reggae Owes Me Money**

(1991) album, which reached #26 on the album charts, also featured such classics as the Earth Wind & Fire sampling anti-heroin track "The Killing" and "18" Speaker" which highlighted the influence of dub on the SUAD sound.

Other successful signings to the label included the militant Rum & Black, indie-kids-gone-dance Codine and Nicolette – whose rave standards "Single Minded People" (1990), which samples George Kranz's cult hit "Din Daa Daa", and "Waking Up" (1991), were some of the earliest tunes to feature Hardcore's trademark speeded-up breaks. Nicolette's Billie-Holiday-as-a-little-girl voice eventually led her to work with Massive Attack, a solo album, **Never Let Anyone Live Rent Free In Your Head** (1996), and a mix compilation for DJ Kicks in which electronicats Plaid did the mixing and she was the selector.

At the end of 1990, Shut Up and Dance released their first album, **Dance Before the Police Come**, which included all of their earlier singles as well as the Terrence Trent D'Arby swipes of the incredibly moody "Derek Went Mad" (which also saw an early appearance of the "Amen" break) and the brilliant "This Town Needs a Sheriff" which pre-dated the strings 'n' funk style of the Wu Tang Clan by a good two years.

The group's and label's biggest success came with "Raving, I'm Raving" (1992) which reached #2 on the British pop charts. The track anchored the duo's second album, **Death Is Not the End**, which also featured the disarmingly simple "Autobiography of a Crackhead". Unfortunately, "Raving..." also signalled the beginning of the end of the label as their cavalier approach to sampling finally caught up with them. "Raving" was based on Mark Cohn's "Walking to Memphis" and the singer-songwriter started legal proceedings, eventually being awarded all of the profits from the sales of the record. Soon afterwards, the label was forced to settle out of court with the Mechanical Copyright Protection Society for their uncleared samples of Suzanne Vega and Ryuichi Sakamoto.

THE ORIGINAL COLLECTION
THE FIRST 20 SINGLES IN FULL 12" VERSIONS

After two years of hibernation, PJ and Smiley emerged with "Phuck the Biz" (1994) on a resurrected SUAD. However, their subsequent **Black Men United** (1995) album was released on Pulse 8. Featuring (cleared) samples of Duran Duran's "Save a Prayer" and Perez Prado's "Guaglione" and forays into swingbeat and lovers' rock, the album failed to generate the excitement of old. Around the same time, Ragga Twins re-emerged with a similarly lacklustre album, **Rinsin' Lyrics** (1995), that showed just how far the mighty had fallen.

Shut Up and Dance's **Got 'em Locked** EP (1999) came closer to the old electricity, but they still had to resort to sampling Portishead.

⊙ **Various Artists Shut Up and Dance Compilation**   SUAD,1990

Although it doesn't have "Raving, I'm Raving", this overview of the label's first twenty singles is the best collection of proto-Jungle you'll find.

Shy FX

When Jungle exploded overground in the summer of 1994, two producers took the brunt of the criticism from the isolationist wing of the Jungle community. M-Beat and Shy FX had allegedly destroyed the drum 'n' bass garden of Eden by turning the music into a hyped-up version of the Jamaican dancehall and creating some of the decade's finest pop tunes. Of course, this is exactly what made Hardcore so exciting in the first place, but this was lost on the sourpusses who insisted that drum 'n' bass was about craftsmanship.

As a teenager from Tottenham, north London, though, the dancehall was in Andre Williams' blood. The budding soundboy made dubplates for local sound systems until he enrolled in a sound engineering course in 1993 and hooked up with the SOUR label. With his taste for Jamaican bad-man tales, Shy FX wired a sample of Ray Liotta in *Goodfellas* to some booyacka-Bobby-Digital drums to create "Gangsta Kid" (1993). It was his third tune, "Original Nuttah" (1994), though, that made him temporary king of the Jungle. Working with MC UK Apachi, Shy made a track that took ragga's soundboy-murderer metaphor as far as it could go sonically without bursting out of the speakers with a spray of bullets. 50,000 copies later, Shy FX was *persona non grata* on the scene.

After a remake of "Gangsta Kid" (1995) with MC Gunsmoke, Shy FX showed how to murder the wack soundboys running Jungle with the mind-boggling "Who Runs 'Tings" (1995). A dizzying collage of Dr. Dre synths, lick-shot drums and Yardie vocal samples, "Who Runs 'Tings" mixed the original delirious spirit of Hardcore with a potent sense of urban dread to create one of Jungle's most criminally underrated tracks. Completely ignored by a media intent on promoting the

latest infinitesimal filter tweak as the sound of the future, his **Just an Example** album (1995) was a good, if single-minded, amalgam of Eric B & Rakim samples, blistering "Amen" runs, dread basslines and sirens.

After splitting from **SOUR**, Shy started his Ebony label with the excellent compilation **The Formula** (1996). Featuring his own "The Wolf", "Call Wait" and "Shotz" as well as tracks from like-minded artists DJ Krust and Potential Bad Boy, **The Formula** was a bruising barrage of familiar dancehall/bad bwoy elements that felt like a clarion call for the gangster boogie as drum 'n' bass got stuck in a seemingly eternal Techstep loop.

The Formula's success was followed up by the Wu Tang funk of "Killer Bees" (1996) and the novel reconstruction of the "Apache" break, "Mad Apache" (1997). His full re-instatement to the drum 'n' bass community, though, came with the release of "Bambaata/Funksta" (1998). Undoubtedly the track of the year, "Bambaata" reconnected drum 'n' bass with its original percussive imperative, while "Funksta" stole the strings from the *Mission Impossible* theme and appended them to a massive horn stab. As 45 Roller, he unleashed "Stomp/Saturday Night Roller" (1998) on his Ivory subsidiary which harked back to Q Project & Spinback's "Champion Sound". "Pandora's Box" (1998), meanwhile, proved that he was flexible enough to create a jazz-groove anthem as well as the hard stuff.

◉ Various Artists The Formula   Ebony,1996

The album that alerted more sensible commentators to the fact that the mainstream coverage of drum 'n' bass' equipment freaks was doing irreparable damage to the heart and soul of the scene.

Talvin Singh

A product of one of the numerous post-colonial Diasporas, producer/percussionist/club promoter/DJ Talvin Singh straddles two worlds. In a country whose most iconic act (drinking tea) is a ritual imported from the Indian sub-continent, Singh is an exotic bit of the other who dresses up "Britain's only home-grown dance music" (itself a product of multi-culturalism) with tablas and sitars. In India, children of immigrants like Singh are as British as the queen. Singh's music – a blend of tribal Punjabi rhythms, cosmopolitan strings and utopian technology – is a perfect encapsulation of this geographical and cultural nether region that trumpeter Jon Hassell has called "the Fourth World".

Born to Punjabi parents in East London, Singh grew up amidst the scattered detritus of his parents' homeland and the magnetic force of Western youth culture. At age five, Singh was sent to India to study classical tabla with Pandit Laxman Singh and returned to play in British jazz-fusion bands during the latter half of the '80s. He got a chance to practise his love for both Indian film music and Electro when Björk asked him to create Bollywood string arrangements for her **Debut** album in 1993. He raised his profile further by supporting Massive Attack on their Protection Tour with his electrified tablas and by appearing on Future Sound of London's **Lifeforms** album, Björk's **Post** and a couple of Adrian Sherwood productions for his On-U Sound label.

Inaugurating a brief media vogue for British-Asian fusion, Singh launched his Anokha Club at London's Blue Note in 1996. Bringing together a like-minded collective of DJs, producers and instrumentalists, Anokha was as much about bridging the gap between electronic programming and improvisation as it was about cross-cultural exchange. Despite occasionally verging on coffee-table exotica territory, **Anokha: Sounds of the Asian Underground** (1997) was an often beguiling album

of dreamy textures, lush strings, tabla freakouts and Junglist breaks that could only have emerged from the double consciousness of London's Asian community.

OK (1998) followed with an even broader sonic and cultural palette. Taking in Okinawan singers, Ry Cooder-style guitar sweeps, reminiscences of the great *qawwali* singer Nusrat Fateh Ali Khan, dub basslines and Chinese water-torture percussion, **OK** explored the narrow streets and back alleys of the same global village mapped out by Jon Hassell and Brian Eno on **Fourth World: Possible Musics Volume 1.**

⊙OK   Island,1998

As a result of Singh's knowledge of the Indian classical tradition and his production chops, this excellent collection of Ambient grooves never becomes mere ethno-trance.

Slammin' Vinyl

U nder the guidance of Red Alert and Mike Slammer, Slammin' Vinyl has been responsible for some of the most intoxicating moments in a genre based entirely on delirium. Slammin's first release was Red Alert & Mike Slammer's **Hold Tight** EP (1993), but they started to make their mark with the intense keyboard stabs of the **Original Bad Boy** EP (1993). "Ruff!!" was nothing but insistent keyboards and a breakbeat that skidded underneath, while "Original Bad Boy" hotwired a classic Italian House piano riff to "Mentasm" stabs, a sinister bassline, a helium James Brown grunt and a ragga chanting "original bad boy, now watch this".

Even more schizophrenic was Red Alert & Mike Slammer's thoroughly awesome "In Effect/Don't Need Your Love" (1993) which flitted in and out of moody bad bwoy attitude, cascading piano chimes and Space Invaders synth stabs to produce a composite portrait of the rave experience in miniature. The lofty esteem in which "In Effect" was held on the scene was reflected by Slipmatt and Sy & Unknown's excellent remixes in 1994 which marked the definitive split between the Junglists and Happy Hardcore. Red Alert & Mike Slammer remixed "In Effect" themselves on their **Fuckin' Hardcore** EP (1993) which was their attempt to explore the dark side, but they fared better in the light and subsequently released the rushy "You Are the One/Let's Do It" and "Feel So Real/Walking on Sunshine" (both 1994).

Fully embracing the bubblier side of Hardcore, Slammin' released Happy Tunes' "Rushin' on Pink Champagne" and Midas' "Imperial March" in 1995. Red Alert & Mike Slammer's "The Ride/Adrenalin" (1995) was a power surge of hot flashes and gushing emotion, while Vinylgroover's "Wishing on a Star" (1996) brought celestial melodics into Happy Hardcore's toytown. Brisk & Trixxy's "Show Me the Way" (1997) squeezed in early Hardcore's breakbeat delirium in between a Vangelis piano line and a bouncy Techno beat, while their "Eye Opener/I Need Somebody" (1997) was all piercing synth stabs and over-the-top diva melodrama with one of the most manipulative breakdowns ever. DJ Stompy's "Give Me Your Love" (1997), on the other hand, updated Human League's android melancholy for bionic cyborgs.

⊙ **Red Alert & Mike Slammer "In Effect"**   Slammin' Vinyl,1993

Hardcore doesn't come much better than this synaesthetic blur of House, Techno and hip-hop. (Available on **Here Come the Drums**.)

Slipmatt/SL2

With the possible exception of The Prodigy, nobody is more representative of the twists and turns of rave culture than Slipmatt. A DJ from Essex who was first really turned on to music by the heavy dub riddims of Jamaican producers like King Tubby and Scientist, Slipmatt has been on the scene since day one and has probably played at every big rave you could name. From generic rave music through breakbeat Techno to Happy Hardcore, Slipmatt has graced each sub-genre with his impressive cutting and mixing skills, building sets that intensify the Ecstasy rush but are equally motivational to chemical-free ravers as well.

As a DJ, Slipmatt is second to none on the Hardcore scene, but his track record as a producer is equally illustrious. Slipmatt and school chum Lime first began to make hip-hop tracks together as SL2 in 1987, but their first proper release was 1990's "Do That Dance". After failing to see any money from the track which sold moderately well, the duo released their next record, "DJs Take Control" (1991), themselves, and quickly sold the complete pressing of 3500 copies. XL Records soon licensed the track and its "Dance when the record spins" and "How's everybody feeling?" samples soon became as anthemic on the early Hardcore scene as its piano breakdown and breakbeat rhythm.

Even more anthemic was "On a Ragga Tip" (1992) which gatecrashed the British Top 10 on the strength of its farting, ragga bassline, skanking piano riff, reggae skatting samples and infectious beats. The follow-up, "Way in My Brain" (1992), was even better. Stealing the computer bassline and a large chunk of vocals from Wayne Smith's dancehall reggae classic "Under Mi Sleng Teng", "Way in My Brain" epitomised Hardcore's pillage of black music to achieve its syncretic, audio analogue of the E-buzz.

As Hardcore was excommunicated from the mainstream dance scene by the House and Techno purists after the chart success of SL2, The Prodigy and The Smart E's, Slipmatt continued to push the more uplifting strains of breakbeat music while DJs like Grooverider and Fabio were being sucked into the vortex of Darkcore. His awesome "Hear Me" (1993), which layered the cheesiest piano riff imaginable and a flute sample on top of an "Amen" break, proved that what would become known as Happy Hardcore could be just as inventive and "intelligent" as their more illustrious drum 'n' bass cousins. "Breaking Free" (1993) followed in a similar style in that it combined a roughneck, sphincter-loosening bassline with impossibly airy, Minnie Ripperton-style diva gushes.

While Happy Hardcore was being blanked by the mainstream dance press even as Jungle was exploding overground, Slipmatt was releasing gaseous breakbeat tunes on his own Benz and Universal labels (naturally, named after his car). When Happy Hardcore was dominated by the 4/4 Gabba kick drum in 1994–95, Slipmatt concentrated on DJing and his own releases became less frequent and less anthemic. With rave nostalgia becoming a significant, if relatively small, market force, Slipmatt's mix CDs have dominated. United Dance's **Anthems** series (1996, 1997) featured Slipmatt's catalytic sets of old-school favourites and new floor-fillers, while Slipmatt's mix for the **Mixmag Live** series (1997) was a 1992 time capsule.

Away from the history lessons, Slipmatt re-united with XL to set up his First Recordings imprint which released his impossibly upbeat collaboration with Eruption, "Sunshine" (1997) – a fitting end to rave's first decade.

○ **Various Artists United Dance**
Presents The Anthems '92–'97   United Dance, 1997

An unimpeachable collection of rave anthems mixed by Slipmatt,
including his essential tracks "On a Ragga Tip" and "Hear Me".

Smokers Inc.

Much of Jungle's excitement comes from the layering of cool
and detached bad bwoy vocal samples from hip-hop and
Ragga over the top of frenetic beats that are the antithesis of cool.
Although criminally ignored by the mainstream, Smokey Joe and his
Smokers Inc. empire have pioneered this strain of Jungle since the
music's earliest days.

With his brother Tobi, Joe Brodie began his career DJing on a
Newcastle pirate radio station at the beginning of the '90s. Using a
Kool & the Gang break and some ragga samples, "Gimme My Gun"
(1993) was released on Hardware Records and was soon picked up
by Labello Blanco Records. Smokey Joe's **Bad Boy** EP (1993) featured "Gimme My Gun" along with the equally devastating "Bad Boy
Riddim" and "Ruff & Rugged" and quickly became a classic with the
puffa jacket set. Similar to both DJ Hype's "Rrrroll Da Beats" and Tom
& Jerry's "Maximum Style", "Special Request" (1994) soon followed
and established Jungle as the sound of a Jamaican dancehall shuffling its way into oblivion.

After the release of "Shining/Four Meg Sound Boy" (1995) for
Labello Blanco, Joe and Tobi formed No Smokin' Records. With

releases like Smokey Joe's "Freakin Wit' Da Cut/Echo Chamber" and "Smokin' Hornz" and B-Jam's Armand Van Helden-inspiring version of the "Think" beat, "Funkula" (all 1995), No Smokin' quickly established itself as one of the two or three most creative jump-up labels around.

No Smokin' became Smokers Inc. in 1996, which also incorporated the Rude & Deadly, Bad Dogz and Evil labels as well. Of the side labels, Evil was perhaps the best, scoring with a series of remarkably militant jump-up tracks like the mind-boggling "Cops Ain't Shit" (1997). The parent label continued to fill jumpier dancefloors with the re-release of Rude & Deadly's 1995 ragga anthem, "Give Me a Dubplate", and The Smokester's wobbling "Bass Come Down" (both 1997). B-Jam followed the trend for blaxploitation funk with "Raid/From the Real", while Babylonian warped Public Enemy with contorted breaks on "Never Had a Gun" (both 1998).

❍Various Artists The No Smoking Selection   Smokers Inc., 1996

Despite its title, this is a non-stop compilation of smoking joints from one of the best jump-up labels including B-Jam's "Funkula", Smokey Joe's "Smokin Hornz" and The Smokester's "Bass Come Down".

SOUR/Emotif/ Botchit & Scarper

F ormed in 1993 by Dave Stone, Sound of the Underground Records was one of the first Jungle labels to attract any kind of above-ground attention. Shy FX's *Goodfellas*-sampling "Gangsta Kid"

(1993) was one of the earliest and best of the roughneck ragga-Jungle tracks that broke Jungle in the mainstream. Even more successful, however, was his collaboration with rapper UK Apachi, "Original Nuttah" (1994), which, on the strength of about a thousand rewinds at the Notting Hill Carnival, made the British pop charts.

Perhaps inspired by the success of "Original Nuttah", SOUR went distinctly pop with "Greater Love" by Elisabeth Troy with Soundman and Don Lloydie (1995). Picking up on the growing trend to incorporate more "musical" elements into Jungle, Soundman and Don Lloydie wrapped Troy's gushing R&B vocals around subdued breaks and the rain-forest squiggle sampled from 808 State's "Pacific State" that would soon come to signify "intelligent" Jungle. Far more underground was T.Power, a producer who claimed he was inspired by the anti-corporate rabble rouser Noam Chomsky. T.Power's debut album, **The Self-Evident Truths of an Intuitive Mind** (1996), was full of autodidact ramblings about the encroaching "police state". Although he may have been correct, the music was often as pleasure-free as his imagined dystopia. More influential was an earlier collaboration with MK Ultra, the half-stepping "Mutant Jazz" (1995).

In the hands of DJ Trace, "Mutant Jazz" lost any vestiges of jazz. The mellow horn riff was replaced by harsh synths and a brutal bassline sampled from Kevin Saunderson's Detroit Techno classic "Another Chance". The success of "The Mutant" inspired SOUR to form an experimental off-shoot, Emotif. While SOUR was releasing killer jump-up tracks like Elementz of Noize's collaboration with MC Det, "Stick Up!" (1996), Emotif was defining the new sound of Techstep with tracks like Rollers Instinct's "The Haze" and "Mid-Town Method" (both 1996). Rollers Instinct was the trio of Trace, Ed Rush and Nico and their tracks were the cornerstones of the epochal compilation **Techsteppin'** (1996). **Techsteppin's** simultaneously detached and angry sound was everything that T.Power's album should have been and its post-apocalyptic feel ushered in the new era of dark tunes that has dominated drum 'n' bass since this compilation's release.

Emotif continued to set the standard for Techstep with releases like Cybernet vs. Genetix's (aka DJ Tonic) "Cyborg 1" (1997), while SOUR formed the Botchit & Scarper label for Down Tempo and funky breaks with releases from Glowball, Raw Deal and Purple Kola. Around this time, though, SOUR folded, leaving only Emotif and Botchit & Scarper. Emotif carried on releasing tracks that walked the tightrope between hip-hop-influenced Hardstep and the heavily metallic Techstep by Click 'n' Cycle and B.L.I.M. Botchit & Scarper, meanwhile, provided fodder for the "nu skool breaks" movement with the acid sub-bass funk of Freq. Nasty's "Boomin' Back Atcha" (1997) and "Underglass" (1998).

O Various Artists Techsteppin'   Emotif,1996

That rarest of records – a compilation that actually defined a sound and wasn't just a haphazard collection of tracks – Techsteppin' created the sound that has dominated drum 'n' bass ever since.

Source Direct

The product of hours spent in front of a computer screen getting the drums just so and the bass sound perfectly tweaked, drum 'n' bass is the music of control freaks. At the forefront of drum 'n' bass' legion of perfectionists are James Baker and Philip Aslett who as Source Direct, Sounds of Life and Hokusai have made the precision and rigour of the producer signify the dysfunctional individualism of post-Thatcher Britain.

A couple of bored suburban teenagers from St Albans, Hertford-shire, Baker and Aslett heard in hip-hop and early Hardcore justifica-tions for their own juvenile delinquency. After run-ins with the law for petty thievery and rave promotion, the two got into production and released "Trust Me" (1993) as Sounds of Life on Certificate 18 Records. Further Sounds of Life records like "Currents/Intellect" and "Hidden Rooms" (both 1994) and releases on Streetbeats as Oblivion like "Night Windows/Lush" (1994) established Baker and Aslett's obsessive-compulsive mutations of Lalo Schifrin's grimy jazz-funk as the blueprint for their creation of atmospheres that were gripped by a sick tension.

With the aid of a Prince's Trust grant, the two set up their own Source Direct label and released "Fabric of Space/Bliss" at the beginning of 1995. More spacious than most of their records, "Fabric of Space" anticipated the melodic "Complexities/Secret Liaison" (1996) 12" that they would release for LTJ Bukem's Good Looking label. Other Source Direct records, however, were less easy on the ears. "Approach & Identify", "Snake Style" and "The Crane" (all 1995) appeared mystical and cosmic on the surface, but there was a dark intensity underneath each of these tracks that was the result of the duo's stated intent to control people with their tracks.

"A Made Up Sound" (1995), their debut for Metalheadz, followed suit with a taxing attention to detail, while the flip, "The Cult", was a foreboding track that warned, "It is defeat that you must learn to pre-pare for". As Hokusai, they released the harrowing "Black Rose" (1995) which was all clenched breaks and taut, coiled energy. Source Direct's "Stonekiller/Web of Sin" (1996) was more of the same, but the melodrama of its brooding, John Carpenter strings slightly undercut the tension. "The Silent Witness" (1996), a track on Mo' Wax's **Headz 2** compilation, continued the dark-alley menace with skin-crawling strings and a rigid deconstruction of the "Apache" break.

Following neighbour and ally Photek to Virgin's Science imprint, Source Direct released a series of singles that recalled the rigid funk and implicit politics of '80s groups like A Certain Ratio and 23 Skidoo. "Black Domina/Two Masks", "Call & Response/Computer State" (both 1997) and "Capital D/Enemy Lines" (1998) were tourniquet-tight tracks of constricted drum 'n' bass that served as bleak soundscapes of Britain's dead cities.

"Call & Response" and "Capital D" both featured on their similarly intense debut album, **Exorcise the Demons** (1999), which also contained the frightening precision of "Mind Weaver" and the fearsome noise blocks of "Technical Warfare".

◉ Controlled Developments   Astralwerks, 1998

A US-only compilation of their singles for Science, this mini-album is a concise introduction to Source Direct's sound of control and dysfunction.

Splatterbreaks/
Terrorcore

M aking the media's presentation of people like Optical and Ed Rush as hard men utterly laughable, the mutant breakbeat freaks making the uncompromising music known variously as "splatterbreaks", "terrorcore" or "harshcore" have turned the drum 'n' bass and Hardcore formulas into vehicles for absolute sonic extremism. With an aesthetic that wires up early '80s Industrial culture to the sensation-for-sensation's sake ethos of Spiral Tribe and the speed-plus-noise breakbeat matrix of labels like Industrial Strength and PCP, producer/theorists like Christoph Fringelli and DJ Scud stick two fingers up at not only drum 'n' bass' gentrification, but at the politics of the growing corporate state as well.

Inspired by Underground Resistance and Paul Virilio, Fringelli's Praxis organisation is the nexus of the scene. Organising the notorious Dead By Dawn parties in Brixton, producing the *Datacide* and *Alien Underground* 'zines and running the Praxis and Subversion labels, Fringelli is deeply committed to the ideals of political interventions and subversive musical practice. Starting in 1992 with the **Scaremonger** EP, the Praxis label has since released some thirty records of gruesome Speedcore that aspires to the sound of violence. While records like Disciples of Belial's Christian-baiting **Songs of Praise** EP (1994) can be perilously close to the cartoony kitsch of death metal, releases like Metatron's **Speed and Politics** EP (1993) and Cyberchrist's **Information Revolution** EP (1995) put the squat politics into practice.

Opening its account with the words "No brain, no power, no future, no hope", DJ Scud's Ambush label is less expressly political than Praxis, although there is no escaping the message behind titles like **Snipers At Work** or the brutal imagery of Ambush's graphics. Jackal & Hide's **Escape From South London** EP (1997) and Aphasic & Scud's **Welcome to the Warren** EP (1997) set the label's basic sound in motion with drum programming that would probably make Matrix scream in agony, septic sub-bass and an acid rain of nasty synth FX. David Hammer's (aka Shizuo) **Give Up**

EP (1997) was accurately described by Scud as a "symphony of stress", while Scud's own **Snipers At Work** EP (1998) connected Techstep's adolescent temper tantrum back to its roots in the Jungle with ragga samples and maelstroms of malfunctioning "Amen" breaks. Scud's best union of post-industrial scuzz, bionic steppers' riddims and rootical reggae was his mind-boggling collaboration with Nomex, "Total Destruction" (1998) on the Maschinenbau label. With a ragga DJ gleefully singing, "Total destruction, the only solution" in the face of searing whiteouts of white noise and escape velocity "Amen" drum shrapnel, "Total Destruction" sounded like a Sam Peckinpah film breaking out in a Kingston dancehall.

2nd Gen's **Noise Sculptures** EP (1998), on the other hand, was the sort of thing that might make Merzbow fans dance (if such a thing was in the realm of possibility). A gratuitously unpleasant maelstrom of noise and fringe-culture titles ("The Art of Self-Abasement") constructed by Wajid Yaseen, **Noise Sculptures** was the aggressive side of Talvin Singh's post-colonial double consciousness. "Ah Ja Shataan" was what you'd think Trip-Hop was if you judged it only by its name: an Aleister Crowley monologue on top of a scurvy low rumble for a bassline, a clanging carillon and some whirling Islamic vocal sounds. A second EP, **Against Nature** (1998), continued with similar themes, but failed to generate the same excitement.

⊙ **Various Artists Dead By Dawn**   Praxis,1997

The soundtrack to the monthly parties of the same name, this collects resolutely brutal tracks by Delta 9, Sonic Subjunkies, Aphasic and Somatic Responses.

⊙ **Nomex & Scud "Total Destruction"**   Maschinenbau,1998

Only available on 7", but worth every effort to track it down if you like your funk obliterated by anarcho-punk chaos.

Spring Heel Jack

Spring Heel Jack are drum 'n' bass at its most eclectic – John Coxon has worked with both Spiritualized and Betty Boo and Ashley Wales used to compose classical music. Elements of Ennio Morricone's spaghetti Western soundtracks, guitar grandstanding, outdated science fiction and Bernard Hermann strings are combined with a dub sensibility to recreate drum 'n' bass in the image of art music. Crucially, unlike any of their contemporaries, Spring Heel Jack are primarily an album act, a fact which says as much about their direction and ambitions as their music.

Coxon and Wales formed Spring Heel Jack in 1994 and released their Ambient-aquatic debut single, "The Sea Lettuce", on Rough Trade. "The Sea Lettuce" was included along with the harp-kissed "Colonades" and the glacial, Nyman-esque "Dereck" on their first album, **There Are Strings** (1995). With almost fully developed melodies and iridescent strings, **There Are Strings** was of course hailed as a model of progression, but the album's best track was a jaunty, Junglist beach anthem called "Lee Perry Part 1" that had nothing to do with complexity and everything to do with rhythmic effervescence.

The duo next hooked up with Everything But the Girl to produce the Top 10 single "Walking Wounded" (1996), which was the first Junglist torch song since Nicolette's "Waking Up". Spring Heel Jack's second album and major label debut, **68 Million Shades** (1996), was an audacious exploration of the possibilities of sampler-based production. Locust hums, Sibelius samples, beats created from speeded-up violins, blues guitars and Miles Davis trumpets peacefully co-existed with cavernous basslines and ricocheting breakbeats to produce an album of kaleidoscopic intensity. **Versions** (1996), a disappointing album of dub remakes, followed a couple of months later.

Perhaps the result of Island's marketing muscle or maybe their self-consciously arty tendencies or maybe the fact that they could cut it live, Spring Heel Jack were hailed in some American quarters as the flag bearers of drum 'n' bass. With the weight of such expectations and the trend towards the toxic atmospherics of Techstep, **Busy, Curious, Thirsty** (1997) was almost inevitably a dud. Tracks like "Casino" and "Bank of America" were meant to be scary, rampaging cyborg Huns, but merely sounded like wannabe hard men who couldn't hide the fact that they were really softies at heart.

❍ 68 Million Shades   Trade 2/Island,1996

One of the more successful drum 'n' bass albums in that it varies mood without becoming mawkish and tries to push the envelope without making a big deal about it.

Spunk jazz

Whatever you want to call it – spunk jazz, Fungle or drill 'n' bass – the combination of double-time drum 'n' bass with impossible-to-dance-to rhythms and toilet humour is the latest playground for computer geeks with no desire or ability to communicate with the outside world. Building on the asocial nerdity of Aphex Twin and µ-ziq, spunk jazzers turn the Jungle into a romper room in which fart noises are still funny, the banging of a square peg against a round hole is a rhythmic innovation and an Ambient, biotic, deodorant-less aroma feels like home.

The archetypal drill 'n' basser is Squarepusher whose first releases came out on Brighton's Spymania label. When it was still known as Nothing's Clear, the label released the **Stereotype** EP (1994) which blended Aphex-style melodicism with obtuse atmospheres and silly breakbeats and "Rumble1/Crot" (1995) which was closer to the typical Squarepusher sound of fusion mayhem. As The Duke of Harringay, Squarepusher continued to pulverise Weather Report with a pneumatic drill on the **Alray Road Tracks** EP (1996) on Spymania proper. The Spymania Allstars' **Avit** EP (1996) featured abrasively brittle avant-Junglist contributions from Si Begg's Cabbageboy project and some joker calling himself Alvis Parsley.

More stale drum caterwauling could be found on Cambridge's Bovinyl label. With even less of a dancefloor conscience than the Spymania clowns, Andy Coleman, Tim Gould, Adam Butler and Richard Watson (aka DJ Tiny Penis) started Bovinyl in 1996 with the release of Gould's **My Toilet Seat** EP under the guise of Milky Boy. Butler's **Broken Breakbeat Bebop** EP (1996) released as Vert followed a similar path with a five-year-old's understanding of syncopation and more textural information than anyone could hope to process. More barely post-adolescent antics, doley farting about and cranky beats could be found on Coleman's Animals on Wheels records. After the Bovinyl release of the **Baits Bite** EP (1996), Animals on Wheels signed to Ninja Tune for the aggressively unpleasant **Designs & Mistakes** album (1997).

Giving the mini-genre its most evocative name, the iLL label's **Spunk Jazz** compilation (1997) was a definitive collection of irritation by the likes of Cabbageboy, Value Ape, Bubbah's Tum and Paddington Breaks. Paddington Breaks' **Smart But Casual** EP (1998) had the scene's requisite dose of hyper-active beats and basslines, but on tracks like "Biztalk" Mr Breaks sounded as if he mellowed out a bit.

⊙ **Various Artists Spunk Jazz** iLL,1997

Not everyone's cup of tea by a long shot, but if you entertain fantasies of wearing oversize nappies and shaking a rattle, then this is your soundtrack.

Squarepusher

The don of the "spunk jazz" movement of too-fast breakbeats and toilet-humour attitude, Squarepusher makes drum 'n' bass of the absurd. While his cheap-gag sensibility can sometimes be a refreshing change from the po-faced ego-tripping that seems to dominate the scene, his pre-adolescent scatology, stubborn refusal to groove and arrogant soap-boxing about "complexity" is unbecoming to say the least. When he feels like communicating with his music, though, Squarepusher can be as inventive as any of the lo-fi nerds who have foisted their bedroom antics on the world since Aphex Twin made it acceptable.

Tom Jenkinson grew up in Chelmsford, Essex, listening to Weather Report's jazz-fusion and falling into their muso cult-of-technique. Around the same time, he attended his first rave and thought it was as hilarious as the broken-down technology he found so kitschy. His love for cheap synthesizers and Weather Report's bassist, Jaco Pastorius, first made itself known on a series of limited-run singles for Brighton's Spymania label in 1994–95, which were later compiled on **Burning'n Tree** (1997). Marked by ludicrously complex drum programming which was probably inspired by another fusion maven, drummer Lenny White, these singles explored the same territory as the funkless electronica of Aphex Twin, Luke Vibert and µ-ziq. Having the same relationship to Jungle as Talking Heads and New Order did to funk and Electro in the early '80s, these smart-alecks effectively erased any trace of the black roots of the music by replacing groove and "tear down Babylon" chants with self-consciously clever programming and "wacky" samples.

Jenkinson followed his Squarepusher recordings with a couple of more industrial releases under his own name for London's Worm Interface label and a couple of more explicitly jazzy releases as the Duke of Harringay. More control-freak drum beats and irritating textures were to be found on his debut album, **Feed Me Weird Things** (1996), which somehow managed to find an audience of 25,000 like-minded juvenilia-obsessed weirdos.

Preceded by the **Port Rhombus** (1996) and **Vic Acid** EPs (1997), his sophomoric sophomore album, **Hard Normal Daddy** (1997), was easily his best release to date. On parts of **Hard Normal Daddy** the laffs actually worked and he actually deigned to play something approaching music on tracks like the blaxploitation pastiche "Cooper's World" and the Electro cut-up "Fat Controller". Thankfully, the Jaco Pastorius and Buddy Rich fetishes only showed up sporadically and his textures approached warmth and phatness. The **Big Loada** (1997) EP, however, retreated back to the schoolyard and his patronisingly kitsch approach to 1991–92 Hardcore.

His third album, **Music is Rotted One Note** (1998), replaced the rhythmic complexity with live drums that Jenkinson played himself. Fulfilling his muso ambitions, Jenkinson played the rest of the instruments as well and toned down his wackiness in favour of a more "mature" abstraction.

⊙ Hard Normal Daddy   Warp,1997

Unquestionably Squarepusher's best record, this works because his
smart-ass tendencies are restrained by almost-funky sounds and the
jokes occasionally work.

DJ SS/ Formation Records

From *Sturm und Drang* rave tracks to the very latest technical
itch, Leroy Small and his Formation Records label have been
at the forefront of the breakbeat continuum since 1990. Small's *nom
de disque* might evoke images of stormtrooper Techno, but DJ SS'
avant-populist records have defined the Hardcore and Hardstep
styles and he never skimps on the funk.

The first release for DJ SS and Formation was **The Psycho** EP
(1990) which, along with Rhythm For Reasons' (also Small) **The
Solutions** EP (1990), created the Hardcore blueprint of crunching
breakbeats and air-raid siren synth riffs. EQ's **Graphic** EP (1990) followed a similar formula, but with a bit more air and that Charvoni
"total ecstasy" sample, while SS' "A New Breed of Ravers" (1992)
and "String of Darkness" (1992) drowned the rave bliss-outs with
desperate vocal samples, descending basslines and synth
grindage.

"Incredible Base" from Oaysis' **Loft Conversion** EP (1992) sampled Chuck D asking, "How low can you go?" on top of a torrent of

manic beats. Megadrive's **Taking Control** EP (1992) and Darkman's **Dark As It Gets** EP (1993) cemented Formation's position at the forefront of Hardcore's deathspin into the dark side. SS' **Breakbeat Pressure** EPs (1993) and Rhythm For Reasons' **Music In Search of the Light (1993)** fumbled for a way out of the darkness by downplaying the synths and stretching out the low end. The **Breakbeat Pressure** EPs set the template for Jungle, but SS wouldn't expand on it until 1995 when he re-emerged from a ragga-enforced hiatus.

"Rollidge" from his **Rollers Convention** EP (1995) was an action painting in sound built around drum splinters, backwards vocal samples, dread bass, centrifugal strings and the timpanis from the *Jaws* theme. With a piano sample from *Love Story* and one of the most infectious basslines ever, Sound of the Future's "Lighter" (1995) was deservedly one of Jungle's biggest anthems. Almost as big was Rhythm For Reasons' "Smokers Rhythm" (1995) which followed a similar theme and a similar bassline. MA2's "Hearing Is Believing/Roller's Music" (1995) blitzed its jazzy breakbeat with a barrage of samples that strafed across its surfaces in waves of dub blades before solidifying into a crashing groove with a severely distended bassline. As if that wasn't enough, SS' unprecedented string of hits continued with "Rampage '95" and Grooverider's phased remix of "Unite" (both 1995).

MA3's "Those DJs" and SS' "Sense of Direction" (both 1996) continued the flow of steppers' anthems with enormous basslines and ascending drum swirls. Formation broadened its sound with its New Identity off-shoot, which kicked-off with Matrix's "Message 96" (1996), and the **Colors** and **Countries** series of 12"s. With the records of John B and By Reasonable Force, Formation followed Techstep to the industrial wasteland, while Mental Power and Tekniq kept things in the mid-range and didn't rock too many boats.

The two **Jazz & Bass Session** albums (1997, 1998) showed that Formation could roll out the jazz-funk flavours as well as the steppers' riddims, while MA4's "Step Into Our World/Bull Terrier" (1998) wrapped a KRS-One sample around a hypnotic bassline that was reminiscent of DJ Krust's "Warhead" and showed that even after eight years of relentless breakbeat pressure, DJ SS could still make a party move at the drop of a hat.

○ **Various Artists Highly Recommended**	Formation,1996

Featuring most of SS' '95 anthems, this is an essential document of Hardstepping Jungle.

Stakka & K-Tee

W hile Brighton may be known as the home of the student antics of Big Beat and drill 'n' bass, it is also the homebase of straightforward drum 'n' bass producers Stakka & K-Tee. With a string of releases for Andy C's Ram Records off-shoot Liftin' Spirits, Stakka & K-Tee were responsible for several floor-filling tracks that followed the label boss' mandate for precision-tooled dynamics.

After a series of white labels as Rhythm N Vibes and FOLS, Stakka & K-Tee's first proper release was "Ruffneck Ragga/The Ladder" (1994) on the Just Dance label. "Brockin' Out/Serious Intention" (1994) followed on Liftin' Spirits which made the duo the toast of the air-horn massive. Tracks like "Living for the Night/After Hours" and "Rugged N Raw/Bad Influence" (both 1995) featured wobbly basslines and high velocity beats designed to create mayhem on the dancefloor. "Danger Zone" and "Ya Don't Stop" (both 1996) followed suit with more crowd-pleasing effects, albeit following the vogue for more mechanical rhythms and darker basslines. "Andromeda" (1997) was their last release for the Ram/Liftin' Spirits family and furthered their reputation for tearing tunes.

The acidic analogue pounder "Titanium" (1997) was the first release for their own label, Audio Blueprint. Even more of a cruncher was their "Motive/Solar Reaction" release (1998) on Trouble on Vinyl. Featuring ringers like Dom & Roland and Hidden Agenda as well as new label artists like Skynet, Lo Life and Psion, the Audio Blueprint compilation **Voyager** (1998) continued the sci-fi paranoia vibe that had become so prevalent in drum 'n' bass to good effect.

⊙ **"Brockin' Out"** Liftin' Spirits, 1994

It might not be terribly original, but it sure wreaked havoc on the dancefloor.

Subject 13

J ungle may have started off as the ultimate revenge of samplers against the rockist naysayers of technological innovation, but with the emergence of the "intelligent" movement it quickly became the preserve of musos who valued "live"-sounding rhythms and "musicality" above all else. Among the leaders of this move towards fusion streamlining were the north London trio Subject 13 who tamed drum 'n' bass with Jean-Michel Jarre vapour trails and Lonnie Liston Smith groovesmanship.

Subject 13 first attracted attention with a couple of records on Basement like "Mystical Flite" (1995) and the Peech Boys-sampling "Can't Wait Tonight" (1996). With atmospheric arrangements recalling

Chick Corea and Larry Heard, "Spiritual Breakdown" (1995) and "Float On" (1996) became firm favourites with Fabio and he signed the band to his Creative Source label.

At around the same time, they formed their own Vibez label and released tracks like their own "Phuture" (1996) and Sirens' "Something/Browns Avenue" (1996), as well as records by Hidden Agenda and future Bukem faves Intense. The Bukem connection continued with "Faith" (1996) which was released on Bukem's **Earth** compilation. "Jazz Style/Loose Flutes" (1997) followed on Creative Source with drum 'n' bass that replicated the grooves and sounds of "real" musicians. "Can You Feel Da Vibez" (1997) was typical of their jazzy vibes and piano tinkling, but the flip, "Blacksteele", showed them branching out into the brooding, acid tracks of Dillinja and Lemon D.

Their debut album, **The Black Steele Project** (1997), for SSR offshoot Selector followed their characteristic blueprint of warm textures and kind of funky rhythms with unfortunate titles like "Dinner Time Jazz". A career supporting Jon Hendricks beckons.

⊙ **The Black Steele Project**   Selector,1997

Warm drum 'n' bass with re-heated jazz flavas for the aerodynamic trainer set.

Swift

Although he was one of the main DJs on London pirate station Kool FM since its early days, Swift (aka Mampi Swift) didn't have a high profile until he hooked up with Suburban Base in 1996. He had released a couple of 12"s for SOUR and Frontline, but Swift made his mark with

"On The Beat/Little Touch" (1996). Even better was "On The Beat (Remix)" (1996) which was a strange low-key affair with multiple breaks, a sapped bassline and occasional "Mentasm" stabs in the background, while its flip, "Old Song", basically worked the same fatigued dynamics with an orchestral sample before breaking down into a jump-up stormer.

"Analogue/Behold" (1996) was more apocalyptic with evil basslines and aggressively chopped-up breaks. He started his Charge label in 1997 and the label's second release, "Feel Good/Just Roll" (1997), introduced his pseudonym The Kraft. "Feel Good/Just Roll" followed his blueprint for minimal rollers with grinding basslines and slightly spacey dynamics. Swift's biggest track, though, was "The One/Journey" (1997) which broke through his usual hypnotic groove with an enormous distorted bassline and stuttering beats.

"Hi Tech/Mission" (1998) continued his new-found ferocity with aggressive bass stabs and big breakdowns, while "Future/Dance" and "War" (both 1998) similarly press-ganged the crowd onto the dance-floor with stomping drums and crunching bassline drops. Even more direct was the 4/4 drum intro to "Sense/Touch of J" (1999) which soon broke into a heaving pulse of tech rhythms.

⊙ **"The One"** Cancel,1997

Despite its tech elements, this pile-driver was constructed with the dancefloor in mind, not Swift's fellow producers.

Sy

With legendary scratching skills at 170 bpm, DJ Sy is Happy Hardcore's most technically proficient DJ. But it's more than just deck virtuosity that makes him one of the scene's most in-demand DJs, though, it's that he injects Happy Hardcore with the energy of escape velocity hip-hop that drove the original Hardcore scene.

Sy's turntable wizardry first made itself known at a residency at Venus in Nottingham which led to bookings at all the major raves of the '93–'94 era. With Unknown, he moved into production with tracks like "Play the Theme" (1994), which featured a slightly sprightlier version of the "Mentasm" synth stab which was the calling card of Darkcore, but worked just fine in a lighter context as well. With Eruption, Sy released the massive anthem "12 Inches of Love" (1995) which seemed like it was the last gasp for the rampant sampladelia that marked Hardcore's early years. Sy and Unknown were also responsible for the Cheddar series which included such unabashedly cheesy crowd movers as Cheddar 2's "Take Me Up" (1995).

As The Vampire, the duo released "Cyclone/Teknostorm" (1995) on Sy's Quosh label which featured a harder sound than the Cheddar releases, while Sy & Unknown's **The Rip-Off** EP (1996) on Sy's Triffic Tunes label was anchored by a couple of hip-hop samples that became their trademark. "Gonna Get Yours/What Is a DJ" (1997) were based around samples of Public Enemy and old-school LA crew Egyptian Lover respectively, while "The Beat Kicks" (1997) melted hip-hop into hyper-speed House. Sy's collaboration with Seduction, "Rushin'" (1997), focused on Sy's scratching skills and a visit from the ghost of rave past with samples and breakdowns aplenty.

Hooking up with Demo, Sy released the enormous "Love and Devotion" (1997) and the even better "Sensation" (1998) which cut up yet another hip-hop sample on top of a ricocheting "Amen" break. Sy & Unknown, meanwhile, indulged in some gangsta posturing, albeit mollified by Happy Hardcore's eternal optimism, with "Listen to the Ace" (1998).

◉ Various Artists Hardcore NRG   Solid State,1996

Highlighting Sy's facility with a pair of Technics, this excellent
compilation of storming 1995/96 Hardcore is less relentlessly matey and
nutty than you might expect.

T.Power

O riginally producing what he called "mindless Hardcore" as part
of Bass Selective, Marc Royal has since insisted that drum
'n' bass is intelligent music, but not in the way most of his contemporaries have gone about it. Bass Selective tracks like "Blow Out"
(1992) might not have been terribly intellectual, but its relentlessly
upful piano riffs and speeded-up Public Enemy sample constituted
an energetic rush of experience and sensation that made intelligence
irrelevant.

After rave's mainstream death, Royal re-emerged as Atomic Dog
with "Step Into the Lite" (1994) and "Natural Born Killaz" (1995) for
Deep Thought Records. With rattling snares and soft-focus diva
murmuring, "Natural Born Killaz" explored the rough vs. smooth
dialectic, while "Step Into the Lite" went deep into the heart of "intelligent" emulsification with insipid horns and wavering strings. As
T.Power, Royal released the harder "Lipsing Jam Ring/Blood From A
Stone" (1994) and the *Planet of the Apes*-sampling "The
Elemental/Chase The Dream/Forbidden Zone Edit" (1995) for SOUR.

A combination of subdued horns and deep, Larry Heard-esque
synth washes, T.Power's collaboration with MK Ultra, "Mutant Jazz"

(1995), brought Jungle closer to the abstract jazz territory of Mo' Wax, but the remix by DJ Trace brought Jungle back to the dark side with its forbidding bassline and synth apocalypse. Where Trace's "Mutant" remix was based on the "Reese" bassline (taken from Kevin Saunderson's Detroit classic, "Just Another Chance"), T.Power's debut album, **The Self-Evident Truth of an Intuitive Mind** (1995), tried to be as melodic as Carl Craig.

While the title of **The Self-Evident Truth of an Intuitive Mind** hinted at an obsession with conspiracy theory, "Police State/Prospects for Democracy/Synthesis" (1996) made this connection readily apparent. Another fusion of Techno and drum 'n' bass that was apparently partially inspired by Noam Chomsky, "Police State" was bludgeoningly single-minded and overbearingly pleasure-free. Typical of an autodidact, T.Power seemed to be unaware of his own contradictions: his music was as sterile as his imagined dystopia, without explicitly setting out to be so. "Symbiosis/Complexification" (1996) followed in a similar style, except that "Complexification" was as preposterous as its title would lead you to believe (it shifted time signatures from 3/4 to 5/4).

Falling out with what he described as the drum 'n' bass mafia and distancing himself from his old sound which he admitted was lame, Royal re-emerged in body-popping mode with Cris Stevens as Chocolate Weasel. The **Music for Body Lockers** EP (1998) was a scrapbook of breakdancing's glory days based on a clever deconstruction of Bob James' "Mardi Gras" break and a dream match of Human League circa *Dare* with Larry Heard and The Time's Monte Moir duetting on keyboards. **Spaghettification** (1998) was more of an electric boogaloo with Monty Python silliness, planet-rocking Electro and Black Dog-style synth work in equal measure.

Reverting to his T.Power alias, but retaining the Chocolate Weasel sound, Royal turned in a fine example of the "nu breaks" sound on "Fuck Dental Hygiene/Who Gives a Funk"(1999).

◉ Chocolate Weasel Spaghettification   Ninja Tune,1998

Light years away from his overbearing work as T.Power, Royal gets stoopid and pumps a little bass on this enjoyable album.

Tee Bone & Stretch

West London's Tee Bone is drum 'n' bass' king of collaboration. With links to the Reinforced camp, Dextrous and nearly all points in between, Tee Bone has worked with many of the genre's biggest names and spanned most of its styles. Tee Bone's penchant for synergy began in 1993 with "Selectors Roll", a ragga-fied Junglist track on Dextrous' Subliminal label.

Tee Bone started his Riddim Track label later that year and released a series of groovy rollers including the excellent "Bump & Bounce" (1995). Riddim Track's finest moment, though, was a devastating slab of Wu Tang jungle called "Shaolin Style" (1996) by Tee Bone & Stretch. The Hong Kong chop-sockie samples might have been received and clichéd, but by the time the equilibrium-damaging bassline and furious drum break kicked in, its lack of originality was wiped aside by a quite stunning momentum.

Stretch had previously produced the **Afterglow Parts** 1 & 2 EP (1994) for Reinforced as Project A-KO and the bad bwoy anthem, "Worries in the Dance" (1994), for DJ Ron's London Some'ting label. As The Guyver, he released the kazoo-sampling **Deep Cover** EP (1995) in collaboration with Mark from Reinforced who was responsible for bringing him together with Tee Bone. The duo also produced dividends as New Skool with "The Natural/Society/Measuring Distance" (1996) for Reinforced.

Tee Bone once again paired up with Dextrous as Fusion Forum for the rolling "Vintage Keys (The Art)/New Beginning" (1996) 12", but really pushed his teamwork skills to the max on the **Collaborated Artists – Strictly Business** album (1997). Calling in favours from people like Goldie, DJ Rap and Shy FX, **Strictly Business** was a sprawling concept album designed to show the world that there was no split within the drum 'n' bass scene and everyone co-existed harmoniously. Whatever the truth of its sentiments, it did produce the killer track "Bruton", made by Tee Bone and DJ Kane.

Tee Bone started his Creative Workz label in 1998 with yet another collaboration, the aluminium jazz of Tee Bone & Leon Mar's "Rezurrection/Passing Phases". Tee Bone continued to pursue a jazz-funk path with "Mr. Bojangles/Born Under a Bad Sign" and "Friday Night at Ronnie Scott's" (both 1998), while Stretch opted for the good old-fashioned tear-out with several releases on his own AKO label.

⊙ **Tee Bone & Stretch "Shaolin Style"**   Riddim Track,1996

A devastating display of five-snare technique and Wu Tang swordplay. (Available on **United Dance Presents The Designer Collection**.)

DJ Trace

Few, if any, records have had as much impact on drum 'n' bass as Trace's remix of T. Power and MK Ultra's "Mutant Jazz". "The Mutant" almost single-handedly created the sub-genre known as Techstep and sucked out nearly all of Jungle's life-affirming funk juices leaving only a gaunt, blood-shot zombie encased in rumbling metal. With co-conspirators Ed Rush and Nico, Trace has gone on to release a series of singles that defines Techstep as the sound of post-industrial urban dystopia.

Duncan Hutchinson was born in Hammersmith in 1974 and almost immediately got into rare groove and jazz through his father who ran a jazz club. By the time he was 15, Trace was DJing for Lon-

don pirate stations like Don FM and Kool FM and working at Lucky Spin Records. After his debut 12", the appropriately named "Inception" (1992), he released the jazzy "Teach Me to Fly" (1993) with LTJ Bukem.

With its sinister bass growls and oppressive atmosphere, "Lost Entity" (1993) marked a 180-degree turn in his style. "Jazz Primitives" (1993), "By Any Means Necessary" and "Vinyl Chapter" (both 1994) followed suit and suggested the brutalist bass distortion to come.

Compared to everything else out at the time, even the allegedly new wave of "dark" released on Goldie's Metalheadz label, "The Mutant" (1995) was the hardest, ugliest thing imaginable – sonic terrorism at its most extreme. The jump-up crew had its chest-caving, Dr. Dre-derived sub-bass, but "The Mutant"'s "Reese bass" (derived from Kevin Saunderson's "Just Another Chance", which he recorded under his Reese alias) was simply punishing, leaning against the listener with all of its weight. In its original incarnation "Mutant Jazz" was an inoffensive little track that just glided by. In Trace's version, any harm done by this rampaging beast was purely intentional. "The Mutant" was the featured track on the style-defining compilation **Techsteppin'** (1996), which also featured Trace's "Haze" and "Mid-Town Method II". With its frugged Wu Tang Clan sample atop drum shrapnel and painful bass distortion, "Mid-Town Method II" was perhaps even more malevolent than "The Mutant".

By this time, Trace had carved a career for himself playing raves in the US and was spending half his time in Philadelphia and half in London. "Amtrack" (1996) was his ode to the American train system that made him habitually late to his out-of-town gigs. Where American blues and country artists imitated train whistles and the chugging rhythm of locomotives as symbols of possibility and freedom, the banging, tumbling "Amtrack" was the sound of the Midnight Special going off the rails. The sample – "Here is the sound of a group trying to accomplish one thing, that is to get to the future" – was accompanied by laughter, suggesting a gruesome *Schadenfreude*.

The clipped drums and gothic synth squalls of "Amtrack"'s flip-side, "Squadron", anticipated the refinement of Techstep's signature elements into the even-less-fun sound that journalist Simon Reynolds dubbed "Neurofunk". Trace's 1998 release on Grooverider's Prototype label, "Sonar", squared the circle by including Trace's Cubase duet with Neurofunk supremo Optical, "Sphere", on the flip.

O Various Artists Techsteppin'   Emotif,1996

This indispensable compilation of sonic art bruit includes three Trace tracks, including the landmark "The Mutant".

⦿ Various Artists Torque   No U Turn,1997

Another essential compilation. This overview of the thoroughly
intimidating No U Turn label includes Trace's "Amtrack", "Squadron"
and "Damn Son" and collaborations with Ed Rush and Nico – "Droid"
and "M.D.M".

Neil Trix

With Doc Scott and Neil Trix, Coventry can lay claim to two of
drum 'n' bass' most influential producers. Running the influential Bangin' Tunes shop, Trix was at the centre of breakbeat developments in not just the Midlands, but all of England. A favourite of
Fabio and Bukem, Trix was one of the leaders of the push towards
"musicality" and his tracks were some of the best of the genre.

Trix's calling card was FBD Project's "Gesture Without Motion"
(1994) which appeared on Reinforced's **Enforcers 7** compilation. A
collaboration with Gavin Wetton, FBD Project's full name said it all:
Future Beyond Dance. This was drum 'n' bass as listening music;
there was nothing functional about it. "Gesture Without Motion" was a
breakbeat epic, but the breaks were swallowed alive by the murmuring tidal drifts that were the track's hallmark. "She's So.../Harploop"
(1995) followed with gently rolling beats, highly developed melody and
someone plucking your harp strings. "Breaking Up", "The Core" and
"Classified Listening" (all 1995) continued Trix's elegant musicality
with shimmering synths and carefully constructed drums.

On his own Bangin' Tunes label, more delicate instrumentals followed in the form of the **Urban Visions** EPs (1996) which continued to

float drum 'n' bass on gossamer wings. After a quiet spell releasing House tracks under his Quivver moniker, he re-emerged on the Funk 21 and Partisan labels as System 4. "Black Cells/Hyperspace" (1998) was another epic of prolonged synth washes and pulsing basslines.

⊙**FBD Project "She's So..."** FBD,1995

With gentle cascades of percussion and swathes of melody, FBD Project's second single is a dreamy artcore classic.

Trouble on Vinyl/ Renegade Hardware

Formed in 1993 by Mark Hill and Clayton Hines, Trouble on Vinyl quickly established itself as one of the premier jump-up/Hardstep labels. Tracks like Code 071's "Ease Up Soundboy" (1993), DJ Kane's "Slave" (1994) and Just Jungle's "Sky" (1994) provided the label with its blueprint of crisp beats, big basslines and hip-hop samples. The **Here Comes Trouble Vol. 2** EP (1995), featuring tracks by Just Jungle, Shogun and IQ Collective (Hines), was a hit with the pirate stations and raves that were ignored by the mainstream media in favour of speed and "intelligence".

The label would really hit its stride, though, with DJ Red's awesome "Devastate" and "Mad PLO" (both 1996). A former pirate DJ also known as Mark O'Neill, DJ Red followed the DJ Hype formula with machine-gun snares, menacing hip-hop samples and enormous portamento basslines. Red followed with the equally roughneck "Enta Da Dragon" (1997), which sampled a Hong Kong chop sockie on top of streamlined beats and a distorted bassline, and "Energize" (1997).

TOV's other star was Kane Fox (aka DJ Kane) who has DJed for both Don and Kool FM. Kane debuted for the label in 1994 with "Izaac's Story" and "Slave", but it was the hypnotising "The Life" (1995) that first got him mainstream attention. "Let's Go to Work" (1996) was little more than a collection of synth stabs and Doppler-effect train samples, but it wrecked havoc on the dancefloor. D-Bridge's "Bring Da Flava/Keep it Real" (1996) and Special K's "The System/Danger" (1997) sampled Craig Mack and Blahzay Blahzay respectively to reassert the label's connection to hip-hop. The showcase compilation, **Code of the Streets** (1997), featured killer cuts from all of the label's main artists as well as ringers like Gang Related (aka DJ Krust) and Future Forces Inc.

With TOV making its name in jump-up, Hill and Hines started Renegade Recordings to provide an outlet for the less straightforward tunes that their artists were producing. Renegade debuted with DJ Kane's "Game Over" (1995) and attracted attention from the "intelligent" set with Shogun's idyllic flute suite, "Pure Alchemy Pts. 1 & 2" (1995). With similar releases on Timeless Records, Shogun became known for his lush, symphonic style and orchestrated a swirling chorus of mermaid strings, dolphin chirps and tidal gushes on records like "Just For You", the **Nautilus** EP, the **Pegasus** EP and the **Ulysses** EP (all 1996). Tertius (aka Danny Coffey of Endemic Void) and Mastermind continued the jazz vibes with "Miracle Switch" and "Imagine/Raw Jazz" (both 1997), while Mastermind took the label into new territory with the pimp strut of "Shaft/70s Flava" (1998).

At around the same time as Renegade Recordings was formed, Hill and Hines created their third imprint, Renegade Hardware, to cater for the return to the dark side instigated by the Techstep onslaught. Perhaps the most successful of the three labels, Hardware was inaugurated with Future Forces Inc.'s "Flash Gordon" and "Intensify/Who's Da Man" (both 1996). Reese basslines, "Amen" drums and ricocheting sound effects characterised these and other Hardware releases by Paradox and Genotype. Following the label's formula, Future Forces' "Dead By Dawn" (1996) became an anthem on harder dancefloors courtesy of a devastating distorted bassline.

Renegade Hardware moved further into the territory of shrieking synths and punishing basslines with releases like Genotype's "Extra Terrestrial" and Future Forces collaboration with No U-Turn's DJ Fierce, "Constant" (both 1997). Mean and metallic, the **Distorted Reality** EP (1997) collected tracks like DJ Kane's acidic hardstepper "System" and Genotype's "Toxic" to produce the label's strongest statement of intent yet. Even better was **Quantum Mechanics** (1998) which featured Optical's remix of "System" and DJ Kane's mighty "Morphis", proving that maybe there was a bit of life left in Techstep.

◉ Various Artists Code of the Streets   Trouble on Vinyl,1997

Straight-up, no-nonsense gangsta stuff from DJ Red, DJ Kane and DJ Krust's Gang Related project.

◉ Various Artists Quantum Mechanics   Renegade Hardware,1998

Unlike most darkside compilations to be released after 1996, parts of this sounded as if there was some urgency left in the scene, as if they meant the sounds they were making.

US drum 'n' bass

A lthough Bronx breakbeats and Brooklyn Techno (Joey Beltram's "Energy Flash" and "Mentasm", Frankie Bones' **Bonesbreaks** records) were key components in the development of Hardcore and Jungle, New York clubbers have never really taken to drum 'n' bass. Despite small rave scenes dotted throughout the US, drum 'n' bass, and electronic music in general, is too diffuse and the personalities too unengaging to ever break out of its fringe ghetto in a market that demands the established cult-of-personality practices of the record industry.

While Southern California was beginning to map out its own permutations of breakbeat with labels like Exist Dance and DJs like Ron D. Core, the arrival of British breakbeat on American shores can probably be traced to New York's NASA (Nocturnal Audio and Sensory Awakening) club in 1992. Run by a British ex-pat DJ, DB, and legendary lighting engineer Scotto, NASA was like the suburban rave experience translated to New York's urban demimonde: *young* kids in bad clothes getting their first exposure to nightlife and drugs with a coterie of Ecstasy dealers for company. The soundtrack, provided by DB and Carlos Soulslinger, consisted mostly of breakbeat Hardcore from England which ran counter to the prevailing sounds of Garage and the more muscular Techno of Bones and Keoki.

With NASA's success, DB took a gig with Profile's Sm:)e imprint licensing British Jungle tracks and releasing the excellent **History of Our World** mix compilations (1994,1996). Soulslinger, meanwhile, opened up the Liquid Sky clothing/record boutique and label. With releases like Soulslinger's "Abducted" (1995), Liquid Sky and its offshoot Jungle Sky was perhaps the first American label to release home-grown Jungle. Compilations like the **This Is Jungle Sky** series have highlighted Yankee drum 'n' bass and introduced producers like Kingsize, 1.8.7, DJ Ani and X Delta X.

In 1996, DB opened America's first drum 'n' bass record store, Breakbeat Science. His partner, Irish ex-pat DJ Dara, was one of the

few US Junglists to release an album, **Rinsimus Maximus** (1998), in addition to his mix compilations like **Renegade Continuum** (1997) and **Full Circle** (1998). As a resident of both of New York's main drum 'n' bass clubs, Jungle Nation and Konkrete Jungle, Dara was one of the country's premier DJs. His main rival was the hardstepping Pittsburgh native Dieselboy whose mix CDs, **Drum & Bass Selection** USA (1997) and **611 DJ Mixseries Volume 1** (1998), made him the new poster boy for American Jungle.

Meanwhile, in Chicago, with its ever-expanding avant community, drum 'n' bass has been taken on by post-rockers like Casey Rice and John Herndon (aka U-Sheen) who have used it to further their exploration of musical space and texture. The city's Junglist mainstay, though, is the Forte label run by 3D and Snuggles which has released fine records by the label bosses, Toronto ex-pat DJ Slak and Kid Entropy. Entropy has also released the excellent "Super Natty/For the Love of It" (1998) on ex-Big Chief Barry Hensler's Chi-Town label, Cosmic Breaks.

◉ Various Artists
The United States of Drum and Bass   Evil Teen,1998

A fine compilation of Yank drum 'n' bass that shifts the focus from the media centres on the two coasts to the scenes where the real action in American breakbeat takes place – the Midwest and Maryland.

⊙ Kid Entropy
"Super Natty/For the Love of It"   Cosmic Breaks,1998

A thoroughly groovy collection of Marcus Garvey shout-outs, street-corner boasting, ridiculously blunt bass bludgeoning, backwards strings, kazoos and rat-a-tat-tat beats makes up "Super Natty", while "For the Love of It" has dizzying Middle Eastern horns that creep in and out of the mix like a celebrity stalker.

Vibes & Wishdokta

A lthough he has garnered more column inches for his Garage releases under his own name, Grant Nelson has gained more fans and more dancefloor time in his Hardcore guise, Wishdokta. Featuring samples of Guns 'n' Roses' Axl Rose screaming, "Do you know where you are?" and D'Borah pumping up the crowd, "Evil Surrounds Us" (1992) on Kickin' Records was his first big track and showcased the cheeky sampling that would characterise his Hardcore career.

In 1993 he hooked up with Shane Levan who also called himself DJ Vibes and recorded the eternal screamer, "Music's So Wonderful". With horror-movie stabs, video game laser effects, a gushing helium diva and a pulse-quickening "Amen" break, "Music's So Wonderful" was a classic example of Hardcore's kinaesthetic delirium. As Ravers' Choice, the duo would record the equally awesome "Ravers' Choice" (1993) which was just as kinetic but relied more on a barrage of swirling, ascendant synth riffs, while Wishdokta's "Rush Hour" (1994) was based around a terrible drug pun and a sample of Tasmin Archer's "Sleeping Satellite".

"Music's So Wonderful" was the second release on Vibes' Asylum label which would also release their "It Feels So Good/Midsummer Mist" (1994) and the infamous "Rave Is a Mystery" (1995). Sampling the intro to Madonna's "Like a Prayer", "Rave Is a Mystery" was a monument to Hardcore's mischievous playfulness and its pure rush aesthetic. More adrenaline overloads followed in the form of singles on Happy Trax like "Gonna Be Alright/Givin' It All I Got" (1995) and the classic "Motorway Madness" (1996).

While Nelson devoted more time to his Garage output, Vibes stayed true to the Hardcore cause with tracks like "Oxygene/Fantastic" (1996) and the Rozalla-sampling collaboration with Seduction, "Free Yourself" (1997), on his own Ravers' Choice label. In 1998 Vibes followed Nelson to the Garage side and spent the summer in Ibiza playing for the Speed Garage massive.

⊙ **"Music's So Wonderful"**   Asylum,1993

Before Hardcore became all bouncy and nutty, the scene produced rushing kaleidoscopes like this. (Available on **United Dance Presents The Anthems '92-'97**.)

Wax Doctor

After being banished from the realm of Techno by Detroit Godfather Derrick May, Hardcore eventually came crawling back, grovelling and begging for forgiveness. Atoning for the petulant zeal of early Hardcore tracks, producers like Wax Doctor aspired instead to the gossamer-winged synth swoops of Techno romanticists like Carl Craig and Dan Curtin. In Wax Doctor's hands, the spiky drum shards and gauche keyboard bombast of Hardcore mutated into ultra-suave "Atmospheric Funk".

Wax Doctor's journey into the breakbeat ether began as Paul Saunders, a child of the Second Summer of Love from suburban High Wycombe. After formative experiences at Acid clubs such as Land of Oz and Sunrise, Saunders hooked up with Reading rave label Basement Records. "New Direction" (1992), a collaboration with Ron Wells, pitted an angelic choir against sharp synth stabs, roiling breakbeats and Belgian synth stabs to generate the kind of meltdown from which he would soon distance himself. With a more regimented rhythm and acidic synth lines, "Unfriendly" (1992) had more to do with hard trance than Hardcore, but the **Dark Matter** EP (1993) redressed the balance with sounds straight out of Grooverider's Rage sets.

Falling under the sway of two of dance music's leading exponents of the lush life, LTJ Bukem and Stefan Robbers, Wax Doctor used the breakbeat format as a vehicle to pursue Detroit's jazz ambitions. In collaboration with Alex Reece, Wax Doctor transported the Motor City's man-machine synths into the Jungle on Fallen Angel's "Hello Lover" (1994); plunged drum 'n' bass into Deep House on Unit 1's "Atlantic Drama" (1994); and all but namechecked Derrick May on Jazz Juice's undulating "Detroit" (1995).

His debut for Metalheadz, "Kid Caprice/The Rise" (1995), introduced the cymbal-riding James Brown break that has become the "Amen" of "intelligent" drum 'n' bass. The horns and flutes from "Kid Caprice" also found their way onto "Atmospheric Funk" (1995) which was released on Gilles Peterson's Talkin' Loud label. The flipside, "Never As Good", continued the Techno emulsion by looping Carl Craig's epic of Novocain bliss, "At Les". His second 12" for Metalheadz, "Spectrum/Step" (1995), was slightly more disjointed, but still concerned itself primarily with the liquefaction of drum 'n' bass' splintered flow.

With the hype surrounding jazzy drum 'n' bass, Belgium's foremost Techno label, R&S, signed Wax Doctor. Of course, the irony of the label that spearheaded Hardcore by releasing the synth rifferama of Joey Beltram and Frank DeWulf signing one of the artists responsible for revising that history was lost on most commentators and probably R&S too. His debut for the label, "All I Need/Finer Things" (1996), was all hotel lounge trumpets, digital warmth and "Kid Caprice" drums. The follow-up, "Heat/Offshore Drift" (1996), was exactly the neon-lit mood piece suggested by the title. After a long absence, the widescreen atmospherics returned on the flute-fuelled "Magnum Fusion/Let It Go" (1998) and Fallen Angels' "Rapier/Biophoric" (1999).

◉ Selected Works   R&S,1998

Collecting "Kid Caprice", "Atmospheric Funk" and "Spectrum" among others, this collection of his jazzy solo records is drum 'n' bass at its smoothest and smarmiest.

DJ Zinc

I t's pretty safe to say that Jungle wouldn't exist without hip-hop and a certainty that DJ Zinc would be a complete unknown were it not for his ear for a catchy b-boy soundbite. Along with Ganja Kru partners DJ Hype and Pascal, Zinc is drum 'n' bass' premier re-interpreter of the wildstyle sound.

A DJ with a succession of pirate stations like Impact and Eruption, Zinc first started to make a name for himself as a producer with the **Swift & Zinc** EPs on Bizzy B's Brain Records in 1993 and 1994. With partner Swift (not to be confused with the other Swift who runs Charged Records), Zinc produced some fifteen EPs of crowd-pleasing breakbeat music that never forgot Jungle's roots in the rave. As Pure on Suburban Base, Swift and Zinc released the original rude bwoy sound of "Anything Test/Positive Steps" (1995) which blended ragga and rare groove with aplomb.

Zinc really started to make a name for himself, though, when he hooked up with DJ Hype and Pascal. As Dope Skillz on Pascal's Frontline label, Zinc released the awesome rumination on Wu Tang hip-hop, "6 Million Ways/Yo Son" (1996), whose sing-song bassline and barrage of percussion effects was unstoppable on the dancefloor. "On Fire Tonight/The Fix" (1996) on Hype's Ganja label was equally anthemic with its "Think" break, bugle riff and shameless rap hooks that led into a wall-crumbling bass roller. Even bigger, though, was the outrageously catchy "Super Sharp Shooter" (1996). Beginning with the Moog riff from The J.B.'s' "Blow Your Head", a rapper proving he could spell, a half-tempo break and a slowed-down pearl of wisdom from Method Man, "Super Sharp Shooter" then erupted into a full-scale Junglist assault with an over-the-top portamento bassline and skull-snapping beats. Of course, the populism of "Super Sharp Shooter" was unilaterally ignored in the mainstream dance press which was foaming at the mouth over the Techstep sound, but history has a way of redressing such imbalances.

"No Diggity", "It's Like That" and the remix of "Reach Out" (all 1997) followed with similar thrill-a-second, G-Funk pastiches and jump-up rhythm dynamics. More take-no-prisoners bassline antics were to be found on "Stretch/Danger" and "Pink Panther/Bad Break" (both 1998), while **The Stronger** EP (1998) saw Zinc collaborating with Hype to create a serious b-boy bouillabaisse.

◉ "Super Sharp Shooter" Ganja,1996

Unquestionably the tune of 1996, this is among the finest examples of hip-hop-flavoured drum 'n' bass.

Down Tempo
and Big Beat

Amon Tobin/Cujo

Originally from Brazil and now a resident of Brighton, Amon Tobin is part of the post-jazz school of breakbeat construction. Splicing together jazz breaks, Latin percussion fills and soundtrack atmospheres, Tobin is representative of a generation that has grown up in an era where the cut-up is the overarching narrative and the sampler is the new electric guitar.

After spending his youth travelling the world, he settled in Brighton and started making music while getting a degree in photography. His first 12" for the HOS label in 1994 under his own name was largely forgettable, but he pricked up ears with 1995's **Curfew** EP as Cujo on Ninebar Records. The **Salivate** EP (1996) was a mish-mash of Middle Eastern strings, blues samples and jazzy drum 'n' bass which established the blueprint of off-kilter stand-up bass jazziness which he would follow on the **On the Track** EP (1996). Cujo's debut album, **Adventures in Foam** (1996), was a further exercise in jazz-based sampladelic quirkiness that was a bit too clever, a bit too blunted and a bit too broad-minded to really work.

Tobin's recordings as Cujo were as predictable as a Stephen King novel. Without an obvious sense of humour, there's only so far you can go with stiff, lugubrious beats and some atmospheric samples. Under his own name, however, and on Ninja Tune, he managed to create some variations on the blunted beatz theme by delving deep into his jazz collection.

Stuffing Lionel Hampton, Art Blakey and Charles Mingus into a compression chamber and sucking the air out of their music leaving only a hint of timbre to colour a wan, but effective, breakbeat collage, Tobin's **Bricolage** (1997) album transcended the aural-wallpaper mediocrity of much Down Tempo . Where so many of his contemporaries used limp bossa nova to add an air of exoticism to their dour collages, Tobin used a killer *bloco Afro* groove on "Chomp Samba".

More be-bop beats followed on **Permutation** (1998), but the production was too reliant on soundtrack eeriness and noirish ambience. His facility with drum 'n' bass was no longer refreshing and the batucada drums were being used by everyone and their funk, soul brother.

⊙ Bricolage   Ninja Tune, 1997

As British breakbeat continued lemming-like towards the edge of the jazz-bore cliff, Tobin showed that there was some potential after all in this star-crossed affair.

Attica Blues

T aking their name from a track by maverick jazz saxophonist Archie Shepp, Attica Blues are one of the few Down Tempo crews whose notion of jazz extends beyond the smooth grooves of Lonnie Liston Smith and Roy Ayers. Formed in 1993 by DJ D'Afro (aka Chris Williams) and keyboardist Tony "T Plays It Cool" Nwachukwu, Attica Blues still have some of the hallmarks of the post-Gilles Peterson British jazz fetishist, but they also have an awareness that jazz is a process and not just a Blue Note label and polo-neck jumper.

Working with singer/songwriter Roba El Essawy, Attica Blues released their debut EP on Mo' Wax in 1994. **Vibes, Scribes 'N' Dusty 45s** included "Contemplating Jazz" which became an instant Down Tempo classic by virtue of its Tricky-esque vibes, string snippets, low-key scratching and smoky subtlety. Their follow-up, the **Blueprint** EP (1995), focused more on El Essawy's vocals which were reminiscent of a huskier Nicolette. There were also more phased electronics on **Blueprint** tracks like "Lonesome Child" and the combination of keyboards and pomo-torch song with jazz breakbeats seemed to be an effort to make hip-hop "beautiful music". A remix EP followed with transformations by Canadian Techno impresario Richie Hawtin and Alex Reece.

Attica Blues' self-titled debut album followed in 1997 and continued down the same path of piano tinkles, strings, mild instrumental stabs, scratching and Cassandra Wilson-style blues laments. Mixes of "Tender" and "3ree (A Means to Be)" by the New York hip-hop crews Organized Konfusion and Anti-Pop Consortium, however, showed that Attica Blues were expanding the parameters of their sound and weren't too arty to pretend that they were above being influenced by the street.

❍ Vibes, Scribes 'N' Dusty 45s   Mo' Wax, 1994

It might not have been as good as Shadow's "In/Flux", but "Contemplating Jazz" proved that Down Tempo beat collage was more than just the bastard offspring of Acid Jazz.

Bassbin Twins

Releasing mostly white labels and recording for a damning number of outlets when he decides to go legal, San Francisco's Pete Houser is a criminally neglected member of the breakbeat fraternity. Like so many of his contemporaries, he was inspired by Charlie Ahern's film, *Wildstyle* to start bombing with aerosol, breaking and making beats with battered drum machines.This soon progressed to a fascination with the sampler and the logic of the cut-up. Following the example of LA's Exist Dance, Houser followed fellow San Franciscan Freaky Chakra onto California's "funky breaks" circuit with a succession of white labels released under his Bassbin Twins moniker.

Making his name with the **Bassbin Twins I, II** and **III** EPs (1995), Houser took the basic California sound, left in the acid basslines, but made it phatter and funkier with more swing and rabble-rousing samples. The **Bassbin Twins Vs. DJ Who** EP (1995) established Bassbin Twins as the best remixer on the American rave circuit, but his biggest hit was probably "A-1 Love" (1995) which ran roughshod over the "funky breaks" formula with a loose-limbed rhythm that bore little resemblance to the ham-fisted bludgeoning that characterised most of the genre.

Remixes of DJ Voodoo's "Everybody Thinks I'm High" (1996) and "Hold Your Wig" (1996) on Bassex followed as did Houser's massive reconstruction of the Electroliners' "Loose Caboose" (1996). "Radioactive Beats Pt. 2" (1997) had the huge acid builds so beloved in Cali, but his best record was his remix of the entire Skint back catalogue, **Two Turntables and a Crate of Skint** (1997). In addition to the requisite "Shack Up" beat and Fatboy Slim snatches, **Two Turntables and a Crate of Skint** managed to take in a bit of **Req**, the World Famous Supreme Team, The J.B.s' "Blow Your Head", Chuck D and Flavor Flav and "Apache", and that was just the first side.

Another soundclash, Bassbin Twins Vs. Doom Selector's "Between the Fro" (1997), followed before the fine singles "Out of Hand" (1997) and "Hell" (1998) definitively established Houser as one of the finest producers working the middle ground between "funky breaks" and Big Beat.

⊙ **Two Turntables and a Crate of Skint**   Skint,1997

With the entire Skint back catalogue as his source material, Pete Houser delivers a party-rocking cut-up in the finest tradition of Double Dee & Steinski and Coldcut.

Bentley Rhythm Ace

B y the middle of the '90s the only emotion that musicians seemed able to express was irony. hip-hop musicians had sampled all of the good records; The Beatles, Rolling Stones, Al Green, Bob Marley and The Ramones had taken all of the good ideas; David Bowie, the Sex Pistols and Prince didn't leave any poses unexplored. The only thing left to do was to scour the charity shops and car boot sales in search of unspeakably naff records consigned to the dustbin of history and wallow in their vulgarity. Of course, this too was nothing new – The Cramps had been doing this for over a decade, except they weren't being ironic. With the possible exception of Beck, no one epitomised this zeitgeist more than a couple of wise-asses from Birmingham naming themselves after a cheap drum machine. Nicking bits and pieces from records so bad that Oxfam wouldn't take them, dressing in shell suits and generally being more sophomoric than a maladjusted 13 year-old computer geek, Bentley Rhythm Ace's entire *raison d'etre* was to get the cheapest laffs possible.

Comprised of ex-Pop Will Eat Itself bassist Richard March and Mike Stokes, Bentley Rhythm Ace formed in 1995 and released their first record, the **Bentley's Gonna Sort You Out!** EP (1996), on Brighton's Skint label once they had accumulated enough low culture detritus. Despite the less than salubrious provenance of the source material, "This Is Carbootechnodiscotechnobooto" was appealingly zany, if too knowing, while the title track sounded like a Carl Stalling hip to Sleazy D. The **Late Train 2 Bentley On C** EP (1996) continued in the same vein with tongue-in-cheek English pastoralism rubbing up against a reworking of "Carbootechnodisco".

Their debut album, **Bentley Rhythm Ace** (1997), was an endless parade of student-friendly hi-jinx: bongos, sirens, horror-movie strings, surf guitars and epileptic beats all bouncing around in a castle. When it was funny, it was charming and endearingly kitsch, when it wasn't it was the musical equivalent of toilet humour.

BRA's drummer, Fuzz Townshend, got in the act with the Small-Faces-tripping-on-broken-beats sound of "Smash It" and "Get Yerself" (both 1998). Although the mixing wasn't anything to write home about, BRA's **FSUK3** (1998) mix was eclectic enough (moving from Jefferson Airplane to Fatboy Slim to Pucho & the Latin Soul Brothers) to redeem their wiseguy antics and any mix with both the Bar-Kays' "Soul Finger" and Pigmeat Markham's "Here Come the Judge" is worthy of your attention.

○ **Various Artists FSUK3**   Ministry of Sound,1998

Even more fun than their own records, this is the acceptable face of vinyl scavenging.

Bolshi

Starting life in 1996 as an off-shoot of Big Life Records, Bolshi is that rarest of dance labels: one run by a woman. Label boss Sarah Francis has fashioned Bolshi into one of the leading lights on the Big Beat scene by virtue of a sampladelic aesthetic that borders on the institutionalisable and an attitude that seems to run counter to the prevailing rabid anti-intellectualism of their Big Beat cohorts.

Bolshi's first artist was Laidback (aka Jason Cohen) whose singles like "Coldrock/B-Boy Noise" (1997) and "Escape" (1998) were derivative, but thoroughly enjoyable, romps through a b-boy's closet. His debut album, **International** (1997), stole samples from De La Soul, looped old funk guitars and worked up a groove that was generally less silly and more professional than the best Big Beat records.

"It's Eggypleptic" (1996), the label's second single and the debut of The Beachcomas, marked Bolshi as one of Big Beat's more creative labels with its clavinet riffs and not-yet-clichéd acid stabs. With samples of people wittering on about fruit and a guitar riff apparently nicked from post-punkers The Mekons, the flipside, "Donuts", sounded like a take on 'Middle England'. The partnership of Matt Austin and Tony Freeman continued to trawl the depths of "Britishness" on their second EP, **Planet Thanet** (1997), which was a messy appreciation of the joys of spending a rainy summer's day at Weston-Super-Mare. Centred around the Pop Group-sampling "Kongball", **The Big Tuddy Sessions** (1998) once again showed that The Beachcomas were the most idiosyncratic act of a genre that prided itself on its eccentricity.

Pelirocco's "Hot Tuna" (1996) never really exited Planet Dust, but it still worked up a lather on dancefloors like The Heavenly Social. LHB's "Bad Magic" (1997) blended '70s-cop-show-soundtrack sounds with Techno filters to create some serious "disco friction". The side project of House producer Ceri Evans, Westway had all the requisite scratches and analogue noises on the **Catfunk** EP (1998), but they sounded too professional.

It was Swedish-born producer Rasmus, though, that fulfilled the label's promise of becoming Big Beat's idiot-savant. His **Mass Hysteria** album (1998) was a delirious cut-up of hyper-speed rappers, the

Beach Boys and movie soundbites that lived up to the title's claims. The **Tonto's Release** EP (1998) displayed Rasmus' virtuosity with the sampler almost as effectively with the vocal hi-jinks on "Nuclear".

◉ Various Artists Donuts   Bolshi,1997

Calling in ringers like Jeep Beat Collective and Lo-Fidelity All-Stars, this fine collection shows off more than just the label's own wares.

Bomb the Bass

As part of the wave of British "DJ records", Bomb the Bass' "Beat Dis" (1988) anticipated the promiscuity of both Hardcore and Big Beat by several years. Constructed by Tim Simenon and originally disguised as a white label import from New York to obscure its British origins, "Beat Dis" was picked up by the Rhythm King label and its wildstyle samplescape that took in everything from *Thunderbirds* to *The Good, The Bad & The Ugly* eventually hit #2 on the British charts.

With the help of vocalists Lauraine Macintosh, Maureen Walsh and DJ/producer Jonathan Kane (later to become Depth Charge), Bomb the Bass' debut album, **Into the Dragon** (1988), featured two other Top 10 singles that captured the cut-up zeitgeist: the raggamuffin chant "Megablast" and the radical reworking of "Say a Little Prayer". Simenon then produced Neneh Cherry's two best singles, "Buffalo Stance" and "Manchild", Adamski's "Killer" and Seal's "Crazy". Suddenly, Simenon was Britain's hottest producer.

Bomb the Bass' second album, **Unknown Territory** (1991), was less immediate, but it did include the proto-Trip-Hop of "Winter in

July" which set an overwrought lament to subdued breakbeats, scratches and minor-key loops. His best fusion of hip-hop, soul and dub, though, was BTB's third album, **Clear** (1995). Introspective and unhinged, **Clear** featured batty contributions from novelist Will Self, Sinéad O'Connor and rapper Justin Warfield and was part of a movement that read hip-hop as the blues of the '90s. Best of all were remixes of "Bug Powder Dust" and "Sandcastles" by Kruder & Dorfmeister, Chemical Brothers, La Funk Mob and the Jedi Knights which linked Simenon's pioneering beat suites to a new generation of samplers.

⊙ Clear   Island,1995

Justifying Simenon's position as the Godfather of Trip-Hop, tracks like "Dark Heart" and "Bug Powder Dust" dragged hip-hop beats and sampladelics into a depressed and paranoid soundscape.

DJ Cam

F rance may have been stuck somewhere in between Uzbekistan and Australia towards the bottom of the world pop league table in the early '90s, but, with the scenes in the US and Britain caught in a state of stagnation, a host of Parisian producers emerged as the saviours of dance music and permanently rehabilitated Gaul's musical reputation. With a legacy that includes the proto-hip-hop of *musique concrète* composers Pierre Schaeffer and Pierre Henry and one of the all-time great breaks – Serge Gainsbourg's "Melodie" – it is perhaps unsurprising that the French would excel at Down Tempo 's abstract hip-hop MO. Along with La Funk Mob, Laurent Dumail led the French invasion of the artier fringes of American and British hip-hop culture.

Taking his name from the French slang for drugs, DJ Cam burst onto the scene with his debut album **Underground Vibes** (1994). Working a similar, but jazzier, terrain to DJs Shadow and Krush, Cam stretched hip-hop beats until they had an emaciated languor and a blood-shot aura. As he showed on the **Sweetest Sounds** EP (1996), though, Cam wasn't a purist and dangled his jazz-flavoured toe into the drum 'n' bass pool.

He displayed his polyglot instincts again on his second album, **Substances** (1996), with the Carl Craig-esque "Sound System Children". Elsewhere, "Hip Hop Pioneers" was exactly the party-jam cut-up you'd expect from the title, while "Innervisions" rocked a harp groove. A compilation for the **DJ Kicks** series (1997) followed a fairly uninspired blunted path, but **Mad Blunted Jazz** (1997) on the American Shadow label faired better. A double-CD affair that included a live disc, **Mad Blunted Jazz** delivered the expected late-night post-hip-hop ambience with flair.

Leading with the collaboration with New York rappers Channel Live, "Broadcasting Live", **The Beat Assassinated** (1998) showed Cam trying to prove that he could keep it real. Featuring not only MCs, but tougher, more New York-style beats, **The Beat Assassinated** was an answer to critics of the Down Tempo movement who thought that the producers were outsiders only interested in stealing hip-hop's thunder. The inclusion of the speed Garage track "Pressure", however, seemed to undermine Cam's argument.

⊙ **Substances**   Inflammable, 1996

With a greater ear for texture and tone colour than most of his contemporaries, Cam's second album is his best and one of the genre's finest.

Catskills Records

That Brighton is the home of Big Beat is not simply down to the fact that the seaside town is the headquarters of Skint and home to their Big Beat Boutique club. Brighton can also count among its residents Adam Freeland who is the figurehead of the "nu-breaks" movement and the very fine Catskills label which specialises in cinematic spins on hip-hop's beats-and-samples formula.

Founded in 1996 by brothers Khalid and Amir Mallassi and Jonny Reggae, Catskills opened its account with Sonorous Star's (the Malassi brothers) **Indian Motorcycles** EP (1996). Featuring droning tamburas, tension-building string obbligatos, Space Age sound effects, exotic percussion and Schifrin-esque beats, **Indian Motorcycles** established the label's blueprint of soundtrack-inspired hip-hop. Sonorous Star's **Bullets & Bad Dreams** (1997) was the label's second release and continued the pattern with acoustic basslines, shuffling beats and hip-hop samples struggling through the instrumental fog.

Bushy's **Spikeback** EP (1997) followed suit, albeit in a slightly more minimal fashion, while Drunken Master's self-titled EP (1998) upped the tempo with ferocious wah-wah licks, scatting hip-hop samples, flatulent synth basslines and breaks reminiscent of '89–'90 hip-hop crowd-pleasers as Masta Ace and Most Wanted. The Mexican's **Fantastic Four** EP (1998) continued the uptempo funk vibe with a combination of old-school hip-hop and wink-wink-nudge-nudge '60s sleazy listening. The label's best release, though, might have been Bushy & Professor's cowbell-heavy **Drop** EP (1998) which rode a Latin-funk break for all it was worth. Finnish trio Pepé Deluxe mixed guitar jingle-jangle, big drums and great scratching to create another dancefloor gem in the form of "Woman in Blue" (1999).

> **◉ Various Artists Straight Out the Cat Litter**   Catskills,1999

A fine round-up of the label's releases that ranged from slowburn to carpet burn.

Chemical Brothers

Big Beat, the reaction against the cults of "complexity" and "intelligence" that is the inevitable result of technological trainspotters telling us how our bodies should react, was unintentionally started by two Mancunian DJs who couldn't mix to save their lives. With their rough 'n' ready sets that consisted of Schooly D bitch-slapping Manic Street Preachers and Orbital, Ed Simmons and Tom Rowlands threw two fingers up at Britain's army of Techno purists and the self-appointed guardians of "proper" House music.

The irony of all this is that the Chemical Brothers started out as the Dust Brothers on Junior Boy's Own, the label of London's House taste-makers *par excellence*, Terry Farley and Pete Heller. With its samples of Public Enemy's siren and This Mortal Coil, Coldcut-style breakbeats and the acid bassline of the Roland TB-303, their debut, "Song to the Siren" (1993), was their usual DJ set in miniature and laid down the framework for the emergence of Big Beat a few years later.

After a spate of remix work for the likes of Lionrock and Leftfield, the duo re-emerged with the **Fourteenth Century Sky** EP (1994) which showed off not only their eclecticism ("Her Jazz" was a reference to riot grrrls Huggy Bear, while "One Too Many Mornings" was a nod to Bob Dylan), but their fetching way with a breakbeat ("Chemical

Beats"). This was swiftly followed by the **My Mercury Mouth** EP (1994) which ensured their future stardom with the title track's rumination on Hashim's breakdance classic "Al Naafiysh (The Soul)", and the drums and grime of "Dust Up Beats". With their hip-hop beats and rock-riff dynamics, the Dust Brothers were the obvious choice as resident DJs at London's Heavenly Social, which under their command would become the birthplace of Big Beat (or Amyl House as PR people were trying to call it at the time).

After a name change forced by the original Dust Brothers (the production team behind The Beastie Boys' **Paul's Boutique**), the duo's debut album, **Exit Planet Dust** (1995), picked up where The Prodigy's **Music For the Jilted Generation** left off. The newly named Chemical Brothers sampled the drum intro of organ grinder Jimmy

McGriff's "The Worm", stole licks from MC5's "Rocket Reducer No. 62" and The Doors' "Peace Frog" and used stadium rock tricks like false endings and sing-along chants to inject a sense of energy into dance music that had been stripped away by too much abstraction and too much "progressivism".

Dig Your Own Hole (1997) disappointingly followed the same template with less flair, but proved to be an enormous success. Where their earlier records only approached rock's riffing frenzy, **Dig Your Own Hole** was explicitly rockist in its outlook with tracks like "The Private Psychedelic Reel" and "It Doesn't Matter" (which sampled psychedelic rockers Lothar & the Hand People!) and it even had the insufferable Noel Gallagher on board. It felt alarmingly like a career move which would be an ignoble end for one of the few truly exciting acts in post-rave dance music.

Brothers Gonna Work it Out – A DJ Mix Album (1998) delayed the inevitable with a fun, if obvious, mix of Willie Hutch's blaxploitation themes, Renegade Soundwave's acidic sampladelia and DBX's Techno.

◉ Exit Planet Dust   Virgin, 1995

They may only have one trick up their sleeve and their collaboration with Beth Orton might sound like a Gordon Lightfoot song, but this is still a great party record.

Coldcut

E ver since Grandmaster Flash unleashed "The Adventures of Grandmaster Flash on the Wheels of Steel" on an unsuspecting world in 1981, hip-hop's cut 'n' paste method of collage has been just about the only musical style worth a damn. With the possible exceptions of Double Dee & Steinski and avant garde pranksters like Negativland and Stock, Hausen & Walkman, no one has done more to bring the mix 'n' scratch style of composition out of hip-hop's occasionally self-enforced ghetto more than Coldcut.

Inevitably, Jonathon More and Matt Black met while record shopping in London's West End. Soon afterwards, the duo could be found slicing and dicing their prodigious record collections in Black's kitchen using an early Casio sampling keyboard. The first of these sampladelic compositions to be released was the staggering "Say Kids (What Time Is It?)" (1987). Heavily influenced by Double Dee & Steinski's "Lessons"

mixes, "Say Kids" was an action-painting in sound comprised of soundbites from Chuck Brown & the Soul Searchers, Trouble Funk, Doug E. Fresh, the *Howdy Doody* television show, Brother D., E.U., *Jungle Book* and, of course, James Brown. Equally kinetic and mind-blowing was the follow-up single, "Beats & Pieces" (1987), which followed the same breakbeat collage blueprint.

The track that really got them noticed, however, was their "Seven Minutes of Madness" remix of Eric B. & Rakim's "Paid In Full" which was, as their intro boasted, "a journey into sound" and reached the British Top 10. Punctuating the mix with spoken word samples from dub maestro Mikey Dread and American TV announcer Dom Pardo, Coldcut extended and messed with the track's groove (based on Dennis Edwards' "Don't Look Any Further"). Even more startling were the samples of Yemenite diva Ofra Haza's "Im Nin' Alu" woven in throughout the song. Apparently, Eric B. & Rakim hated it, but the mix remains irrefutable proof that sampling is an art and not digital theft.

After signing to Big Life Records, Coldcut hit the British Top 10 with "Doctorin' the House" (1988) which kick-started the career of vocalist Yazz. Reggae singer Junior Reid's Top 40 single, "Stop This Crazy Thing", followed suit shortly thereafter. Both tracks were included along with their brilliant collaboration with Lisa Stansfield, "People Hold On", on Coldcut's debut album, **What's That Noise?** (1989). Despite the presence of The Fall lead singer Mark E. Smith, **What's That Noise?** and their ensuing albums, **Some Like It Cold** (1990) and

Philosophy (Arista, 1993), were predominantly in the optimistic post-Acid House style that has characterised British dance music since 1988.

Below the cheerful surfaces, however, discontent was brewing. Free thinkers and playful tinkers like Black and More have always had rocky relationships with major labels and the corporate culture of Big Life and Arista did not suit them at all. After a trip to Japan, where they picked up on Ninja

iconography, the duo formed their Ninja Tune label when they returned to England in 1990. Among the label's first releases was **Jazz Brakes Vol. 1** which More and Black released as DJ Food. Conceived as DJ tools to be looped and mixed in a set, the jazzy hip-hop samples and grooves of the **Jazz Brakes** series were appreciated on their own merits and became one of the cornerstones of the British blunted hip-hop scene.

Further adventures into abstract music came with Mixmaster Morris' remix of their "Autumn Leaves" (1994) which did away with beats altogether in favour of Ambient washes of sound. Coldcut's contribution to Britain's flourishing Ambient scene was solidified by their Solid Steel show on London's KISS FM where they championed such outré music as Steve Reich's **Music For 18 Musicians** and John Cale's **Church of Anthrax** as well as the more expected hip-hop and Jungle.

More and Black's eclecticism made their contribution to the **Journeys By DJ** (1995) series, without a doubt one of the best records of the decade. Taking in Boogie Down Productions, ex-Dead Kennedy Jello Biafra and everything in between, their "70 Minutes of Madness" mix showed just how little imagination most other DJs working in Britain had. Coldcut achieved a similar feat with Ninja Tune material on their half of the mix-tape battle with DJ Krush, **Cold Krush Cuts** (1997). Black applied this cut-up philosophy to his Hex multi-media project which attempted to bring ideas of randomisation, post-humanism and political awareness into the usually content-free world of rave visuals and video games.

The roots of the cut 'n' paste method in Dadaism and William Burroughs became apparent on Coldcut's 1997 album **Let Us Play**. Rants from Salena Saliva and Jello Biafra made their beat manipulation more expressly political, while the détourned samples of "Atomic Moog

2000" linked Coldcut to the pranks of the Situationists. Other shenanigans included a vocoded voice reading extracts from Omar Khayyam's epic poem *The Rubaiyat*, music generated by a software program, an ode to the lunatic Moog experiments of Jean-Jacques Perrey and Steinski's history of the sex manual. While the music didn't quite live up to Coldcut's high standard, the accompanying CD-ROM remains far and away the most creative and cheeky example of music-based interactive technology yet.

Their political belief in the democratisation of technology continued with the inclusion of their video/audio sequencing program Vjamm on the remix album, **let us replay** (1999). Still not quite hitting the highs of their previous work, collaborations with, and remixes by, Grandmaster Flash, Carl Craig, Shut Up and Dance and Cornelius did manage to put a fresh spin on some of the material from **Let Us Play.**

⦿ Seventy Minutes of Madness

Journeys By DJ   Journeys By DJ,1995

Easily the best commercially available mix compilation. If you've never experienced a DJ epiphany, then get this mix.

Compost

Dedicated to furthering the jazz spectrum, Munich's Compost Records is Germany's answer to Talkin' Loud. Encompassing the lush tones of lounge jazz, bossa nova, Detroit Techno, Deep House, hip-hop and drum 'n' bass, the output on Compost comprises a stoner wonderland of Down Tempo beats and dreamy textures.

Compost debuted in 1994 with A Forest Mighty Black's "Candyfloss/Fresh In My Mind" 12". The brain-child of Freiburg-based Brazilian music fiend Bernd Kunz, A Forest Mighty Black sounded like a Down Tempo version of one of LTJ Bukem's wet dreams with the Amazonian-rainforest keyboards and textured beats. The mainstay of Compost's roster, AFMB have since defined slacker jazz with records like "High Hopes/Tides" (1996) and their **Mellowdramatic** (1997) album.

Label boss Michael Reinboth, along with Jan Krause and Tobias Meggle, got in on the act with Beanfield's "Charles" (1995). As well as being the label owner, Reinboth was a critic who dubbed his brand of Down Tempo Electro-jazz and made connections with such pioneers of electronic music as Karlheinz Stockhausen, Pierre Henry, Jean-Jacques Perrey and Miles Davis producer Teo Macero. Such Space Age references were extended with the galactic phonk of **The Dr. BJ Harris Experience** EP (1997), which was named after the first black astronaut. Reinboth was also partially responsible for the supine hip-hop of Knowtoryus whose "Bomberclad Joint" (1995) came complete with second-hand black consciousness rhetoric and a Kruder & Dorfmeister remix.

The real proselytising, however, was saved for the **Future Sound of Jazz** series of compilations which were broadsides against the media's definition of Trip-Hop. With tracks by Compost regulars as well as Jimi Tenor and Wagon Christ, **Volume 1** (1995) represented what Reinboth called "Hybrid-System-Music" – analogue sounds manipulated digitally. It was a lot of conceptual baggage to foist upon such impressionistic music, but the compilation succeeded in shattering the dope-addled mindlessness of a lot of Down Tempo music. Imagining a community comprised of American post-rock experimentalists Tortoise, Nightmares on Wax, μ-ziq and Midlands Junglists

Back 2 Basics, **Volume 2** (1996) was even better and made Reinboth's points more strongly. **Volume 3** (1997) was equally far-reaching, but by the time of **Volumes 4** and **5** (1998) the future sound of jazz had become a stifling consensus.

Before such unanimity was in place, Compost helped introduce the radio-interference sound of Funkstörung. Both the **Funkentstört** (1997) and **Sonderdienste** (1998) EPs bore strong similarities to Aphex Twin and μ-ziq, but with less of the grating little-boy tantrums that can often mar their work. While Compost continued to release challenging music from the likes of Funkstörung and Move D, the label also retreated into the formulaic drum 'n' bass of Fauna Flash, who were one of the few foreign drum 'n' bass acts to be well received in England, and the lame Latin boogie of the Rainer Trüby Trio.

⊙ Various Artists Future Sound of Jazz Volume 2   Compost,1996

It might be a bit old hat now, but at the time this compilation defined the zeitgeist of musical experimentation.

Norman Cook

With the possible exception of art Junglists Spring Heel Jack and Boymerang, Norman Cook (né Quentin Cook, July 31, 1963) is assuredly the only person in this book to have been spotted wearing a cardigan in public. The former bass player with twee Christian indie band The Housemartins, Cook has since established a career as dance music's most versatile entertainer under a plethora of cheesy sobriquets.

While remixing avant-funkers A Certain Ratio, indie jangle meisters Aztec Camera and hip-hoppers Digital Underground, Cook released his first two singles, "Blame it on the Bassline" and "For Spacious Lies" (1989), under his own name. Although it featured the immortal line "Freedom is just a song by Wham!", "For Spacious Lies" was outdone by his work as Beats International. **Let Them Eat Bingo** (1990) was a hodge-podge of soul, reggae, African music and hip-hop and included the British #1 single, "Dub Be Good to Me", which borrowed heavily from The SOS Band and The Clash.

Excursions into House as Mighty Dub Katz and Pizzaman followed, as did another #1 single, "Turn On, Tune In, Drop Out" (1994), with his funk pastiche troupe, Freakpower. Recording as Fried Funk Food with Ashley Slater, Cook explored blunted beats territory with the **In Dub** EP (1994), which coated some Freakpower instrumentals with hash resin and sticky breaks.

Changing genres as quickly as he changed aliases, Cook assumed his Fatboy Slim identity for "Santa Cruz" (1994), the first release on Skint Records and Cook's first to use the guitar feedback and breakbeat formula of Big Beat. Inspired by clubs like The Heavenly Social and Big Kahuna Burger, and records like Josh Wink's "Higher State of Consciousness", Fatboy Slim's "Everybody Needs a 303" and Fried Funk Food's "The Real Shit" (both 1995) echoed the hedonistic abandon of early Hardcore with acidic synths, hip-hop and soul samples plus basslines and breakbeats that knocked you into the next room.

With a cheesy Hardcore keyboard and a sample of blues slide-guitar on "Song For Lindy" and the guitar riff from The Who's "Can't Explain" on "Going Out of My Head", Fatboy Slim's **Better Living Through Chemistry** (1996) album revealed Big Beat as the unholy love child of purist dance music's two sworn enemies: rave and rock.

While **Better Living Through Chemistry** was the soundtrack to Britain's better parties, Cook extended his good-time monopoly of the summer of 1997 with Mighty Dub Katz's "Magic Carpet Ride", whose ersatz Latin feel made it one of the anthems of Ibiza.

A #1 spot somehow eluded Fatboy Slim's awesome "Rockafeller Skank" (1998), but Cook appeared in the lofty heights of the pop chart with his remixes of Cornershop's "Brimful of Asha", while his mix of Wildchild's "Renegade Master" (both 1998) wasn't far behind. Cook debuted his remixes at Brighton's legendary Big Beat Boutique club where he presided over inebriated chaos every fortnight, an atmosphere he captured on his sterling mix collection **On the Floor at the Boutique** (1998). **You've Come A Long Way Baby** (1998) included not only "Rockafeller Skank", but the Top 10 "Gangster Trippin'" and the #1 "Praise You", as well.

⊙ You've Come A Long Way Baby   Skint,1998

No pretences of "intelligence" or complexity here, just breaks, basslines and synths arranged in such a manner that they wouldn't feel entirely out of place on an AC/DC album.

Crystal Method/ City of Angels

P robably doomed to be called "the American Chemical Brothers" for eternity, Crystal Method are America's most high-profile breakbeat act. Peddling a streamlined version of the standard acid-funk sound, Ken Jordan and Scott Kirkland have burst out of LA's rave ghetto to sign with Geffen subsidiary Outpost and shift some 300,000 units.

Originally from Las Vegas, Jordan and Kirkland skipped town as soon as they could and got involved with Los Angeles' nascent rave scene in the early '90s. The duo's first single, "Now Is the Time/The Dubeliscious Groove" (1994), came out on the local label set up by British ex-pats Justin King and Steven Melrose, City of Angels. With beats both lumpy and lumpen bumping below some rising analogue acid riffs, "Now Is the Time" established the trademark flatulent bounce of City of Angels. "Keep Hope Alive/More" (1995) followed with another sort-of funky breakbeat loop and tweaking Roland 303 patterns and became the anthem of the American breakbeat scene.

After a seemingly endless series of remixes of "Now Is the Time" and "Keep Hope Alive", Crystal Meth's debut album, **Vegas** (1997), arrived on Geffen's Outpost imprint. Filled with the same single entendre drug references and hip-hop samples as British Hardcore, but without the speed-demon exhilaration, **Vegas** sold by the ton but failed to make "funky breaks" the underground riposte to the Limey Electronica invaders that Garage rock was to the first British Invasion.

Although their major act left, City of Angels continued to define the "funky breaks" genre with the **Space Kadet** EP (1995) and **Botz** EP (1996) by LA-based producer Überzone. One of the mainstays of the SoCal scene, Simply Jeff, released the "My Planet/Godzilla Funk" (1997) 12" and the two scene overviews, **Funk-Da-Fried 1 & 2** (1997, 1998), on the label. Venturing out of the local talent pool, City of Angels made connections with British Big Beat producers like Fatboy Slim and the Freestylers for their **White Noise** (1997, 1998) compilations and signed UK MCA rejects Lunatic Calm for the abrasive funk of their **Metropol** album (1998). Überzone, meanwhile, took a lesson from their British counterparts and made the beats more fractured and more funky on their fine **The Freaks Believe In Beats EP** (1999).

◉ Crystal Method "Keep Hope Alive"   City of Angels,1995

For a couple of years it seemed as if this track was a cottage industry unto itself with its umpteen remixes, but unlike most Yankee breakbeat, it was worth the effort.

Cup of Tea Records

G rowing out of the club of the same name in Bristol, Cup of Tea Records put out intermittently potent brews of Bristol swing that ranged from Down Tempo collages to full-on Junglism. Beginning in 1994 with Junk Waffel's "Mudskipper/Sub Strata", Cup of Tea would really announce their arrival with Statik Sound System's languorously dubby **Revolutionary Pilot** EP (1995).

"Trout" from Monk & Canatella's **Fly Fishing** EP (1995) was an early traveller on the now overly familiar cop-show soundtrack path, while Grantby's **Timebooth** EP (1995) was more allied to Jerry Goldsmith's extraordinarily trippy *Planet of the Apes* and *The Omen* soundtracks. Ben Dubuisson and Scott Hendy's Purple Penguin project followed with the compressed Fender Rhodes sounds of "Pressure" (1995).

A Compilation (1996) collected together some of the finest moments from these EPs as well as the jazzier sound of Spaceways and The Eff Word. Purple Penguin's dubby "Mountain" (1996) and Elvis-sampling "Memphis" (1997) expanded the label's sound palette, while Mr. Scruff's **Large Pies** EP (1997) brought a hint of his Mancunian eccentricity to the Avon. Jaz Klash's bass-heavy drum 'n' bass number "BQE" (1997) was the result of a collaboration between More Rockers' Rob Smith and Peter Rose with LA-based producer Angel.

Monk & Canatella's **Care in the Community** and Statik Sound System's **Tempesta** albums (both 1997) followed with slightly loopy variants on the standard Down Tempo blueprint. Following this same template as slowly as possible, Grantby compiled the **Coffee Table Music** compilation (1998) from impossibly supine grooves and strange C&W passages. As their abstract hip-hop and dub moves began to wear thin, Cup of Tea licensed tracks from leftfield lunatics Experimental Pop Band and Cincinnati hip-hop doomsayers Mood to inject some life into a genre which was rapidly running out of steam.

◎ Various Artists A Compilation   Cup of Tea, 1996

Featuring some of the best moments from EPs by Grantby, Monk & Canatella and Statik Sound System, this shows the label in the best possible light.

Death in Vegas

A round 1995 when even drum 'n' bass was running out of ideas, some art-school smart alecks started cutting and pasting lame records they bought at car boot sales to produce the ultimate music for the Age of Irony. While the often pernicious "dance music for indie kids" genre may have been started by Primal Scream and Andy Weatherall (if not PiL or The Clash), this new genre of big beats, undergraduate insouciance and scrumpy hi-jinks that aspired to the hedonism of a Black Sabbath produced by Lee Perry was made by Heavenly Socialites turned on by the Chemical Brothers.

Richard Fearless was a graphic artist-turned-DJ who spun Dr. John and Augustus Pablo records at the Sunday Social and The Job Club when he hooked up with BBC radio engineer Steve Hellier to produce "Opium Shuffle" (1995) as Dead Elvis. With its dubadelic feel undercutting the chipper French vocals, "Opium Shuffle" was more downbeat than most Social-associated records. Just like the Chemical/Dust Brothers, Fearless and Hellier were forced to change their name to Death in Vegas when they discovered a record label that was named after the deceased king of rock 'n' roll.

Even though it sampled the *Woodstock* soundtrack, "Dirt" (1996) had nothing to do with hippies playing their bongos in the mud, thanks largely to its cod-Tony Iommi guitar riff and Roxanne Shanté "Unless you get a fuckin' gun butt to your gut" sample. Sounding like a post-rock Krautrock cover band saddled with someone's kid brother playing out-of-tune digi-dub basslines, "Rekkit" (1997) was a less agreeable take on rock dynamics.

Both singles were featured on **Dead Elvis**

(1997) which showed that, "Dirt" aside, they were attempting to remake Big Beat in the sombre image of Trip-Hop: "I Spy" mutated a sitar sample into an eerie Ennio Morricone guitar riff, while "Amber" was as unexciting as either the colour or the porn star from which it took its name. The dub excursion "Rematerialised" and the ska pastiche "GBH" kept **Dead Elvis** from being nothing but a collection of textures in search of a context.

They followed "GBH"'s reggae inflections with a cover of The Beat's "Twist and Crawl" (1997) that came complete with Rankin' Roger reprising his original toasting. Like "Dirt", "Twist and Crawl" showed that when Fearless and Hellier wiped the smug smirks off their faces they could be as much fun as their contemporaries.

◉ Dead Elvis   Concrete,1997

Most of this is a turbid mess of "dark" atmospherics, but when they decide to groove on "Dirt", "GBH" and "Rematerialised" almost all is forgiven.

Deejay Punk-Roc

Bursting on to the Big Beat scene with "My Beatbox" (1998), Brooklyn native Deejay Punk-Roc perfectly captured the old school hip-hop zeitgeist with an LL Cool J sample, retro-Electro Bambaataa-isms and a vocoded chorus. His instant success didn't come without a price, however. The press started a rumour that he was a front-man for a white British producer looking for some street-cred.

DeeJay Punk-Roc **My Beatbox**

Whoever the real Deejay Punk-Roc was, "I Hate Everybody" (1998) followed in swift succession with the same party-rockin' imperative and virtually the same stock of samples on beats. "Far Out" (1998) had even more swipes from Mantronix, but it was made even better by Swedish producer Rasmus' remix which added acid basslines, strings and an interminable snare roll from Josh Wink's bag of tricks.

Punk-Roc's debut album, **Chicken Eye** (1998), included all the singles as well as the Electro jam "All You Ladies", and a pseudo-bossa nova loungecore track, "The World Is My Ashtray". All of which failed to clarify anything about Deejay Punk-Roc's identity. Even more confounding was Punk-Roc's fierce collaboration with hardcore hip-hoppers Onyx on "Roc-In-It" (1999).

◉ Chicken Eye   Independiente, 1998

The were some alarming lapses of judgement, but the singles were undeniable party jams, whoever was making them.

Depth Charge

A dedicated b-boy since day one, Jonathan Saul Kane is generally credited as the person who mutated hip-hop into something that made more sense in Britain's grey and unpleasant land: the
bleak and somnambulent feel of Trip-Hop. As Depth Charge, Kane
made instrumental hip-hop populated with samples from the kung-fu
and exploitation flicks he's made a side-career out of watching. As
Octagon Man, he made grim, punishing Electro that seemed to com-
press an entire decade's worth of British b-boy obsessions into five
minutes of twisted funk.

Kane first began to attract attention with Depth Charge's "Goal"
(1990). One of the two or three great football-themed songs, "Goal"
took advantage of the Latin-American tradition of over-the-top commentary by layering a sample of a Brazilian commentator screaming,
"Gooooallll", over some mild breakbeats for the duration of the track.
Under his Octagon Man guise, Kane also released the stripped-down
proto-nu-Electro tracks "Free-er Than Free" and "The Demented Spirit" in 1990.

Kane's Hong Kong chop-sockie and B-movie obsession began to
pay off with the ridiculous film dialogue samples of "Depth Charge
(Han Do Jin)" (1992) and "Bounty Killers" (1993). Picking up on the
undercurrent of kung-fu terminology in early hip-hop at the same time
as the Wu Tang Clan turned it into their own pseudo-science, Kane's
Shaw Brothers fetish was writ large on Depth Charge's **Nine Deadly
Venoms** (1994). The album's rampant sampladelia and beat collaging
made it a huge influence on the emerging downbeat scene, while the
breakneck breaks and feedback of tracks like "Shaolin Buddha Finger" taught the Chemical Brothers a thing or two.

The sampling swordplay continued on the first release for his DC Recordings imprint, Depth Charge's **The Legend of the Golden Snake** EP (1995). DC Recordings was also the home to the stunning sampling wizardry of Deadly Avenger whose "Milo's Theme" and "Coney Island Baby" (1995, 1996) are classics of post-Double Dee & Steinski sound-bite manipulation.

DC also released the definitive and throughly essential early hip-hop compilation **Beat Classic** (1997) – which contained what is probably the Rosetta Stone of Trip-Hop, Rammelzee and K-Rob's 1983 single "Beat Bop" – and re-issued Alan Tew's legendary **The Hanged Man** soundtrack (1998), devaluing the record collections of beat collectors world over in the process.

The Octagon Man re-emerged in 1995 with **The World According to...**, an album of brutally minimal Techno-phunk that married the chilling bleakness of Finnish electronic crew Panasonic with the austere groove of LFO. The stunning **The Rimm** EP (1996) followed with a very warped take on art-house Junglism. The darkness of Kane's Octagon Man releases crossed over into his Depth Charge persona as recent tracks like "Disko Vixen" (1997) and "Blue Lipps" (1998) pummelled the life out of House music. "Romario" (1998) attempted to do for France '98 what "Goal" did for Italia '90, but like the striker of the title, it wasn't quite fit enough. Nonetheless, Kane's ragged production style and keen ear for a sample means that he remains the *sifu* of beat collage.

⊙ Nine Deadly Venoms   Vinyl Solution, 1994

Along with the early Ninja Tune records, this collection of Kane's Depth Charge EPs is one of the original, and one of the best, Down Tempo records around.

Double Dee & Steinski

Probably the greatest and most important artists you've never heard of, Double Dee & Steinski took hip-hop's cut 'n' paste logic to its furthest possible extremes and ushered in the era of sampladelia. Picking up where "The Adventures of Grandmaster Flash on the Wheels of Steel" left off, studio engineer Doug DiFranco and advertising jingle producer Steve Stein diced and spliced breakbeats, song snippets, movie fragments and mass media soundbites into audio collages that were potent critiques of the information society, but were also as exciting as any James Brown song. Even if they were more concerned with play than detachment, Double Dee & Steinski's complex, but populist, beat suites are the foundation of the blunted beat style of labels like Ninja Tune and Mo' Wax.

The winner of a contest held by Tommy Boy for mastermixes of G.L.O.B.E. & Whiz Kid's 1983 single "Play That Beat Mr. DJ", Double Dee & Steinski's "The Payoff Mix" (1984) became an enormous cult hit in New York by virtue of its prescient reading of sampling as the modern equivalent to the call-and-response that characterised African-American music. Despite the fact that you couldn't hear the joins or edits, however, "The Payoff Mix" was not the product of sampling technology, but the result of endless hours in the studio literally cutting and pasting tape together. Encompassing Spoonie Gee, "Soul Power" chants courtesy of Bobby Byrd, Funky Four Plus One's "It's the Joint", the World Famous Supreme Team radio show, Incredible Bongo Band's "Apache", Culture Club, Little Richard, exercise routines, Humphrey Bogart, Herbie Hancock's "Rockit", The Supremes' "Stop in the Name of Love", Grandmaster Flash, Chic and about a hundred other things, not to mention "Play That Beat Mr. DJ", "The Payoff Mix" remains one of the most audacious records ever made.

Following its success, DiFranco and Stein applied their mastermixing touch to the Hardest Working Man in Showbusiness on "Lesson Two: The James Brown Mix" (1984). A few years before Eric B. & Rakim heralded the age of hip-hop's JB idolatry, Double Dee & Steinski recognised the Godfather of Soul as the progenitor of hip-hop. Another promiscuous mixture of sounds, "Lesson Two: The James Brown Mix" sandwiched Mr Please-Please's greatest hits next to Bugs Bunny, Dirty Harry, Junior's "Mama Used to Say", Sly Stone, "Double Dutch Bus" and G.L.O.B.E. & Whiz Kid.

"Lesson Three: The History of HipHop" (1985) appeared with the other two on an EP that was scheduled for release by Tommy Boy, but was blocked by corporate copyright robber-barons who demanded compensation for the samples. With an info-slipstream comprised of Herman Kelly & Life's "Dance to the Drummer's Beat", Dennis Coffey's "Scorpio", "Starski Live at the Disco Fever", *Mars Needs Women*, original cut 'n' paster Dickie Goodman, a late-night talk show announcer, Baby Huey, Newcleus, Kraftwerk, Lauren Bacall, human beatboxing courtesy of the Fat Boys and Groucho Marx, "Lesson Three" was as mind-boggling as the first two and was a perfect summation of hip-hop culture.

Although the multi-nationals put a halt to the duo's multi-textual nefariousness, Steinski continued his guerilla media pranks while DiFranco returned to engineering. Credited to Steinski & Mass Media, "The Motorcade Sped On" (1987) was a stunning comment on the assassination of President Kennedy. A cut-up of the news coverage with beats, a snippet of Bob James' "Mardi Gras" and Queen thrown in for good measure, "The Motorcade Sped On" held a mirror up to the face of post-modernism with its utterly ambiguous flurry of signifiers. Far less nebulous was the post-Gulf War call to arms, "It's Up to You" (1992), which was a lot funnier and less facile than most left-wing Bush bashing. After contributing to the **Producers for Bob** (1993) project which consisted of cut 'n' paste artists having their way with speeches emanating from The Church of the Sub-Genius, Stein continued to write music for adverts, produced an excellent radio show for New Jersey's WFMU station and contributed an ode to the sex manual for Coldcut's **Let Us Play** album in 1997.

◉ Various Artists No Rights Given Or Implied:
The Original Samplers Bond Street, 1992

Given the litigiousness of copyright owners, none of Double Dee & Steinski's work is easy to find. This brilliant compilation which includes all the "Lesson Mixes" as well as "The Motorcade Sped On" and "It's Up to You" is probably the easiest to track down.

Dub Pistols

One of those scenesters who seem to have made a career out of partying, Barry Ashworth has been involved with dance music in one form or another since 1988 when he started promoting events like Déja Vu, Monkey Drum, Westway and Eat the Worm around London. With ex-Woodentop Rollo, Ashworth was part of Déja Vu who were signed to Cowboy Records and had dancefloor hits with "Why Why Why" (1992) and "Never Knew the Devil" (1993).

In 1996, Ashworth started the Dub Pistols with "There's Gonna Be a Riot" for deConstruction off-shoot Concrete whose title and knock-about dynamics took its lead from the thug aesthetics of punk rock. The bad boy quasi-Junglist sub-bass of "There's Gonna Be a Riot" was echoed on the follow-up single, "Westway" (1997). More hooligan jump-around followed on "Best Got Better/Blaze the Room" (1997).

Featuring New York rapper Kid TK Lawrence, "Unique Freak" (1998) took the Dub Pistols out of the back alleys with an attitude and sound that evoked more than just a lager-lout's Saturday night. "Cyclone" (1998) followed with a hard-man version of the legless party-ska that Fatboy Slim and Lionrock specialised in. The Dub Pistols' debut album, **Point Blank** (1998), followed with exactly the sort of bludgeoning beats, acid riffs and hip-hop samples you'd expect from such Big Beat ne'er-do-wells. It wasn't so much the formulaic sounds that were the problem, it was more that Ashworth and co. didn't stop bullying you for a second.

◉ Point Blank   Concrete, 1998

The album was a bit like being caught in the middle of a screaming fight between Big Daddy and Giant Haystacks, but it did feature early singles like "There's Gonna Be a Riot" which sounded decent enough on their own.

Dust 2 Dust

Massimo Bonaddio's first label was Dust, which he formed in 1995 to nurture the anything-goes eclecticism that was growing among people tired of club culture's increasing tendency towards niche-marketing and narrowcasting. Records like Lee Van Cleef's **1/4 of Solid** EP (1996) were collages of head-nodding beats, high-pitched synths and piano samples lifted from DJ Premier's Akai.

Dust was reborn as Dust 2 Dust in 1996 with Danmass' (Bonaddio and Dan Carey) "Breakout" which piled a tweaking 303 bassline on top of rough and ready breakbeats. The **Big Beats** compilation (1996) featured one-offs from artists like Funky Monkey, Unsung Heroes, Red Myers, The Mellowtrons and other people who'll probably never be heard from again, but it was capable of rocking the dancefloor with the best of them.

Moog's "Moog Attacks" (1997) was exactly what its title suggested, while Danmass' **Drugs and Hospitals** EP (1997) sampled the *Taxi* theme. Even less tasteful was the **Porno Beats** compilation (1997) which had incredibly lame and gratuitous samples from John Holmes flicks on top of mild hip-hop beats and samples from Italian sex farce soundtracks, not to mention a cover of Serge Gainsbourg's "Je T'Aime... Moi Non Plus". Danmass' "Gotta Learn" (1997), however, was a pretty awesome collage of old-school samples, rough scratching and a mother of a synth hook.

The **Dust 2 Dub** and **Sunday Best** (both 1998) compilations took the tempo down a bit with slowburn versions of their usual party-hardy shenanigans. Moog's fab organ groover "What Is a Party?" (1998) picked up the tempo, however, while Mr. Dan's **Strange Skies** EP and **Cab Riding** EP (both 1998) continued Danmass' cut-up momentum. Lee Van Cleef's **The Final Spliff** EP (1998) was a couch potato's life in miniature, while Danmass' collaboration with Afrika Bambaataa, "Mind Control" (1998), was the old-school sample-fest you'd expect. **the planet of breaks** compilation (1999) highlighted the genre's reliance on '80s street funk on tracks like Felonious Phunk's "Hoodlum Hustle" and the haphazard approach to sampling on Danmass' "The Beast".

⊙**Moog "What Is a Party?"**   Dust 2 Dust, 1998

Maybe the organ sample is a bit too facile and a little obvious, but it sure does move something fierce.

DJ Food

As if the multiple aliases that plague dance music weren't enough trouble, the identity of DJ Food is dependent on the situation. Originally, the pseudonym of Coldcut, DJ Food can now be a collaboration between Jonathon More and Matt Black of Coldcut and Patrick Carpenter and Strictly Kev if they are making a record, or just Carpenter and Kev if DJ Food is mixing it up live.

DJ Food began life as the beat connoisseur behind the **Jazz Brakes** (1990) collection of doped-out breakbeats designed to be looped and cut up by producers and DJs. With the phenomenal depth and breadth of More and Black's record collections, the **Jazz Brakes** series extended to Volumes 2 and 3 (1991, 1992) and became key components in the emergence of Trip-Hop with their bleary sparseness and blood-shot tempos. **Jazz Brakes** Volumes 4 and 5 (1993, 1994) emerged with Patrick Carpenter on board and

fleshed out the collection of recyclable breakbeats concept with textural detail, pharmacological ambience, Latinate swing and almost-hooks so that they almost seemed like albums in their own right.

DJ Food emerged as a fully fledged artist with "Peace Pts. 1 & 2/Dark Blood/Well Swung" (1994). **A Recipe For Disaster** (1995) soon followed with b-boy collages, stoner stabs at Jungle and more bad puns than a lifetime of Bob Hope concerts. **Refried Food** (1996), a collection of remixes, featured an excellent line-up, but, with the exceptions of The Herbaliser's nu-blaxploitation mix of "Mella" and Wagon Christ's e-z listening send-up of "Turtle Soup", largely failed to deliver anything but re-heated leftovers. With the exception of "Cosmic Jam" on the **Ninja Cuts: The Joy of Dex** (1996) compilation, DJ

Food has largely been absent on wax since, concentrating instead on their four-turntable live routines.

⊙ Jazz Brakes Volume 3　　　　　　　　　　Ninja Tune, 1993

Perhaps a bit dated now, but this collection of beats and pieces was one of the building blocks of Down Tempo.

Freestylers

As The Kingsmen and Otis Day & the Knights were to frat houses of the '60s, The Freestylers were to Freshers' Fairs of the late '90s. After striking it big with Strike's Top 10 chart hit "U Sure Do" (1995), Matt Cantor hooked up with Aston Harvey to form The Freestylers. With Public Enemy samples, crowd-pleasing Jungle and funky beats for the breakdancers, their debut EP, **Uprock** (1997), quickly became a party-rocking staple on the Big Beat scene. Even better, though, was the **Adventures in Freestyle** EP (1997) which featured the awesome "Feel the Panic" which sampled Aerosmith's "Walk This Way" as well as the massive "B-Boy Stance". Stealing riffs from Oasis and the bassline from reggae's eternal "Stalag 17" riddim, "B-Boy Stance" rocketed the group to fame and had their label's lawyers working overtime.

"B-Boy Stance" was inevitably remixed without the offending riff in 1998, but The Freestylers compensated with infectious scratching from J-Roc and timestretched ragga vocals from Tenor Fly. "Ruff-neck" (1998) followed suit with Junglist MC Navigator chatting on top of dancehall gun shots and ska from Fatboy Slim's trash can. Navigator also graced the guitar-led Aphrodite-style Junglism of "Warning" (1998) with his verbal skills.

These party antics were writ large on their debut album, **We Rock Hard** (1998). There were old-school references aplenty – especially with appearances from the Soul Sonic Force on "We Rock Hard" and the Electro cut-ups, "Drop the Boom" and "Breaker Beats Part 2" – and riotous, anthemic choruses everywhere you looked. Cantor and Harvey applied a similar logic to their DJing sets, a facsimile of which can be heard on their contribution to the FSUK series (1998).

◉ We Rock Hard   Freskanova, 1998

It might not have the original version of "B-Boy Stance", but the one on the album is still pretty irresistible as is most of the record.

Fretless AZM

Despite its sleepy reputation, there's more to the Isle of Wight's music scene than Level 42. Dotted amongst the retirees, there exists a small community of like-minded post-everything musicians centred around the ambit of Max Brennan. With an aesthetic not entirely different from obO, Brennan makes organic, live-sounding music that wants to be Techno. Fusing influences that range from James Brown to Sun Ra to Jeff Mills, Brennan churns out track after track of individual mélanges of House, funk, disco, jazz, Down Tempo and Techno under his umpteen aliases (Fretless AZM, Maxwell House, Universal Being, OH Krill and Max).

Debuting in 1995 with the **Breeze** EP on Holistic as Fretless AZM, Brennan quickly set out his MO of denuded '70s funk, jazz textures and Deep House keyboard washes put together with more than a hint of psychedelectation. Brennan's debut album, **Ultimate Maxploitation**

(1996), followed suit with what sounded like Weather Report's jazz-fusion played by a hipper Tortoise. At the same time, in collaboration with former session musician Rupert Brown, Brennan released the **Holistic Rhythms** album (1996) as Universal Being. Slightly more cinematic in both scope and approach, **Holistic Rhythms** also introduced a Jon Hassell-esque fourth world aspect to Brennan's soundworld.

Fretless AZM's **From MARZ With Love** (1996) continued with Brennan's trademark combination of chicken-scratch guitar riffs and Detroit synth washes. As Maxwell House, he released the **Maxwell House One** album (1996) for Peacefrog and as OH Krill he released the **The Landing** EP (1996) for Beau Monde, both of which translated dance music's uplifting groove into the scribbled-code nonsense verse of a lonely boy's diary.

Yet more jazzual Detroit-style Techno that wanted to be a blaxploitation soundtrack – or was that mellow jazz-funk that aspired to the electronic lullabies of Larry Heard? – followed in the form of Fretless AZM's **Astral Cinema** LP (1997), while Brennan's occasional drummer Paul Butler released the solo **Comfy Club** EP as Pnu Riff and the dubby **Lost Arks** album (both 1997) as Delta T with Pat Watson, Colin Brocquillion and Kate Smith.

Jazzual, Detroit-style techno came in the form of Max Brennan's **Alien to Whom?** album (1998) for Japanese label Sublime, while Pnu Riff's album, **The Cat Scratch** (1998), continued to blaze a trail totally incomprehensible to all but the most acid-fried.

◉ Various Artists Holistic Reflections　　　　　　Holistic, 1998

A collection of the Isle of Wight's finest – including tracks from Fretless AZM, Universal Being, Delta T and Pnu Riff.

Fused and Bruised
Records

Popular music, especially dance music, approaches the revolutionary only when it's at its most heterogeneous, so you have every reason to be wary of purists whose rhetoric sounds alarmingly similar to religious leaders and social engineers. Standing in resolute opposition to the House fascists and drum 'n' bass progressivists, the musicians on Big Beat labels like Fused and Bruised throw everything together to see what sticks.

Formed by Simon Lewin and Shack in 1996, Fused and Bruised had a self-stated aim to "release a free-style jam culled from the worlds of instrumental hip-hop, Electro, Jungle, funk, Techno; all united by the broad base of the booming beat." The label's first release, pHrack R's **Catch 22** EP (1996), lived up to the manifesto with a collection of nervous rhythms, gurgling synths and liquid bass. fUtUrEcOrE's **Bus, Dinner, Jam** EP and **Combat Squad** EP (both 1996) followed the same lines with darker hues and acid-washed chromatics.

Fused and Bruised's dancefloor breakthrough came with the release of the **Mainframe Wrekka** EP (1997) by a South London graffiti artist calling himself Elite Force. **Mainframe Wrekka** was an unholy alliance between the white noise of the Chemical Brothers and the cheeky sampladelia of Renegade Soundwave that generated a pandemonium. More sedate beatfreakery was offered on the **Point Five** series which featured the supine grooves of Silverkick.

It was the uptempo tracks, though, that were the label's stock in trade and pHrack R's **Sigh Co.** EP and the **This Is Latin Amyl** collections (both 1997) pushed the right buttons. Even more of a kick was the Mild Mannered Janitors' "Q Babs" (1997) which approached the mastodon stomp that hadn't been heard since the glory days of Black Sabbath, Grand Funk Railroad and Black Oak Arkansas. More hooligan jump-up appeared in the form of Surreal Madrid's **The Devil's Tingle** EP (1998) which was rather more formulaic than previous releases.

Day Trip to Brisco (1998) was a compilation album that claimed to fuse disco and breakbeat. While the glitterball shone on Environmental Science's "Brisco Sucks", the most obvious touchstone was old Hardcore as most of the tracks revolved around sped-up hip-hop breaks and enormous synth riffs. With releases by Junior Blanks, DJ Scissorkicks and Lunatic Calm, the label's commitment to no-nonsense party tunes looks set to continue until any hint of millennial angst has been long since forgotten.

☉ Various Artists Day Trip to Brisco   Fused and Bruised, 1998

Perhaps a bit on the laddish side, this compilation is the sound of a bunch of guys getting drunk and thrashing around a room.

Genaside II

ailing from South London, Genaside II represent breakbeat music at its bleakest and most Hardcore. Producers Kao Bonez and Chilli Phats are obsessed with intimidation and use tried and true tactics like thug life tales, gothic keyboards and dragging beats to get their point across. Like most self-aggrandising hard men, however, their bark is often worse than their bite and rarely has their music matched their criminally minded words.

One of a seemingly infinite number of anonymous white label 12"s that marked Hardcore's arrival in the early '90s, Genaside II's "Narra Mine" (1991) was a classic of post-Thatcher roughneck attitude and post-Summer of Love adrenaline rush. Credited by The Prodigy's Liam Howlett as "the people who invented Jungle", Genaside II went on to provide a tearing remix of "Jericho" (1992) for the band.

After a series of very low-profile bootlegs like "Death of the Kamikaze" (1992), Genaside II returned in 1996 with their debut album **New Life for the Hunted.** Featuring such luminaries as reggae legend Eek-A-Mouse, former Soul II Soul vocalist Rose Windross and various Wu Tang Clan hangers-on, **New Life for the Hunted** found the band working a distinctly slower version of the breakbeat Hardcore with which they had made their name and largely fell flat on its face. The one bright spot was a re-appearance of "Narra Mine" which was released as a single with rather sub-par mixes by both Armand Van Helden and the Wu Tang Clan.

With lyrics like "We're fucking fucked, we live that kind of life" from MC Killerman Archer, **Ad Finite** (1998) ditched the celeb cameos in favour of a horror-flick ultra-violence schtick. Aiming for the epic, but ending up resembling an early George Romero movie without the special effects budget, the music failed to live up to such titles as "Paranoid Thugism" and "Bullet Proof Jumper".

⊙ **"Narra Mine"**   Passion Music, 1991

Later re-released on London, this is the one time Genaside II managed to convey their urban verité in both music and boasts.

Global Communication

Taking dance music's obsession with multiple aliases to its logical extension, Mark Pritchard and Tom Middleton have their fingers in just about every musical pie available. Located in deepest, darkest Somerset, Pritchard and Middleton are able to pursue whatever direction they choose without adhering to the dictates of fashion from the dance capitals of London, Manchester or Bristol.

They might be the poster boys of dance music's intelligent set, but their beginnings were slightly less esoteric. As one third of Shaft,

Pritchard was responsible for the sandbox Hardcore of "Roobarb and Custard" (1991) – one of the toytown rave tunes that signalled the beginning of the end of rave as a cultural force. Middleton, on the other hand, was the other Aphex Twin, working with Richard James on the **Analogue Bubblebath** EP. Pritchard and Middleton started their Evolution label in 1991 with their Techno collaboration as Reload. Reload's debut album, **A Collection of Short Stories** (1993), was made up of industrial found sounds layered with crunching breakbeats and Ambient synth harmonies.

Global Communication was christened in 1992 and in 1993's "Obsilon Mi Nos", the duo made their finest record. A gorgeous, shimmering track of chiming synths and tick-tock percussion, "Obsilon Mi Nos" was mournful (it was inspired by the death of Middleton's uncle)

and uplifting at the same time. "Obsilon Mi Nos" also appeared on Global Comm's debut album, **76:14** (1994), which was that crystalline sound writ large.

Swiftly changing gears, Middleton and Pritchard recorded the Bukem classic "Amazon Amenity" (1994) as Link. A crucial track in drum 'n' bass' move away from the rave and the Jungle, "Amazon Amenity" caressed mellow breakbeats with Fender Rhodes licks, soothing synth washes and a sample from *Ferris Bueller's Day Off*. The duo also spun drum 'n' bass tunes as the Chaos & Julia Set.

As Jedi Knights, Pritchard and Middleton created an old school bricolage of Mantronix, Man Parrish and P-Funk. Their **Noddy Holder** EP (1995) was the first release on Clear Records and helped pioneer the Electro revival. **New School Science** (1996) ushered in the era of the kitschy remembrance of swing past with a collection of tracks that a shell-toed Monty Python would have made. Even more homages to 1980s New York appeared on their "Catch the Break" (1997) 12".

They renamed their label Universal Language in 1996 and released both perverse obscurantism from Wish Mountain (aka Matthew Herbert) and perverse polymorphism from The Horn. Meanwhile, Pritchard moonlighted for Danny Breaks' Droppin' Science label as Use of Weapons with the "Mojo Women" (1998) single.

⊙ Global Communication "Obsilon Mi Nos"	Evolution, 1993

One of the few true classics of the armchair Techno genre, this moved more than just your head. (Also available on Global Comm's **76:14** where it is called "14:31".)

◉ Jedi Knights New School Science	Universal Language, 1996

Heralding the retro-Electro movement, this album looked back to the days when technology was silly and charming, not threatening.

Grand Central

No MC who speaks the Queen's English will ever pass a "keep it real" test, so British hip-hop heads have concentrated instead on beat construction. One of the few such British hip-hop producers to get props from his American cousins, Mancunian Mark Rae founded his Grand Central label in 1995 as a conduit for the city's under-appreciated hip-hop scene to showcase its wares. While the label's output has occasionally strayed too far into the awkward realm of "real" songs, Grand Central is one of the few mostly instrumental hip-hop labels whose records aren't smug or completely detached from their surroundings.

In addition to running the Fat City record shop, Rae was the prime mover behind Manchester's Feva club nights which were the focus of the city's hip-hop community and where most of the label's talent emerged from. Grand Central's first release was **Central J. Parlay** (1995), an album of beats and loops made by Tony D, an American producer who had previously worked with the Poor Righteous Teachers. Recording as First Priority, Rae and Ross Clarke released the jazzy hip-hop of the **Pure Arithmetic EP** (1995) which also appeared on the **Fryin' the Fat** (1995) compilation.

More jazzy sampladelia appeared in the form of Aim's **Pacific North West EP** (1995) which was the work of a kid named Andy Turner jamming in the basement of his father's music shop in the Cumbrian backwater of Barrow-in-Furness. Straight outta Bradford, the Funky Fresh Few (scratch DJ Damon Savage and producer James Folks) debuted with the excellent **Slow For Focus** EP (1995) which featured the low-slung grooves of "89".

Rae's junglist excursion "Free Rollin'" (1995) marked Grand Central's shift from purist hip-hop towards a more broad-based breakbeat approach. Aim's Kool & the Gang cut-up, "Souldive" (1996), maintained the hip-hop flavour, but Only Child's "Electric Chair" and Andy Votel's "If Nine Was Six" (both 1996) ventured into more cinematic territory. Rae & Christian's "Northern Sulphuric Soul" (1996) threw Brazillian *batucada* drums into the mix, but their hip-hop sensibility never let the track dissolve into Gilles Peterson-style suavity.

"Souldive" and "Northern Sulphuric Soul" both appeared on the very fine **Central Heating** (1996) compilation. The post-Portishead/Lamb torch songs didn't work very well, but the instrumental tracks all showed an attention to textural detail and momentum that was all too often missing from Down Tempo beat collage. Highlights included Funky Fresh Few's collaboration with Jeru The Damaja associate Afu Ra, "Through These Veins", Aim's "Loop-dreams" and his cut-up of the Evel Knievel album, "Original Stuntmaster". The ultimate proof of the label's cool quotient, however, was Andy Votel's Trip-Hop cover of Black Sabbath's "Hand of Doom", which succeeded against all odds.

After nearly a year of remix EPs of material from **Central Heating**, Grand Central released Tony D's **Pound For Pound** (1997) album which brought the label closer to the American hip-hop community. After **Central Reservations** (1998), a collection of remixes and unissued tracks, Grand Central released Rae & Christian's debut album, **Northern Sulphuric Soul** (1998), to critical acclaim. Cuts like the motivational "Divine Sounds", the stunning "Now I Lay Me Down" and collaborations with Jeru the Damaja, the Jungle Brothers and members of the JVC Force proved that maybe there was some life in Down Tempo beats after all.

◑ Various Artists Central Heating   Grand Central, 1996

A very solid collection of beat collage that avoided most of the pitfalls of the abstract bluntedness scene.

**⊙ Rae & Christian Northern Sulphuric
Soul**   Grand Central, 1998

There are perhaps too many lame songs which feature the likes of
Texas, but this is worth owning just for YZ's amazing Bible-bashing on
"Now I Lay Me Down".

Headrillaz

Although Darius and Caspar Kedros have made jazzy dub as
Slowly for Ninja Tune and House as Tranquil Elephantiser for
Language, their real love is testosterone-fuelled rock and roll which
rears its ugly head in their recordings as Headrillaz. While thrashing
about a room drunkenly is the *raison d'etre* of all Big Beat, the Headrillaz's records often sound like just that.

After a couple of tracks as Slowly and "Low Down" (1995) as Tranquil Elephantiser, the Kedros brothers debuted as the Headrillaz for
Pussyfoot with "Hot 'n' Bovvud/Weird Planet" (1996). Welded metallic
wah-wah riffs to stomping beats, Headrillaz sounded like the Bomb
Squad after a couple of fifths of Jack Daniels. Their mini-album **Coldharbour Rocks** (1997) added some spy-flick cut-ups to the distortion
overload to create their most listenable record.

Solidifying their line-up with MC Saul and drummer Steve, Headrillaz signed to Virgin subsidiary V2 for "Dawn of the Dead/Yeah
Right... Nice Clothes" (1998). More frenzied breakbeats and sub-punk
snottiness, the single failed to expand on their rowdy hooliganisms.
"The Right Way" (1998) used some live instrumentation to move them

ever-so-slightly out of the Roland 303-guitar-obvious beats ghetto that they had occupied for so long.

○ Coldharbour Rocks   Pussyfoot, 1997

Named after the street in South London in which all the band members live, Coldharbour Rocks aimed a pile-driver of distortion straight at you in order to get you to dance.

The Herbaliser

Members of the legion of southwest London hip-hop trainspotters, Ollie Teeba and Jake Wherry have largely avoided Down Tempo's standard M O of turning hip-hop into a soporific by maintaining close ties to the parent genre. Honouring both DJ Premier and Coldcut, The Herbaliser attempt to blend the best of American and European DJ culture.

The duo emerged from the netherworld of Twickenham, London in 1994 with their debut 12", "The Real Killer/Blowin' It" on Ninja Tune. Knowing that hailing from the world capital of rugby is about as "real" as Snoop Dogg in drag, The Herbaliser took their clues from crews like Organized Konfusion and recast hip-hop as head music. With tracks like "Repetitive Noise" and "Scratchy Noise" which emphasised hip-hop's beat re-manipulation, their debut album, **Remedies** (1995), was awash in sticky jazz toffee and narcotic atmospheres.

The Flawed hip-hop EP (1996) introduced MCs into their soundworld, but the skewed jazz dynamics of "Mr. Chombee Has the Flaw" and the wading-through-quicksand feel of "40 Winks" re-affirmed their Down Tempo credentials. Their second album, **Blow Your Head-**

phones (1997), was a soundclash between the suavity of Lalo Schifrin, the smooth lyrics of MC What What, old English eccentricity and B-movie zaniness; proving that the best Trip-Hop was simply British hip-hop made in the face of a severe lack of half-decent MCs.

The Herbaliser's most successful re-write of hip-hop's original blueprint was unsurprisingly the one that did the least re-writing. Despite its title, which payed homage to the invincible turntablist crew the Invisbl Skratch Piklz, **Wall Crawling Giant Insect Breaks** (1998) was not a DJ battle record. Instead, it was the Ninja Tune record that most lives up to the bosses' cut 'n' paste heritage since they released Steinski's "It's Up to You" in 1993. The title track was a more frenetic version of DJ Shadow's "In/Flux", while the rest of this excellent EP was comprised of breakbeat collages so fleshed out and sprightly that you'd never remember that they used to call this stuff "abstract hip-hop" or "blunted beats".

◉ Wall Crawling Giant Insect Breaks　　　　Ninja Tune, 1998

Incorporating both well-executed live material and one of the great sample collages, this is Down Tempo about as uptempo as it comes.

David Holmes

O nce known almost exclusively as "that Irish Techno DJ", David Holmes has since pursued a path of single-minded eclecticism. Beginning his DJing career playing Northern Soul and disco to Belfast's party people, Holmes' first shot at notoriety came with "De Niro" (1993), a House classic recorded by him and fellow traveller Ashley Beedle as The Disco Evangelists. A legendary remix of

Sabres of Paradise's "Smokebelch" (1994) followed as did releases as Death Before Disco and 4 Boy 1 Girl Action, but Holmes wouldn't truly make a name for himself until he got over his identity crisis with his first solo album.

Despite the forced title, **This Film's Crap, Let's Slash the Seats** (1995) was one of the first dance music records to explicitly explore the "invisible soundtrack" motif that is so central to recent Down Tempo beat collage. His House and Techno past crept in here and there, but the album largely concerned itself with post-narcotic blues and nods to John Carpenter and Ennio Morricone.

The product of a trip to New York with a sampler and lots of DATs, **Let's Get Killed** (1997) featured more excursions into soundtrack territory, including an excellent cover of Serge Gainsbourg's "Don't Die Just Yet". More uptempo and just plain funkier, but just as effective, were "My Mate Paul" and "Headrush on Lafayette". Holmes' soundtrack aspirations were fulfilled in 1998 when he scored the George Clooney vehicle *Out of Sight*. A combination of moody downbeat collages and blaxploitation pastiches, Holmes' soundtrack was an admirable translation of Trip-Hop's cinematic influences.

The culmination of Holmes' peripatetic musical path, though, was his **Essential Selection Mix** (1998). Taking in rare groove organ grinder Googie Rene's "Smokey Joe's La La" (the track that "My Mate Paul" was based on), the kitsch sitar funk of Ananda Shankar and the old-school reminiscing of Jurassic 5, **Essential Selection Mix** proved that Coldcut didn't have a monopoly on bizarre juxtapositions.

◉ Essential Selection Mix   ffrr, 1998

Moving from the rock histrionics of Rare Earth to the ultra-mellow electronics of Skylab, this is a virtuosic rendering of Holmes' record collection.

Howie B

With the rise of the sampler has come the rise of the producer/engineer as an artist in his or her own right. Producer to the stars, Howie B is probably the most well-known figure of this phenomenon, creating "vibes" for artists like Björk, U2 and Sly & Robbie.

The erstwhile Howard Bernstein was born in Glasgow and moved to London in the mid '80s where he worked in a studio, eventually engineering a couple of tracks for Soul II Soul, Siouxsie & the Banshees and Massive Attack. As Nomad Soul, he released one record, "Candy Soul" (1991), for Island and then hooked up with James Lavelle's Mo' Wax where he recorded a few tracks. In 1994 he formed his Pussyfoot label and released tracks like "Breathe In/Dew in June" under his own name and "The Fourth Way" (both 1994) as Daddylonglegs.

1994 also saw him collaborate with Mat Ducasse and Tosh and Kudo from Major Force as Skylab. Their album, **No. 1** (1994), was a Down Tempo masterpiece that bore little resemblance to either the Ambient Techno or Trip-Hop vogues of the time. Howie's solo project **Music For Babies** (1995) was his response to the birth of his daughter and wove jazz, calypso, Latin timbales and dub into a rich soundscape that grooved on textures rather than beats.

With these Ambient classics under his belt, Howie naturally progressed to working alongside Brian Eno, Nellee Hooper and Flood on U2's **Passengers** (1995) and **Pop** (1996) projects. Meanwhile, Pussyfoot was releasing occasionally excellent records by the likes of Dobie ("B-Boy Anthem/Luv 'n' Hate/Original Heads" [1995]) and Luke Gordon's Spacer project (the **Atlas Earth** album [1996]). The **Howie B. EP** (1996) was centred around "Butt Meat", a masterpiece of overload that encompassed a hip-hop beat that was too fast, a big bass sound, lots of distortion and a fuzzed organ that might have been what Sly Stone sounded like from the back row of Shea Stadium circa 1969.

Turn the Dark Off (1997) followed the **Howie B. EP** with big beats and bigger samples and extended Howie's list of collaborators with "Take Your Partner By the Hand" featuring Robbie Robertson from The Band. Unexpected links were also forged with peripatetic producer and collaborator extraordinaire Hal Willner. His brilliant, staggeringly original **Whoops, I'm an Indian** album (1998) was released by Pussyfoot to almost complete neglect by the press. Howie's own **Snatch** (1999) was less gob-smacking, but featured plenty of moments of production genius.

⊙ Skylab No. 1   L'Attitude, 1994

Hovering in a netherworld between Trip-Hop, Brian Eno, Silver Apples and Faust, this explored the less travelled corridors of Down Tempo's sonic museum.

⊙ **Hal Willner, Whoops, I'm an Indian**   Pussyfoot, 1998

Easily the best record Pussyfoot's ever released, this beautiful, moving
sampladelic journey through a mythical America, where Hank
Williams, old gospel singers and Jewish street-corner philosophers
move to a Junglist beat, is a criminally neglected future classic.

Jimpster

Given that his father was the drummer for lite jazz-funksters
Shakatak, it is unsurprising that Jamie Odell's Jimpster project has updated their sound for post-House Britain. Odell combines
Down Tempo and sorta-Junglist rhythms with flutes and jazzy atmospheres in the same way his father's band combined post-disco beats
with flutes and jazzy atmospheres. Unfortunately, like many other
Electronica artists, Odell has been seduced by the illusion that jazz-
fusion never sacrificed groove for virtuosity.

Somewhere along the line, someone decided that slow, smooth
jazziness replaced the profundity of Jamaican dub as the stoner
groove of choice and Jimpster's debut, the Initial EP (1996), was
aimed at this new market of blunted sofa surfers. Coming across like
fusion keyboardist Chick Corea and Kruder & Dorfmeister playing ele-
vator music, the Initial EP laid down the Jimpster blueprint. The Martian Arts EP (1996) expanded the Jimpster formula with Bukem-esque
drum 'n' bass, but still contained plenty of creamy jazz licks and
sounded like Acid Jazz might have if its practitioners had actually
taken acid.

After collaborating with Coldcut on their **Let Us Play** album (1997), Odell released the **Facing the Future** EP (1997) as Audiomontage. Further expanding his repertoire, the EP's "Mind Painting" introduced Brazilian *batucada* rhythms into his sonic palette alongside the live-instrument Junglism. The **Perennial Pleasures** EP (1997) followed with more drum 'n' bass for lounge lizards, which Jimpster proved by playing live gigs as a band with bassist Cheyne Towers, flautist Roger Wickham and drummer Dave Walsh.

The **Interconnect** EP (1998) continued the supine jazz-electronic-breakbeat hybrid and provided the foundation for Jimpster's debut album (1999) which did its best to prove that jazz was no longer an improvised music in the eyes of post-House musicians. "Jazz" had become simply a set of stock sound effects to sprinkle liberally over an anonymous production to give it a vague sense of legitimacy. No longer a process, jazz was merely a cult of the object.

⊙ **Martian Arts**   Freerange, 1996

Thankfully, this EP isn't as bad as its punning title, but its muso sensibilities can try the patience.

Klute

While most drum 'n' bass artists moved along a path that began with hip-hop and progressed through Acid House and rave to drum 'n' bass, Tom Withers took a rather different course. In 1981 Withers formed The Stupids, a punk band that took its cue from that other musical hardcore, Californian hardcore punk, and garnered enthusiastic press in the inkies. After such gems as "Retard Picnic" and "Peruvian Vacation", Withers moved to the US and discovered the sampler. Returning to the UK in 1993, he hooked up with a neighbour who was calling himself Photek and started making his own drum 'n' bass tracks.

After a couple of tracks as Tom & Tom and Dr. Know, Withers swiped an alias from a Donald Sutherland/Jane Fonda flick and emerged as Klute on Certificate 18. "Right Or Wrong/Work It Out/Ram Raider" (1996) ran the gamut of drum 'n' bass' range: moody, precision-tooled future funk to jazz-lite to "Amen" floor-burner. "Leo 9" (1996) and "Perception" (1997) followed suit with sharp, bright electronic melodies and glistening textures. Meanwhile, Withers recorded Down Tempo tracks as Override for Ninja Tune, recorded as Phume with Ubik's Danny Campbell and teamed up with Endemic Void's Danny Coffey for a release as Brass Wolf on Moving Shadow.

With metallic cricket chirps, processed wah-wah licks and a sample of Miles Davis' "Black Satin", Klute's **Total Self** EP (1998) was a compelling update of '70s fusion's extra-terrestrial funk melting pot. On "Hang-Up" and "Blow: Cold" paranoiac whispers were appended to crushing rhythms to remake the hazy, spook world suggested by Francis Ford Coppola's *The Conversation* in the image of Techstep's groaning assembly line. Klute's debut album, **Casual Bodies** (1998), explored superficially similar terrain, but tried too hard to be all things to all people and failed to deliver the claustrophobia that made **Total Self** so compelling.

⊙ Total Self   Certificate 18, 1998

One of 1998's better drum 'n' bass records, this succeeded because its model of jazz-fusion was Miles Davis and not the Yellowjackets.

Kruder & Dorfmeister

W hile Vienna may be in thrall to its traditions of classical music, liver dumplings and rich pastries, a growing underground of producers and scenesters have made Austria's capital one of the world's more creative dance music centres. Pranksters like the Mego and Sabotage labels and Techno wiseacres like Patrick Pulsinger and Erdem Tunakan have raised the profile of Austrian humour, but it is the production duo of Peter Kruder and Richard Dorfmeister that has attracted the most attention to the shores of the Danube.

Kruder and Dorfmeister both used to play in dodgy pop bands, but strayed towards DJing in the early '90s. They met in 1993 and immediately recorded the classic **G-Stoned** EP, released the following year on their own G-Stone label. Tracks like "High Noon" and "Deep Shit Parts 1 & 2" revealed their indebtedness to the blues, Ambient pioneer Brian Eno and Brazilian tropicalistas Airto Moreira and Edu Lobo as well as the beat science of New York hip-hop. While the music was more blunted and detailed than run-of-the-mill Down Tempo beat collage, it might have been the cover's parody of Richard Avedon's photo for Simon & Garfunkel's **Bookends** album that made the EP emblematic of the stoner aesthetic and knowingly kitsch sensibility that pervades Down Tempo music.

Their best track, "Young Man", was released exclusively on Wall of Sound's **Give 'Em Enough Dope Volume II** in 1995. Featuring snatches of blue-eyed blues singer Mose Allison and EPMD, "Young Man" was one of the first tracks to show the startling affinity between the ramshackle atmosphere of the blues and the moody beats of hip-hop. Constructed largely out of an answering machine message, the slomo "A Track For Us" featured on Talking Loud's **Multidirection** compilation in 1995. Other compilation exclusives included the piss-taking "Shakatakadoodub" on Ninja Tune's **Flexistentialism** (1996), "Out of the Blue" on **Freezone Volume III** (1996) and "Black Baby" on their contribution to the **DJ Kicks** series (1996). Kruder & Dorfmeister's **DJ Kicks** album was an exceedingly mellow foray through their own brand of abstract beats, the ultra-tasteful drum 'n' bass of Aquasky, second-hand dub from the 2 Kool and Cup of Tea labels and the proto-Big Beat of Hardfloor's "Dadamnphreaknoizphunk".

The underground success of the **G-Stoned** EP led to a flurry of

remix activity. Especially noteworthy were their reworks of Bomb the Bass's "Bug Powder Dust" (1995) and Alex Reece's "Jazzmaster" (1996) which they did in a tongue-in-cheek exotica style. Other recipients of Kruder & Dorfmeister overhauls include David Holmes, Lamb, UFO and, bizarrely, Bone, Thugs & Harmony. Their best mixes were collected on **The K&D Sessions** (1998).

Dorfmeister has also recorded as Tosca with school-friend Rupert Huber. Their "Chocolate Elvis" (1995) single was based around a recording of a New York street musician claiming he was the "chocolate Elvis" and its sparse lo-fi aesthetic set it apart from the glut of Down Tempo product that emerged that year. **Opera** (1997) followed suit with more gritty social realism and mini-documentaries of urban life, often sounding like a beat-head version of Gavin Bryars' art-music classic **Jesus' Blood Never Failed Me Yet**. Proof positive that indica indulgence and "content-free" music doesn't necessarily imply air-headedness.

⊙ **G-Stoned EP**   G-Stone, 1994

One of the more original documents of blunted beat movement by virtue of its affective music and cheeky cover. Also seek out their excellent "Young Man" on Wall of Sound's **Give 'Em Enough Dope Vol. 2.**

DJ Krush

Unlike the often insipid jazz flavours of his Down Tempo contemporaries, DJ Krush, at his best, actually picks up the grainy textures of the urban underbelly that the genre's beatnik jazz clichés are meant to evoke. Not that he doesn't slip every so often into the streamlined "coolness" that the slumming jazz-funkers can't escape when they slow down their Acid Jazz tempos – it's just that his love of hip-hop's obsession with "realness" keeps his productions grittier and less aspirational than his cohorts.

Like so many other non-Americans, Tokyo-based Krush was originally inspired to get into hip-hop by the film *Wild Style*. Through his DJing he became connected with Japan's jazz fetish scene and the Miles Davis copyists in Jazzy Upper Cut who graced his debut single, "Slow Chase" (1993), with Blue Note organ vibes and a febrile electronic trumpet solo that could have been from **Bitches Brew**. "Slow Chase" caught the attention of Mo' Wax impresario James Lavelle and appeared along with collaborations with vocalist Monday Michiru on Mo' Wax's **Jazz Hip Jap** (1993) overview of the Japanese jazz scene. **Bad Brothers** (1994), basically an album of remixes of material by jazz guitarist Ronnie Jordan, featured Krush's beats in an airy, loose-limbed environment. This easy-swinging jazzy flavour was writ large on his eponymous 1994 debut album, a hint of the more effective monochromaticism which was to come.

Mo' Wax issued Krush's next release, the epochal "Lost & Found/Kemuri" (1994) split single with DJ Shadow, which heralded the arrival of the abstract, blunted beat generation with its low-slung beats and scratches. The flute-led "Kemuri" was the highlight of his second album, **Strictly Turntablized** (1995), which was constructed exactly as its title said it was. The tubercular atmospheres and wheezing bass of the record's best tracks showed that the Down Tempo beat crew was capable of evoking something other than their own ganja-soaked hipness. **Strictly Turntablized** was followed by DJ Shadow's excellent "89.9 Megamix" which cut up samples from the album and layered them over a big bassline and scratching for ten minutes. At around the same time, Krush also added scratches to

Howie B's remake of the *Wild Style* theme as Olde Scottish on Mo' Wax's **Headz** (1995) compilation.

On **Meiso** (1995), Krush proved his hip-hop credentials by working with rappers C.L. Smooth, Guru and members of The Roots. Better than the tracks featuring MCs, though, were his standard instrumental collages, which featured geometric bass pulses, asthmatic beats and a duet with Shadow on "Duality" which was basically a scratch marathon over the beat from U2's "Sunday Bloody Sunday". The collaborations continued on **Milight** (1997) with guest appearances from the leading lights of New York's hip-hop underground, Shawn J. Period and Mos Def, and blunted Frenchman DJ Cam. Where the previous two albums had been tense, grimy affairs portraying the physical and moral deterioration of the inner city, **Milight** was relaxed and spacious.

Krush hadn't lost his taste for congestion and compression, however, and his half of **Cold Krush Cuts** (1997), a mix of tracks from Ninja Tune, was fuzzed and fugged – a bit like being hit on the head by a blunt instrument. His own megamix of his greatest hits, **Holonic** (1997), was similarly bleary, but with a bit more turntable gymnastics thrown in. Far cleaner was Krush's album with Japanese jazz giant Toshinori Kondo, **Ki-Oku** (1998), which blended the neon warmth of movie soundtrack jazz with mellow hip-hop beats.

◉ Strictly Turntablized   Mo' Wax, 1995

Krush's most minimal, least jazzy, dirtiest and, therefore, most original album.

Lamb

Perhaps the best of the "next Portishead" that emerged in 1996, Lamb injected an aesthetic of disjunction into the heart-break poesy of the post-modern torch song genre instigated by Björk, Portishead and Everything But the Girl. Combining a love of wordplay with a play of textures, Lamb made the Celtic folk song swing with the sashaying grace of jazzy drum 'n' bass and swoop to the narcotic depths of a morose DJ Premier.

Andy Barlow had previously recorded the Ramsey Lewis-inspired, proto-Big Beat funk fest "Anafey" (1995), as Hip Optimist for Skint and Louise Rhodes had contributed vocals for 808 State before the duo were put in contact with each other by Garage producer Elliot Eastwick. Their first single, "Cotton Wool" (1996), flitted between off-kilter Beatles mellotron patterns, warped pitch-bended beats, Ennio

Morricone dust-bowl guitars and skewed cellos. Even better than the original was an excellent epic mix by Fila Brazillia, which used synth-washes the way they were meant to be used – to suggest a detached, narcotised bliss.

"Gold" (1996) featured textured beats, a vibes riff, electronic malice and plenty of strings to put its tale of sexual ecstasy as madness across. "Gorecki" (1996), meanwhile, touched its cap to the minimalist composer while beats surged against a fragile piano sample. Their eponymous debut album (1996) was similarly fractured with cuts like the forbidding "Transfattyacid" lying side by side with the cellos of "Zero" and the mariachi horns of "Merge". **Lamb** was that rare album that explored the sensuality of not only rapture, but rupture as well.

◉ Lamb   Fontana, 1996

One of the better documents of post-modern blues, this debut album rose above the rest of the genre by virtue of a broader, more experimental sonic palette.

Lionrock

Britain's dance culture may be dominated by elitist purists who have turned the demotic impulses of raving into an industry of leisure, but thankfully there are people like Justin Robertson whose eclecticism has led him to embrace the tunesmithery of The Beatles, the high energy of Detroit punks The MC5, rude boy ska from the Studio 1 label, Acid House, Detroit Techno and hip-hop. He's even gone so far as to buy a round of drinks for speed metal pioneers Slayer. While the music of Robertson's polyglot group Lionrock may never be more than the sum of its parts, at least their heart's in the right place.

Raised on a diet of Northern Soul and Laurel Aitken bluebeat records, Robertson fell under the sway of House while at university, where he DJ'ed parties by mixing with two stereos (ie, turning the volume down on one while turning the volume up on the other one). During his stint behind the counter at Manchester's Eastern Bloc record shop, Robertson started the Spice Night, which has become one of those clubs that is talked about in reverential tones even though few people actually went there. Even more legendary was Robertson's

Most Excellent club, which spread Balearic eclecticism outside of London and was one of the few places on Earth where a DJ could spin Nitzer Ebb without being laughed off the decks.

The Rebellious Jukebox continued this adventurous spirit with an anything-goes policy that encouraged DJs to spin Curtis Mayfield next to The Stooges, thus influencing Big Beat's ground zero, The Heavenly Social, where Robertson would later DJ. During this time, Robertson released his eponymous debut single as Lionrock in 1992 and was busy remixing The Shamen, Happy Mondays, New Order and Erasure. Featuring raps from MC Buzz B, "Packet of Peace" and the MC5-sampling "Carnival" (both 1993) both hit the British charts with a strange blend of music that existed in some nether region between House and hip-hop.

With an enduring love for the live excitement of rock, Robertson decided to blend live instrumentation with samples and turntables on Lionrock's next single, "Straight at Yer Head" (1995). Named after a song by The Fall, **An Instinct For Detection** (1996) marked Lionrock's debut as a fully fledged band with Robertson, Buzz B, engineer Roger Lyons, Mandy Wigbey (keyboards) and Paddy Steer (bass). Taking its inspiration from *The Man From U.N.C.L.E.*, "Fire Up the Shoesaw" sampled Nancy Sinatra's "These Boots Are Made For Walking", while sampled dialogue from Sherlock Holmes movies served as bridges between songs. An EP of outtakes, **Project Now** (1996), followed with more ska-rap-House-hip-hop-spy-theme grooves.

After a series of live gigs that attempted to integrate "real" instruments and knob twiddling even further, Lionrock recorded, aborted, then re-recorded their follow-up album. **City Delirious** (1998) was another audio collage of an imagined London or Manchester as a multi-cultural hipster paradise. An ode to wanton diversity, **City**

Delirious included nods to Electro, Derrick Morgan, John Barry, Duane Eddy, Kraftwerk and Kevin Yost. It was a fine summation of their polymorphously perverse influences, but not much more than that.

○ **City Delirious** Concrete, 1998

A well-produced pastiche, this album is less uptight and swings a bit more than their debut.

Major Force

L ong before the first MC got on the mic to laud his DJ, hip-hop music was nothing but a series of breaks and tunes that the DJ thought were cool segued together. Inspired by the cut 'n' paste antics of Marley Marl, Double Dee & Steinski, DJ Red Alert, The 45 King and Coldcut, Toshio Nakanishi and Masayuki Kudo tried to bring hip-hop back to its roots as a purely instrumental form. Master-mixing James Brown breaks, '60s organ runs, jazz solos and easy listening textures, the records released on their Major Force label are clear antecedents of the Trip-Hop and Down Tempo genres that followed half a decade later, even if they were more about the play of textures and sounds than the latter's desire to disengage from reality.

Major Force first attracted attention with DJ records like "Thumpin'" and "Return of the Original Art-Form" (both 1988) which were recorded by Kudo, Hiroshi Fujiwara and DJ Milo from Bristol's Wild Bunch. "Thumpin'" was an extraordinary track that fused hip-hop's cut-up logic with the breakneck 4/4 pace of House, while "Return of the Original Art-Form" retained more of a breakbeat feel even as it propelled the funk towards escape velocity. Takagi Kan's records like Tiny Panx's "Last Orgy" and The Orchids' "Yes We Can Can" (both 1988) picked up where Double Dee & Steinski left off with loopy edits and crazy juxtapositions, not to mention many of the same breaks.

Tycoon Tosh's "Get Happy!" (1988) slowed down the pace significantly and sampled Chakachas' "Jungle Fever" and Eric B & Rakim on its way to becoming the godfather of Down Tempo beat collage, particularly as it gave Massive Attack one of its grooves. Tosh's "Economic Animal in Concrete Jungle" (1989) made the breaks and samples format even more subdued and evocative.

Major Force's peripatetic sound palette ranged from the New York Dolls sample on Tosh's "Love & Peace" (1988) to the lovers' rock of "Tribe of Love" (1989). By 1990, though, the enthusiasm that characterised their initial output had largely deserted them and Major Force descended into the fashion statement that they had always threatened to become. There were exceptions like DJ Doc Holiday's MC5-sampling "Club of Steel" (1990), but by and large records like Takagi Kan's "Meet the Rhythm" (1991) and SDP's "Santastic Mix" (1991) were little more than unctuous sax and lame piano loops on top of a stagnant breakbeat. Hooking up with Mo' Wax in 1993, Tosh and Kudo went headlong down this path of tasteful jazziness and never looked back. With a preponderance of soft-focus jazzisms, theremins and Moogs, **Major Force West** (1998) collected Toshi and Kudo's work in London for their Mo' Wax subsidiary label.

◉ Major Force: The Original Art-Form   Mo' Wax, 1997

With the infinite collectability of the original Major Force records, this compilation is not only the best overview of the label/crew, but probably the only record you'll be able to find.

Massive Attack

nspired by Charlie Ahearn's pseudo-documentary of hip-hop culture, *Wild Style*, Grant Marshall (aka Daddy G), Robert Del Naja (3D), Andrew Vowles (Mushroom), Nellee Hooper, Milo Johnson and Claude "Willie Wee" Williams formed the Bristol hip-hop collective The Wild Bunch. Accused by some of destroying the city's live music scene because of the popularity of their parties, The Wild Bunch would epitomise the sound (an agglomeration of hip-hop, rare groove, soul, reggae and rock influences) and organisation (loose affiliations of multi-media artists) of music groups in post-hip-hop Britain despite releasing only one single during their five-year lifespan, "Friends and

Countrymen/The Look of Love" (1987). While the Wild Bunch are largely myth and legend to those who lived outside Bristol, their legacy lives on in the group that grew out of the collective, Massive Attack.

With a core of Daddy G, 3D and Mushroom, Massive Attack formed in 1988 after the break-up of The Wild Bunch and released a cover of Chaka Khan's "Any Love", which was produced by fellow Bristolians Smith and Mighty. Their real calling card, however, was "Daydreaming" (1990). With Tricky and 3D quoting *Fiddler on the Roof* and The Beatles while floating on a stream-of-consciousness detachment, background inhalations and exhalations, creeping bpms and Shara Nelson's blues whispers, "Daydreaming" was all about the doped-out headspace that results from "living in my headphones". Backed with Larry Heard's gorgeous remix of "Any Love", the single heralded the arrival of "the Bristol sound" and presaged the development of Trip-Hop.

Their debut album, **Blue Lines** (1991), was quite simply epochal. Incorporating Bristol's laconic take on hip-hop, reggae vocalist Horace Andy, the jazz-fusion of Billy Cobham, the James Brownian motion of funk, symphonic '70s soul and the "death disco" of Public Image Limited, **Blue Lines** was the first representation of a certain kind of syncretic Britishness that would define the island's music for the next decade. Just as The Rolling Stones and Led Zeppelin re-read African-American blues as the soundtrack for the sexual liberation of Swinging London, Massive Attack reworked the ganja crawl of reggae and bloodshot atmospheres of hip-hop as the sound of post-Thatcher disengagement from society: "There's no sunshine in my life because the way I deal is hazy"; "Are you predatory? Do you fear me?"; "Just be thankful for what you got"; "Excommunicated from the brotherhood of man".

When **The Massive Attack** EP (1992) was released, Nelson and Tricky had more or less drifted out of the group and the one new track, "Home of the Whale", featured vocals from Caroline Lavelle. With Tom-Waits-produced-by-Danny-Elfman music and the ethereal, almost folk vocals, "Home of the Whale" prefigured the direction that Massive Attack would take on their next two records.

Three years and a copious amount of spliffs on from **Blue Lines**, **Protection** (1994) was released to much fanfare. Aside from the gor-geous title track with stunning vocals from Everything But the Girl's Tracey Thorn, though, the album was a further retreat into paranoiac inner space and mari-juana fog, with less to offer in terms of hooks and swing. Although the album was already wrapped in a cloud of bass and a patina of rust, dub producer Mad

Professor mixed the album into a vortex of quicksand gravity on his dub version of the album, **No Protection** (1994). Despite being beaten at their own game by neighbours Portishead and exile Tricky, the album was received rapturously and led to them working with Madon-na on her cover of Marvin Gaye's "I Want You".

"Risingson" (1997) heralded their third album with an edgy, dis-comfiting, guitar-led sound. **Mezzanine** (1998) was all jagged edges, morose textures and brooding menace. The only respites were the tracks featuring Cocteau Twins singer Elizabeth Fraser, whose airy vocals brought a vague sense of peace to the gothic *Sturm und Drang* of the album. **Mezzanine** nearly caused the band to split during its prolonged and painful recording and it was the sound of a comedown. When the highpoint was as saturnine as **Blue Lines**, **Mezzanine** was a long way down.

An eleven-CD collection of their past singles and remixes wrapped in heat-sensitive packaging, the **Singles Collection** (1999) was meant to prove that they were the most important British band of the '90s, but its almost mercenary capitalism left a sour taste.

⊙ Blue Lines   Circa, 1991

Probably the best, certainly the most important, album of the decade, **Blue Lines** defined the sound of Britain's carcass after Thatcher had finished with it.

Mo' Wax

As a hipper-than-thou agent provocateur and mogul who has a gift for translating avant garde abstraction into semi-popular fashion statements, Mo' Wax head honcho James Lavelle is the figurehead of a mini-generation of hip-hop iconoclasts.

The "Holygoof" started out writing about lame jazz-funk records for the Gilles Peterson-worshiping *Straight No Chaser* magazine and releasing records of the same quality by the likes of Raw Stylus and Palm Skin Productions in the early '90s. It was his discovery of DJs Shadow and Krush that shifted his label away from the bearded fringe and towards the skatewear-clad cutting edge of which his label is now the avatar. Krush first appeared on the **Jazz Hip Jap** (1993) compilation with the jazz pastiche of "Slow Chase" and in collaboration with vocalist Monday Michiru. Shadow's debut, "In/Flux" (1993), was more auspicious. A mind-boggling cut-up of a small portion of Shadow's prodigious record collection, "In/Flux" was the first of a series of peri-

odic coups pulled off by Lavelle that heralded the dawn of the abstract beat generation.

La Funk Mob's **Tribulations Extra Sensorielles** EP (1994) was another cut 'n' paste jazz-funk-disco mash-up that signalled that France had finally reversed its inability to produce a musician more contemporary than Johnny Hallyday. Their "La Doctresse" and "Motorbass Wants to Get Funked Up" were included along with "In/Flux" and "Slow Chase" on **Royalties Overdue**

(1994) which surveyed the transition from jazz fetishism to "abstract musical science" that occurred during Mo' Wax's first two years. With cover art by graffiti artist Futura 2000 and "16 instrumental excursions from the hip-hop avant garde" by the likes of Nightmares on Wax, Autechre, Howie B., Tranquility Bass and DJ Shadow, **Headz** (1994) made this transition complete.

Lavelle made his own recording debut in tandem with Tim Goldsworthy as UNKLE with **The Time Has Come** EP (1994) – "A trib-

ute to Sun Ra and all things fucked up". With its air-raid sirens, huge beats, background insect buzz and distortion, Beastie Boy associate Sam Sever's "What's That Sound?" (1995) was an early Big Beat classic. Another Beasties crony, Money Mark, provided the label with a leftfield hit with his down-at-heel album of lo-fi scribbles and twee songs, **Mark's Keyboard Repair (1995)**.

While too many Mo' Wax records had an annoying, self-regarding attitude that threatened to obviate the music, Lavelle occasionally released records that were more than just hype. Dr. Octagon (a collaboration between ex-Ultramagnetic MC Kool Keith, The Automator and Invisbl Skratch Piklz turntable maestro Q-Bert) released one of the most stunning records of the decade with **Ecologyst** (1996). More than just an amusing diversion from hip-hop's obsession with "realness", **Ecologyst** was a mind-bending, scatalogical twist on hip-hop's old "dropping science" metaphor that showed just how limited the imaginations of most musicians who claimed they were making sci-fi music really were. Mo' Wax's re-release of Innerzone Orchestra's (aka Detroit Techno producer Carl Craig) "Bug in the Bassbin" (1996) was equally revelatory. Whatever the veracity of the legend that "Bug in the Bassbin" was played by Grooverider and Fabio at their proto-Jungle Rage club, Carl Craig's "Jazz Mix" was one of the rare examples of a "jazzy" track that seemed to hear jazz as a process and not just a Fender Rhodes lick.

With DJ Shadow's masterpiece of cinematic hip-hop, **Endtroducing** (1996), Mo' Wax seemed to be overcoming its terminal hipness, but the **Headz 2** (1996) compilation confirmed old prejudices. Two double-disc packages with de rigueur graffiti art that sold for crazy amounts of money, **Headz 2** was a collection of largely disagreeable Down Tempo-music-by-numbers that would have made PT Barnum proud. Far better and more low-key was a collection of material from Mo' Wax's Excursions imprint, **Excursions** (1996), that included Io's smooth-grooving classic "Claire" and The Groove Robbers' excellent "Hardcore hip-hop".

After a couple of lacklustre albums from Luke Vibert and California's easy-listening piss-takers Sukia, the label redeemed itself with an excellent compilation of early '80s New York avant garde funksters Liquid Liquid (1997) that showed just how unoriginal the supposed "abstract" and "blunted" innovations of '90s beatniks really were. It was a feeling that was magnified by the hype-overdrive surrounding UNKLE's stunningly underwhelming **Psyence Fiction** album, which tried to disguise its paucity of ideas with a glittering cast of thousands featuring bit parts from various Beastie Boys and Radioheads and anyone else whose name was worth dropping in 1998.

Despite the success of the UNKLE album, Mo' Wax was thrown into disarray with the closure of the label's parent company, A&M. The Mo' Wax name transferred to Island, but Lavelle himself moved to XZ – a situation which leaves the status of downbeat's most famous label up in the air.

⊙ Dr. Octagon Ecologyst   Mo' Wax, 1996

Despite the pointless porn samples, this is an album of rare vision and daring that is one of the finest examples of black culture's long association with mad scientists (see also Mad Professor, Elijah Muhammed, Parliament-Funkadelic).

⊙ DJ Shadow Endtroducing   Mo' Wax, 1996

Like Dr. Octagon, Shadow moulds hip-hop to his own ends in this beat collage fantasy world.

Moloko

Taking their name from the milk drink in *A Clockwork Orange*, Moloko are not your everyday average Trip-Hop band. Vocalist Roisin Murphy and knob-twiddler Mark Brydon blend '80s funk, Junglism, hip-hop beats and off-kilter Acid Jazz with a surrealism and desire to be difficult appropriated from art-school.

After kicking around with influential Sheffield bands like the Forge-masters, House Arrest and Cloud 9, Brydon hooked up with Irish ex-pat Murphy and released "Fun For Me" (1995). With synth scribbles and an elastic bassline appropriated from '80s funkateers Yarborough & Peoples, "Fun For Me" created the Moloko template which was writ large on their debut album, **Do You Like My Tight Sweater** (1995). In among the chubby, if not phat, basslines, drum 'n' bass touches and post-hip-hop beats, though, was a kitsch sensibility that overwhelmed the music. Unlike, say, Deee-Lite or Fatboy Slim who managed to make wallowing in vulgarity fun and not merely the result of jaded boredom, Moloko tried to be clever with their kitsch – the original sin of music in the '90s.

Their shenanigans worked better in single form and "Where Is the What If the What Is in the Why?/Party Weirdo" (1996) had a liquid bump-and-grind groove that made you forget the gratuitous tongue-twisting. "Dominoid" (1996), meanwhile, was a slinky, sorta Junglist slow jam with typically kooky vocals and nonsensical lyrics.

"The Flipside" (1998), which featured an enormous remix from the king of jump-up Aphrodite, was another art-damaged torch song that was the lead single from their second album. I Am Not a Doctor (1998), though, played down the weirdness-for-weirdness' sake mannerisms and tracks like "Caught in a Whisper" and "Should've Been Could've Been" were straightforward pop tunes that signified something beyond Murphy and Brydon's cleverness.

◉ I Am Not a Doctor   Echo, 1998

Still wilfully bizarre, but they took their mucked-up hipster camouflage down every once in a while to make tunes and grooves.

Money Mark

As strange pop success stories go, you can't get much more bizarre than that of Mark Ramos-Nishita. Working as a carpenter in 1989, Nishita was called to repair the front gate of the Beastie

Boys' Los Angeles compound at around the time they were finishing up their **Paul's Boutique** album and building their own studio. After helping them finish their studio, he adopted the persona of Keyboard Money Mark and contributed keyboards to their Meters-esque **Check Your Head** (1992) album.

After laying down more old-school licks on the Beasties' **Ill Communication** album (1994), he hooked up with James Lavelle's Mo' Wax operation and released the **More Shit From the $ Man** EP (1995). A collection of songs he recorded in his bedroom before his rise to fame with the Beastie Boys, **More Shit** heralded Money Mark as the lo-fi poet of stoner melancholy and analogue weirdness. The album **Mark's Keyboard Repair** (1995) followed with grooves constructed out of cruddy Hammond organs, Fender Rhodes and dinky Casio keyboards rescued from local thrift stores and soldered back together. Tracks like "Insects Are All Around Us" featured ridiculous samples, "Have Clav Will Travel" was little more than a funky-butt clavinet riff and a ramshackle beat, while "Cry" featured Nishita's humorously maudlin vocals.

Mark's Keyboard Repair was a surprise success and showed that Down Tempo had a larger emotional range than ragged torch songs and stoned detachment. A mini-album, **Third Division** (1996), followed the same blueprint, but his second album, **Push the Button** (1998), was a dramatic change of direction. Instrumental fusions of Jimmy McGriff, Tonto's Expanding Headband and Jean-Jacques Perrey still abounded (check the awesome instrumental "Trust"), but the production was much slicker and naïfs like "Cry" had become polished pop songs like "Too Like You" and "Tomorrow Will Be Like Today". Like the rest of the leftfield music community of the late '90s, Money Mark's polystylism became rampant and left him with too little of his own personality.

⊙ Mark's Keyboard Repair   Mo' Wax, 1995

As wiggy and kooky as any album from a decade where wigginess and
kookiness were everything, this odd bedroom-studio affair neatly
encapsulated most of the obsessions of the *fin de siècle* music scene.

Monkey Mafia/
Jon Carter

For all of the alleged eclecticism of Big Beat, the music can
often be little more than a re-heated acid bassline with the
drum break from Banbarra's "Shack Up" or Jimmy McGriff's "The
Worm" and a hip-hop sample. With the possible exceptions of Fatboy Slim or Rasmus, no one lives up to Big Beat's claims of stylistic
promiscuity as much as Jon Carter. With a music background that
includes engineering apprenticeships at No U-Turn and various reggae studios, Carter has done his best to expand the parameters of
Big Beat.

After playing in a couple of reggae bands in Southampton, Carter
hooked up with the Wall of Sound label and released "Dollar" (1995)
as Artery. He followed this bit of downbeat nonsense with "Blow the
Whole Joint Up" (1995) on Heavenly under his more familiar pseudonym, Monkey Mafia. This combination of hip-hop exhortations, wah-
wah licks, acid-dub basslines and a lengthy loop of The Who's "Out in
the Street" was a big hit on the dancefloor at the Heavenly Social
where Carter was a resident.

Testament to Carter's party-hardy DJ style at the Social could be found on his **Live at the Social** mix album (1996). Featuring Monkey Mafia's Patra-sampling "Work Mi Body" (1996), **Live at the Social** moved from hip-hop to ragga to hoary breakbeat clichés with the grace and ease of a drunk football hooligan. The **15 Steps** EP (1997) was a similarly inebriated crawl through a puddle of samba and hip-hop effluence that beat your head and body into submission.

With reggae vocalist Dougie Reuben, scratch DJ First Rate, bassist Tom Symmons and drummer Dan Peppe in tow, Carter turned Monkey Mafia into a live band and released **Shoot the Boss** (1998). Despite a crazy wack version of Creedence Clearwater Revival's "As Long as I Can See the Light", **Shoot the Boss** was a mindlessly enjoyable romp through the Jamaican dancehall while listening to an Acid House mix-tape on the Walkman and wearing a sleeveless denim vest with Billy Squier album art painted across the back.

○ Live at the Social Volume 1   DeConstruction, 1996

With its sloppy eclecticism, this mix compilation did its best to recapture the vibe at the landmark Heavenly Social club.

Mr. Scruff

With a zany eclecticism that rivals Bentley Rhythm Ace, Mancunian Down Tempo funkologist Mr. Scruff rewires hip-hop for people more comfortable with Dr Who than Dr. Dre. Former fine art student Andy Carthy adopted the alter-ego of Mr. Scruff in his bedroom and started making pause-button mix-tapes in the early '90s that were comprised of thrift store flotsam, world music esoterica and chunky hip-hop beats.

One of these tapes fell into the hands of Pleasure Records who released it as the **Hocus Pocus** EP (1995). It was the follow-up, **The Frolic (Part 1)** EP (1995), however, that brought him attention. The highlight, "Chicken in a Box", had the kind of cod tribal beat reminiscent of crusties playing patchouli bongos underneath the Brighton pier hoping to get recruited by Stomp.

The **Limbic Funk** EP (1996) followed with hopelessly silly puns like the "arms, legs everywhere" sample on the title track and soothing jazz-funk. Some collaborations with Grand Central's Mark Rae followed, including the fine post-modern soul of "How Sweet It Is" which was included on the **Central Heating** (1996) compilation. The "Large Pies/Mexicanos" (1997) 12" for Bristol's Cup of Tea label highlighted Scruff's loony pan-stylism with mariachi horns and Andean pan pipes.

His eponymous debut album was a collection of his first three EPs which had an alarming preponderance of neutered beats and tracks that relied on non-sequitur puns like a dopey voice intoning, "The largest sea mammal is a whale", on "Sea Mammal" or the "Bless my whalebone corset" sample on "Wail". Too many of the beats were as rigid as baleen (if he'd sampled John Bonham's drumming on "Moby Dick", he might have gotten somewhere) and the stale, cocktail-piano jazziness was about as thrilling as scrimshaw. Scruff's stuff was great in a club environment, but all too often at home it was as engaging as plankton.

Signing to Ninja Tune, Scruff released the **Chipmunk** EP (1998). The title track sounded like Pete Rock playing the mighty Wurlitzer organ at a Blackpool working man's club, while "Fish" was jazzier and dafter.

⊙ The Frolic EP   Pleasure, 1995

Featuring his signature tune, "Chicken in a Box", this EP shows Scruff at his grooviest with his penchant for geekish lunacy reined in.

Nightmares on Wax

Back when club culture was as innocent as a smiley face, styles and genres cross-pollinated on the dancefloor without attracting the wrath of the guardians of taste. The "bleep music" of Unique 3 could ride atop breakbeats, plangent Techno could melt into lachrymose soundtrack strings, flutes could float into Belgian Nu-Beat drums, a rapper could rhyme to a steel drum riddim, American rocker Steve Miller could be the instigator of a trippy bass odyssey, the dub of Scientist could share space with the instrumental hip-hop of the 45 King and all of this could happen on the same album. Unlike their more austere Warp labelmates and E'd-up contemporaries, Nightmares on Wax saw Techno as an outgrowth of the funk and hip-hop scenes and approached it with a herbalist's mindset. The resulting music was one of the building blocks of both Down Tempo and Jungle.

The duo of George Evelyn (aka E.A.S.E.) and Kevin Harper (aka Boy Wonder) released their first single in 1989 on Warp, the Sheffield label famous for their bleak industrial electronica. "Dextrous" was as fiercely minimal as the rest of the label's output, but the track's rhythmic dexterity suggested a range of influences not shared by their labelmates. "Dextrous" was swiftly followed by "Aftermath/I'm For Real" (1990) which fulfilled the promise of the debut. "I'm For Real" followed the Techno-soul blueprint of Kevin Saunderson brilliantly, but it was "Aftermath"'s sparse breakbeat pattern and devastating sub-bass that was truly remarkable. By reducing sound to pure sensation and by suggesting drug paranoia with its spooky "there's something going 'round inside my head" refrain, Nightmares on Wax laid down what would become the blueprint of Hardcore's dark sound of 1992–93.

Evelyn and Harper would continue to influence the future course of British dance music with their debut album, **A Word of Science – The First and Final Chapter** (1991). Tracks like "Nights Interlude", "Playtime" and the Steve Miller-sampling "Back Into Time" were little more than audio scribbles, but their intensely doped-out atmospheres and breakbeat foundations mark them out as the foundations of Down Tempo beat collage. Elsewhere, the awesome groove of "A Case of Funk" saw Detroit Techno as the inheritor of disco's spirit, "B.W.T.M." made the connection between human beatboxing and Techno's Roland 808 drums and "How Ya Doin'" was one of the earliest examples of jazz's influence on electronic music.

Aside from a couple of remixes and a couple of jazzy House tracks on Nucleus Records, Evelyn was not to be heard from until the re-emergence of a Boy Wonder-less Nightmares on Wax album in late 1995. **Smokers Delight** began where the first left off in that the tracks were even less well defined and the dope fog even thicker. "Nights Interlude" from the debut re-appeared as "Nights Introlude" and things continued in the same vein with supine jazzy vibes, lazy hip-hop beats and deracinated '70s funk samples. It was all very well produced, but the eclectic

excitement of the first album was gone and **Smokers Delight** seemed like just another Trip-Hop album.

Still Smokin', a remix EP released in 1996, rectified matters with versions by Mr. Scruff, Rae & Christian, DJ Food and a Junglist mix of "Stars" by Evelyn himself. The highlight was Rae & Christian's hip-hopped version of "What I'm Feelin'" which obliterated the soporific pace of the original with motorvational horn samples, heart-stopping scratches and manic exhortations from KRS-One. It's a model Evelyn would do well to follow if he wants to regain the brilliance of his debut.

◉ A Word of Science	Warp, 1991

The kind of album we'll probably never hear again as it's so full of the innocent joy everyone's scared to show in this age of ludicrous image-consciousness and po-faced taste-makers.

Ninja Tune

Ninja Tune has been at the vanguard of abstract hip-hop and Down Tempo beat collage since it was founded in 1990 by Coldcut's Jonathon More and Matt Black as an antidote to major label indifference to experimentation and artistic development. With the notion of play as its guiding principle, Ninja Tune has used puns, bricolage, beats, multi-media terrorism and "tricknology" as weapons in a DIY guerilla war against the bloated House mainstream of body fascism, designer-label fetishism and formulaic music.

The label kicked off by creating what is widely regarded as the DNA of "Trip-Hop", the **Jazz Brakes** series, in 1990. Sampled and orches-trated by Coldcut and released under the DJ Food moniker, **Jazz**

Brakes Vols. 1, 2 and 3 were collections of loops intended to be DJ tools, but were fleshed out enough to be listened to at home. The **Jazz Brakes** series was followed by the **Breakbeats And Grooves** series credited to **DJ Toolz** which featured such cheeky titles as **Toolz Gold**. While these snippets of More and Black's awesome record collections were DJ favourites, the first Ninja Tune release to make a splash with club punters was NW1's "The Band Played the Boogie" (1992).

As students of the science of mixology, More and Black paid homage to their mentor, cut 'n' paste pioneer Steinski, by releasing his plea for people to pick up the means of media production, "It's Up to You", in 1993. Although Coldcut's last official single for the label for several years was 1994's Ambient classic, "Autumn Leaves", More and Black released material not only as DJ Food, but under such aliases as Hex (the name of Black's multi-media collaboration with Rob Pepperell), Illuminati of Hedfuk and Clusterfunk.

While the label bosses went on a bit of a sabbatical, Ninja Tune released important Down Tempo records by 9 Lazy 9, Funki Porcini, The Herbaliser, Up Bustle & Out and the London Funk All-Stars, which were collected on the label's first compilation, **Funkjazztickle Tricknology** (1995). **Refried Food** (1996), a collection of remixes of DJ Food material that featured blunted blues classics like the Fila Brazillia remix of "Consciousness" and the MLO mix of "Dark Blood", and the excellent compilation **Flexistentialism** (1996) proved that Ninja Tune was one of the few Down Tempo labels, if not the only one, to have a sense of humour as well as a surfeit of sensimillia.

The label expanded the boundaries of Down Tempo funk with Funki Porcini's comic and cinematic **Love, Pussycats & Car Wrecks**, the hip-hop *concrète* of DJ Vadim's **USSR Repertoire** and the brilliant Jungle one-off from Quincy, "Bruce Lee MC" (all 1996). Ninja Tune's Stealth Club at London's Blue Note put their ideas about collage, multi-media and experimental technology into practice with four-turntable DJ sets, ludicrous eclecticism and DJs jamming with graphic artists.

Although it didn't quite succeed, Coldcut's **Let Us Play** (1997) attempted to break those boundaries altogether by introducing computer randomisation into the mix. More successful were Kid Koala's awesome scratchadelic turntablist throwdown "Skratchhappyland" (1997), and Chocolate Weasel's (aka Junglist T.Power) **Spaghettification** (1998) which fit in perfectly with the retro-electro craze that was raging in Europe at the close of the millennium. Neotropic (aka Riz Maslen) kicked Electro until it was only a dark, angry shell on **Mr. Brubaker's Strawberry Alarm Clock** (1998). The label closed out a disappointing 1998 with the re-release of an undisputed classic of New York underground hip-hop, East Flatbush Project's "Tried By 12", while Funki Porcini indulged in some jazzy ska shenanigans on his **Rocket Soul Music** EP (1999).

⊙ **Flexistentialism: The Joy of Dex**   Ninja Tune, 1996

Featuring Coldcut's "Atomic Moog 2000", Luke Vibert's "Get Your Head Down" and 2 Player's "Extreme Possibilities", this represents the best of not only Ninja Tune, but the entire Down Tempo genre.

⊙ **ColdKrush Cuts**   Ninja Tune, 1997

Ninja Tune's output in its mixological milieu. Coldcut's mix is more fun and more daring, while DJ Krush's follows his usual formula of polluted textures and grimy beats.

obO

One of the more interesting projects from the electronica-jazz melting pot, Allan Riding's obO is the mirror image of most electronic music. Instead of making Techno or drum 'n' bass or House that wants to be jazz, Riding makes jazz that wants to be as looped and rinsed out as Techno. Equally influenced by John Coltrane and Andrew Weatherall, Riding's music is, when he gets it right, the most effective jazz-electronic collision this side of Carl Craig's "Bug in the Bassbin".

The rub is that, like most UK jazz-obsessives, his taste in jazz has been cultivated under the influence of trainspotters like Gilles Peterson and Russ Dewbury; thus Riding's first incarnation as 8 Up was marred by the self-consciously bohemian tendencies and the love of silkiness that characterises the British jazz-dance scene. After three EPs and an album, **Lie Down** (1994), for the Soul Jazz label which were ignored by a dance media bent on following the wretched excesses of pre-DJ Shadow Mo' Wax and the tail-end of the Acid Jazz movement, Riding contributed brass and woodwinds for the like-minded Red Snapper.

Riding left the band after their **Hot Flush** EP (1995) and started releasing material as obO. In a flurry of activity, obO released six albums in a year and a half that were not so much chill-out as lovers' rock – electronica as quiet storm. Albums like **Mall** and **Slide Burn** (both 1996) were what Dr. Dre records might sound like if he actually liked the women he slept with, while **Fut!** and **Fut! II** (both 1996) were the sound of James Bond, martini in hand, undressing Pussy Galore with his eyes. Unlike the upwardly mobile fantasies of most jazzy drum 'n' bass, Techno, House and Down Tempo, however, Riding eschewed the trappings of luxury and his records were resolutely lo-fi affairs that tried to recapture that atmosphere of obscure '70s soul records for a time when nearly anyone could afford a state-of-the-art home studio set-up.

Dashing (1997) was less syrupy than previous efforts, but it was still sugary make-out music for copy shop assistants too stoned to leave the couch. **Diamond Loser** (1998), on the US Shadow label, was a compilation of some of the highlights from his previous records. obO's best record, however, was an obscure 7", "1-Locks/Far Canal" (1998), which abandoned his occasionally fey jazz tendencies while still being smooth but not smarmy.

⊙ **"1-Locks/Far Canal"** obO, 1998

"1-Locks" had a vaguely Eastern European cello weaving its way through synth loops, while "Far Canal" was basically a wah-wah guitar riff that wanted to be a Jeff Mills filtered synth pattern.

The Orb

Doubters of the power of Ecstasy should rewind their minds to the fallout of Britain's second Summer of Love when ex-punks like Dr. Alex Paterson, Jah Wobble, Primal Scream and The KLF dropped their anomie and became, for all intents and purposes, hippies. Paterson, who used to be a roadie for Killing Joke and an A&R man at Brian Eno's EG label, turned on to the pharmacological components of the rave experience in the early days of the Acid House explosion and formed The Orb in 1988 with Jimmy Cauty, who would soon become a member of rave pranksters The KLF.

Their first release was a track on an obscure compilation album called **Eternity Project One** (1988) that was put together by Killing Joke's drummer, Youth. **The Kiss** EP (1989) was built around samples taken from New York's KISS FM radio station and led Paul Oakenfold to hire Paterson as the chill-out room DJ at his Land of Oz club. The Orb's breakthrough track, however, was "A Huge Ever Pulsating Brain That Rules From the Centre of the Ultraworld" (1989) which was labelled as "Ambient House for the E generation". Based around a sample of '70s soul diva Minnie Ripperton's "Loving You", the track was a twenty-plus minute trip across a luminous, psychedelic countryside.

"Little Fluffy Clouds" (1990) followed in a similar vein with a sample of Rickie Lee Jones reminiscing about the "little fluffy clouds" of her childhood and was included on The Orb's debut album, **The Orb's Adventures Beyond the Ultraworld** (1991). Almost two hours long, **Adventures Beyond the Ultraworld** was the pastoralism of "Little Fluffy Clouds" made as big as the wide open country it pined for. Largely constructed by Paterson and another former punk, Thrash (aka Kris Weston), the nods to space rock (the cover pastiched Pink Floyd's **Animals**, there was a track called "Back Side of the Moon" and Gong's Steve Hillage helped out on a couple of tracks), the dub influence and the undercutting of hip-hop beats with incongruous bits of sonic whimsy presaged many of the trends that would characterise much of the decade's music.

Taking their tendency to "stretch out" as far as it could go, "Blue Room" (1992) was a forty-minute marathon of aquatic vibes pushed

along by Jah Wobble's post-punk skanking bassline that made the British Top Ten. **UFOrb** (1992) was more dubby than the debut and was a further move towards making dance music the head music of the '90s. But unlike dub, The Orb's head music and the Trip-Hop that would partially come in its wake was vehemently apolitical and anti-significance. It seemed to be the internalisation of Thatcher's claim that "there is no such thing as society".

But there was a society of Orb lovers, as 1993's quadruple LP **Live 93** proved, as did **Pomme Fritz** (1994) and **Orbus Terrarum** (1995) which both reached the Top 20 album chart. By this point, however, the band's MO had been seized more effectively (and affectively) by the Trip-Hoppers who stripped their chill-out blueprint of any remnants of Ecstasy's positivity. Kicking off with their brilliant remix of

Material's "Praying Mantra", **Auntie Aubrey's Excursions Beyond the Call of Duty** (1996) was a collection of The Orb's remix work that served as the swansong for the band's relevance.

> **⊙ The Orb's Adventures Beyond the Ultraworld**   Big Life, 1991

It seems dated now, but the dub vapour, blissed languor and daft jokes suggested something very special at the time.

Palm Skin Productions/ Chris Bowden

As a member of Talkin' Loud's K Collective and a session player for D-Note, Jhelisa Anderson, Mother Earth and Neneh Cherry, Simon Richmond has done more than most to foster Britain's nu-jazz scene. Taking his polo-necked sensibility over to Mo' Wax, Richmond formed Palm Skin Productions and helped foment Down Tempo's production style.

Palm Skin Productions' first single, "Getting Out of Hell/Like Brothers/A Little Skin" (1993), featured the molasses groove and dub percussion of "Like Brothers" which became one of the cornerstones of the early Down Tempo movement. "The Beast/In a Silent Way" (1994) nodded towards Miles Davis in both its title and its Ambient jazz and featured the soprano sax of Chris Bowden. Bowden would also blow a Coltrane tribute on the fusion freak-out "Spock With a Beard" (1994).

"Slipper Suite" (1995) was an epic that took in hip-hop, Junglism and free-ish jazz blowing that appeared on Mo' Wax's **Headz** compilation and showed that Richmond was capable of more than dishing out oily variations on "Expansions" or "Laying in the Cut". "Condition Red" (1996) marked his shift to Hut Records and saw Richmond combine live instruments with flipped breaks.

Palm Skin's debut album, **Remilixir** (1996), represented one possible route of escape from both the smugger-than-thou Mo' Wax school of abstraction and the bone-dry pool of jazz-funk cliché. Exploring the variegated terrain of tone colour, **Remilixir** featured severely mutated trumpet doubled by high-pitched transformer scratching on "Fair Seven"; Ennio Morricone guitars re-arranged so they sounded like the Guo Brothers' zithers on "How the West Was Won"; bubbling and hissing keyboards on "Trouble Rides a Fast Horse" and a set of pieces featuring Ambient washes caught in the doldrums.

Meanwhile, Richmond's erstwhile collaborator, Chris Bowden, was getting out-there with a series of astro-jazz pastiches. "Mothers and Daughters Now Mothers" (1996) was a chilled-out Gil Evans freestyle, while "Life Support System" (1996) was galactic string dub. His debut album, **Time Capsule** (1996), was reminiscent of Barry Adamson's wannabe soundtrack manoeuvres, while the **In Orbit** EP (1996) imagined how aliens might communicate if they were given access to a wah-wah pedal. With those other astral travellers, 4 Hero, Bowden released the wispy, saccharine fusion of "Lullabuy/Hero" (1997) to almost universal acclaim.

◉ Palm Skin Productions Remilixir   Hut, 1996

One of the few Down Tempo albums of its time to try to find its way out of the Trip-Hop cul-de-sac.

◉ Chris Bowden In Orbit   Soul Jazz, 1996

It could have used a bit more Mtume to go along with its Herbie Hancockisms, but this was fine future jazz nonetheless.

Pork Recordings

O perating out of deepest, darkest Kingston-upon-Hull, Pork Recordings has ploughed a singular furrow in the world of Down Tempo beats since its inception in 1991. Eschewing the formulaic blueprints of both Trip-Hop and Ambient, the most successful Pork releases somehow manage to evoke the best of both genres without falling into the trap of stylistic fence-sitting.

The narcotic lockjaw and strange numbness that most Pork records exhibit can be traced to the obsession with conspiracy theory shared by the label's main movers – label boss Pork and the man behind the majority of the sty's music, Steve Cobby. As a member of Sheffield's industrial-funk scene in the '80s, Cobby in particular holds no illusions about the realities of the music industry or the limits of radical politics. As a result, Pork and Cobby refuse to have their pictures taken, grant very few interviews and insinuate rather than proselytise.

The record that really got the label noticed in spite of their best efforts to be ignored was Fila Brazillia's "Pots and Pans/The Sheriff" (1994). Produced by Cobby and Man, "Pots and Pans" was a stunning mixture of the Brazilian funk of Jorge Ben, the vocoded bass of Graham Central Station and House tempos, while "The Sheriff" added some of dub's spatial awareness to Balearic House's functional groove. These two tracks anchored Fila Brazillia's debut album, **Old Codes New Chaos** (1994), which also included fine earlier singles like "Mermaids" (1991) and "Fila Funk" (1993). The same Ambient-you-can-dance-to/House-you-can-relax-to vibe of **Old Codes** appeared on Heights of Abraham's (Cobby, Slim Lister and Jake Harries) "Sportif/EVA" (1994) single which was one of the first records to exploit the rediscovery of '70s Moog maestro Jean-Jacques Perrey.

Cobby's three **Losing Patients** EPs (1995) released under his Solid Doctor alias and collected on **How About Some Ether** (1995), however, changed the label's output towards a more anaesthetic direction where the music's digital veneer was an analogue of the blunted bliss symptomatic of a pill-popping culture. Despite a rabble-rousing sample of American come-dian Bill Hicks, Fila's **Maim That Tune** (1995) followed a similar path as did Heights of Abra-ham's **Electric Hush** (1995) and Solid Doc-tor's **Beats Means Highs** (1996).

New artists like Baby Mammoth (Mark Blissenden and Andrew Burdall) and Bullitnuts followed the same blueprint of wrap-ping Techno's glacial timbres, quasi-hip-hop beats and gentle Junglism in a jazzy sensibility. Fila's **Black Market Gardening** (1996) added whispers of Salsoul disco into the mix, while Baby Mammoth's excellent **Bridging Two Worlds** (1997) incorporated Sly Stone and someone ordering soul food with their synth washes. Continuing to add new artists like Akotcha and Gerd to the label, Pork celebrated their fiftieth release with the fine **Sty Wars** compilation in May 1998.

○ **Fila Brazillia Old Codes New Chaos**   Pork, 1994

Including the utterly brilliant "Pots and Pans", this is the prolific label's best release.

◉ Baby Mammoth Bridging Two Worlds   Pork, 1997

A close second, this album manages to be both soothing and uplifting at
the same time.

Portishead

While the fazed beat collage that would eventually be called
Trip-Hop may have been around since New York rappers
Rammelzee and K-Rob dropped the utterly surreal "Beat Bop" in
1983, nobody has been more associated with the term or better
codified the style than Portishead. Named after a tiny seaside
town outside of Bristol, Portishead existed on the periphery of the
Wild Bunch-led scene that eventually gave Bristol its trademark
sound, but their scratchy atmospheres and languid beats are as
emblematic of the Bristol swing as the music of any of their neighbours.

Portishead's ideas man, Geoff Barrow, got his break in music
when he landed a job as a tea boy at Bristol's Coach House Studio in
1991, just in time to help programme and carry tapes around for the
sessions that became Massive Attack's **Blue Lines** album. Barrow
also helped produce Neneh Cherry's "Somedays" and Tricky's first
solo track while fetching beverages at the studio. Through the studio
he met engineer Dave McDonald and jazz guitarist Adrian Utley, but
Portishead's sound really came together when Barrow met pub singer
Beth Gibbons on an Enterprise Awareness Day. With Barrow's
school-friend and DJ, Andy Smith, in tow, the band's first release was

a ten-minute black and white homage to spy flicks like *The Ipcress File* and *Get Carter*, called *To Kill a Dead Man* (1994). While the film itself was pretty shoddy, Portishead's soundtrack featured the same intriguing blend of slow and moody looped beats, John Barry guitar and tormented torch song vocals that marked their debut singles, "Numb" and "Sour Times" (both 1994).

The Mercury Prize-winning album **Dummy** (1994) followed soon after and notched up sales of 200,000 copies in the UK with its zeitgeist-capturing blueprint. **Dummy**'s crackling sound was achieved by recording the live instrumentation onto acetates and then scratching and blending them while the tracks were being mixed. The tape hiss and snap-crackle-pop of the production worked perfectly with the ragged blues of Beth Gibbons' vocals, which recalled the female singers of the classic blues era, but without their often playful sexuality or transcendence, just the pain. Capitalising on Down Tempo's potential for creating sepulchral soundscapes, Barrow surrounded Gibbons' racked vocals in catacombs of oppressive bass pressure, slowed-to-a-crawl beats and a Johnny Ray sample drawn out until it had the consistency of phlegm.

After **Dummy**'s success came the deluge of torch-singing groups using the same formula, but with less artistry. As a result, Portishead kept a low profile while their once-unique sound became a genre unto itself. When it did come out, their follow-up album, **Portishead** (1997), failed to capture anything like the buzz that accompanied their debut. Three years had gone by, but all they could come up with was a slightly darker, less hooky version than their first record and it seemed as though no one was particularly interested any more.

PNYC (1998), a document of a 1997 concert at New York's Roseland Ballroom, featured a thirty-piece orchestra and went a little way

in restoring their reputation. Andy Smith's **Document** (1998) mix compilation didn't exactly hide the joins, but it was an enjoyable romp through crowd-pleasing hip-hop, cheesy listening and good old-fashioned stadium rock.

◉ Dummy   GoBeat!, 1994

One of the decade's landmark records. Barrow mixed up slow 'n' low hip-hop beats and Lalo Schifrin samples before, and better than, anyone else.

Propellerheads

N ow that seemingly every record in the world has been picked clean in the search for even the slightest hint of a break, beat collectors the world over have been forced to get ever more creative in their break sourcing. The cod-funky soundtracks of the late '60s and early '70s have replaced obscure funk and jazz records as the choice fodder for sample scavengers, even inspiring a sub-sub-genre of Down Tempo/Big Beat, "spybeat", in the process. Taking their cues from the incidental music from James Bond flicks composed by John Barry and David Arnold, Propellerheads are the most high-profile act of this rather specialised field.

Propellerheads' head-spinning journey through *Ipcress File* atmospheres and Beastie Boys momentum began in Bath when Alex Gifford (organ, bass, turntables), a journeyman musician who had worked with Van Morrison, The Grid and The Stranglers, met up with Will White (drums, turntables, human beatbox), who had previously recorded for Cup of Tea. Their first Wall of Sound release, the

Dive! EP (1996), harked back to the days of breakdancing on dis-
carded refrigerator boxes and was eventually used in an advertise-
ment for athletic footwear. The follow-up, the Richard
Nixon-sampling "Take California" (1996), made the lower reaches of
the British pop chart on the strength of its enormous bassline and
judicious scratching.

"Spybreak" (1997) capitalised on the simmering mini-craze for Lalo
Schiffrin arrangements with its *Get Carter* vibe and poked its head
into the Top 40. The duo reached the Top 10 with their next effort, a
remake of the *On Her Majesty's Secret Service* theme (1997), which
led to them working with David Arnold for the score of *Tomorrow
Never Dies*. Other remakes have included fine remixes of Luscious
Jackson's "Naked Eye" and 808 State's "Lopez".

Their most bizarre collaboration, however, was the soundclash
with Shirley Bassey on "History Repeating" (1997) which pushed their
007 fetishism to the limit. All of their singles were featured on the Top
10 album **Decksandrumsandrockandroll** (1998), which also included
the Bible-bashing "Bring Us Together" and the zipper-loosening "Vel-
vet Pants". Their commercial instincts are second only to Fatboy
Slim's, but as Big Beat and secret agent music gradually gets as
saggy as Roger Moore's jowls, will Propellerheads be able to keep
up?

The **Extended Play** EP (1999) showed that they might. While the
reworking of Brian Fahey's E-Z listening landmark "At the Sign of the
Swingin' Cymbal" was hopelessly obvious, hooking up with the Jungle Brothers and De la Soul for "You Want It Back" and "360 Degrees
Oh Yeah" was inspired.

◉ Decksandrumsandrockandroll   Wall of Sound, 1998

Throw-away dance music that recognises that that's all it is – and all the
better for it.

Q-Burns Abstract Message

O rlando, Florida is probably the world's most unlikely stronghold of rave culture. Despite its being the favourite destination of families the world over, one of America's biggest dance scenes has emerged in the shadow of Walt Disney's sprawling empire. Although he is not entirely representative of the city's style, Orlando's dance ambassador is Mike Donaldson (aka Q-Burns Abstract Message). Taking his *nom de disque* from the damage that DJs do to their records (cue burn), Q-Burns Abstract Message makes records that are Big Beat admixtures of House hedonism, Electro funk, hip-hop grooves and world music eclecticism and represent a DJ set in miniature.

After moving to Florida from the Cajun country of Louisiana and playing in punk and rockabilly bands, Q-Burn moved towards dance music and debuted with "141 Revenge Street/Mess of Afros" on San Francisco's Mephisto label in 1995. Picked up by British labels like Wall of Sound and Delancey Street, "141 Revenge Street/Mess of Afros" heralded the emergence of an American breakbeat sound that existed apart from, but in parallel to, the scene in Europe.

Donaldson started his Eighth Dimension label with his own "Uncertain T/Vibe Checkin'" that same year. Sounding like hip-hop from a Moroccan casbah, "Enter/Other" (1996) was Q-Burns at his most frenetic, while "Toast" and "Pools in Eyes" (both 1996) saw him combining Balearic sunrise House with breakbeats and slide guitar. "Flava Lamp/A Song For Peace" (1996) upped the funk quotient and created a sound that was not altogether different from the formula Fatboy Slim would use a couple of years later to take over the British pop charts.

Unlike most of the studio boffins who dominate breakbeat music, Q-Burns could cut it live and proved it on his contribution to the **Deep Concentration** (1997) collection of DJ tracks, "Book of Changes". Signing to the American dance giant Astralwerks, Q-Burns released compilations of both his own releases – **Oeuvre** (1997) – and the output of his Eighth Dimension label – **Selected Material** (1997) – in advance of his debut album. Working with Jon Curtis (aka Pimp Daddy Nash), Q-Burns' **Feng Shui** (1998) was a triumph of breakbeat eclecticism. Including a cover of Krautrock band Faust's "Jennifer", **Feng Shui** combined House's swooning bliss with breakbeat's uptempo transcendence to create a rare album that managed to feature dance music's twin poles of ecstatic release.

◉ Feng Shui   Astralwerks, 1998

With funk and shimmering melodies in equal measure, this album was the best of both worlds in dance music.

Red Snapper

Formed in 1993, Red Snapper are Down Tempo's oddballs. Largely eschewing both the turntable and the sampler and inspired by the teen-beat of drummer Sandy Nelson, the dub reggae of Augustus Pablo, the composed improvisation of jazz bassist Charles Mingus, the strip-grind sax of Sam Butera and the surf guitar of Dick Dale, Red Snapper make some of the most engaging abstract music around.

With help from Aloof collaborator Dean Thatcher, drummer Richard Thair, guitarist David Ayers, bassist Ali Friend and wood-wind player Allan Riding released the minimal, dubby funk of the **Snapper** EP (1994) on Thair's own Flaw label. This was followed swiftly by the more detailed **Swank** EP (1994) and Red Snapper had established their own unique musical terrain that existed in the nether-world between hip-hop and Bernard Herrmann. The **Hot Flush** EP (1995) and the brilliant Dr-Who-in-a-beatnik-film Sabres of Paradise remix of the title track truly got the band noticed and they were signed to Warp, who released the **Reeled and Skinned** compilation (1995) of their releases.

By the time of the release of their first proper album, **Prince Blimey** (1996), Riding had left to become obO and was replaced on brass by Ollie Moore. With honking, strip-joint sax blares, neat pro-duction tricks, twanging tremolo and a Billy Stewart sample, **Prince Blimey** padded their warped spy-flick jazz sound with more textural detail and sounded like the Saint in a gritty chase scene scored by Roland Kirk, The Chantays and King Tubby.

More consistently funky than their previous records, **Making Bones (1998)** never became the abstract mess that was their bane on previous releases. They managed to embrace everything

from Slam Stewart stand-up bass trickery to Junglist toasting without the album seeming like a précis of their record collections.

◉ Making Bones   Warp, 1998

By downplaying the guitar which often got them into awkward territory, they came up with the best record of their career.

Renegade Soundwave

Dubbed "Chas 'n' Dave with a beatbox" by some wag in the music press, Renegade Soundwave had the highest profile of any of the old punks who turned on to the power of the sampler. Originally a trio comprised of Gary Asquith, Danny Briottet and Karl Bonnie, Renegade Soundwave's grating, industrial take on the sound of the cut-up is a hidden precursor to the cut 'n' paste collages of Hardcore, Down Tempo and Big Beat. Like fellow traveller Meat Beat Manifesto, Renegade Soundwave's loops of chunky beats and enveloping bass have been influential to a generation of British break-beat manipulators while the art-school-Shaun-Ryder vocals of Asquith have been consigned to the dustbin of history.

Renegade Soundwave's first two "transgressive" singles, "Kray Twins" and "Cocaine Sex" (both 1987), appeared on Rhythm King Records and attracted the kind of notoriety once reserved for Frankie Goes to Hollywood records. With a bassline swiped from Wayne Smith's Jamaican dancehall classic "Under Mi Sleng Teng" and a rhythmic sensibility that was two parts Kool DJ Herc and one part King Tubby, the "Sub Aqua Overdrive Dub" of "Cocaine Sex", however, marked them out as something other than a media-prank novelty. Tracks like "The Phantom" and the "Funky Nassau"-sampling "Ozone Breakdown" (both 1988) followed the same dub-meets-breakbeat logic.

Their debut album, **Soundclash** (1990), was unfortunately dominated by Asquith's thinking-man's-thug poetry, right angles and stiff beats. **In Dub** (1990), though, was deeper, wider and far more interesting. Prescient glimpses of early Hardcore can be heard in tracks like "Biting My Nails (Bassnumb Chapter)" which layered the horn line from Amii Stewart's version of "Knock on Wood" over a speeded-up break, drum machines and a dub piano that sounded like proto-rave synth. "Thunder", meanwhile, seemed to predate groups like Trans-Global Underground and Loop Guru by several years and its foundation of melancholy strings over a huge bassline and breakbeats laid the groundwork for Trip-Hop even if it was about fifteen bpms faster.

By the time their follow-up, **Howyoudoin?** (1994), came out, their formula had been pushed to the limits elsewhere and their previously rampant sampladelia had been reined in by the intellectual property lawyers. **The Next Chapter of Dub** (1995) had its moments, but compared to the drum and bass mutations happening in Jungle, it seemed to be a bit of a retrograde step.

With yet another version of "Cocaine Sex", Asquith re-emerged as Dragon Bass in 1998, but it was evident that his best days were behind him.

⦿ RSW 1987–1995   Mute, 1996

Not an ideal compilation (it's got too many naff raps and not enough dub), but it's just about everything worthwhile they've ever done.

Req

As the eternal search for British hip-hop seemed to have settled on the jump-up Jungle of Aphrodite and DJ Hype or the Big-Beat exploits of Norman Cook as solutions, a more intriguing, and possibly more "British", twist on beat construction was being developed amidst the cracking paint and tatty charm of Brighton. Rather than using the attenuated and enervated drum loops of DJ Vadim, Req's explorations of decay sounded like the bedrock foundation of hip-hop being buffeted by gusts of sea mist and covered in a layer of carcinogenic chip grease.

Req first began exploring hip-hop culture's limitations as a graffiti artist in 1984 and he has since developed into one of Britain's most celebrated aerosol bombers, designing covers for Mo' Wax and collaborating with spraypaint legend Futura 2000. His recording career began with EPs for local labels Skint and Ultimate Dilemma. Req

Garden and **Miracles** (both 1996) were some of the most compressed records ever made – there was absolutely no high or low end – and sounded like the ghost of hip-hop past haunting England's ravaged industrial wasteland.

Comprised of rigid, pinched, funkless drum programming and horn samples that were barely perceptible because they were entombed in the mix, his debut album, **One** (1997), had similarly squashed dynamics and cantankerous atmospheres. Unlike nearly every other Down Tempo record, **One** didn't slow down hip-hop to

express an insouciant, stoned languor. Instead, the scratches, beats and cut-ups were desperate stabs at communication from underneath a suffocating force. **One** was music left to rot like the inner city.

With its grotty timbres and congested atmospheres, his second album, **Frequency Jams** (1998), felt like a meditation on compression and pollution. In a fashion similar to his work as a graffiti artist, the collage of ancient drum machines, obsolete synthesizers, crackling textures and disembodied hip-hop samples made an art form out of the dismal conditions of everyday life.

◉ One   Skint, 1997

In a different universe entirely from the rest of Skint's output, this album is a brilliant exploration of the decay of the inner city.

DJ Shadow

O f all the people who have been inspired by the original hip-hop cut-ups of Grandmaster Flash and Double Dee & Steinski, no one, with the possible exception of Coldcut, has taken the cut 'n' paste aesthetic as far as DJ Shadow. Growing up as an isolated hip-hop junkie in suburban Davis, California, allowed Josh Davis to take the music in any direction he wanted without the constrictions of having to "keep it real". Hip-hop became the music of his fantasies and the largely instrumental beat collages that he would soon make were all characterised by a bleary, dreamy quality.

Shadow's first release was an explicit update of Double Dee & Steinski's "Lesson Mixes", "Lesson 4" (1991), which appeared on the b-side of a single by The Lifers' Group, a hip-hop crew comprised of ex-cons. Another mind-boggling sampladelic collage hidden away on the b-side of a lame record really made beat heads take notice. "The Legitimate Mix" (1992), on Zimbabwe Legit's eponymous EP, established his skills not only with the sampler but on the decks as well, with a flurry of transformer scratches.

"The Legitimate Mix" prompted Mo' Wax's head honcho, James Lavelle, to sign Shadow and the immediate result was the stunning collage of the vinyl dustbin, "In/Flux" (1993). Like its source material (obscure '70s soul records), "In/Flux" was a gloomy meditation on a society in transition that didn't mope and was never dragged down by its heavy vibes. Equally impressive was his debut for his own Solesides label, "Entropy" (1993), which was a seventeen-minute discourse on why hip-hop culture was dying.

His next release on Mo' Wax, "Lost and Found" (1994), plunged further into the depths of the sampler. Largely built around one of the decade's most inspiring feats of beat archeology (the martial drums from U2's "Sunday Bloody Sunday") and keyed on a deceptively loony spoken-word sample about being true to yourself, "Lost and Found" showed that Down Tempo beat collage could be more than the aural equivalent of bong water. "What Does Your Soul Look Like?" (1995) was another beat suite about self-actualisation, but perhaps not quite as effective as his earlier efforts.

During this time Shadow was also producing records by members of his Solesides crew, Blackalicious and the MCs who would soon become Latyrx, but his forte would remain the largely instrumental compositions with which he made his name. "Midnight in a Perfect World" (1996), one of those rare tracks that sounded exactly like the utopia they described (a dusty record shop cluttered with undiscovered breaks), was his most emotive track yet. **Endtroducing...** (1996) may not have had his two best tracks, but it was still an often blinding album that suggested that, despite the money, hip-hop did *not* suck in '96.

While Shadow kept a low profile in 1997 and 1998 (aside from his production of Latyrx's excellent debut album and UNKLE's dead duck of a debut, **Psyence Fiction**), Invisbl Skratch Pikl Q-Bert's "Dog Sled Camel Race" (1997) was a remarkable display of turntable skills that transformed some of Shadow's greatest beats out of Morpheus' realm and into a scratch orgy of Dionysian excess.

◉ Endtroducing... Mo' Wax, 1996

An album that proved that Trip-Hop or instrumental hip-hop or blunted beats or whatever else you want to call it wasn't just an excuse for bohemians to drop out.

Skint

For a town with so many students and state-funded slackers, Brighton has a surprisingly low profile in British musical history. While "London-by-the-sea" can boast indie nightmares Spear of Destiny and the scourge of England's property owners, The Levellers, it is the AC/DC-meets-The-45-King-inna-acid-bath sound of Skint Records that will be Brighton's legacy to the tradition of Anglo-American musical miscegenation. Unlike the po-faced artistes who dominate the more fashion-concious corners of dance music, Skint musicians have their tongues firmly embedded in their cheeks as they wed hip-hop beats with rock decadence to create the joyously inebriated sound of Big Beat.

Skint's crusade against musical puritanism began in 1994 when journalist/Arsenal fanatic/DJ/ex-record store clerk/ex-manager of Loaded Records Damian Harris released Fatboy Slim's affecting mix of buzzing guitars, phat beats and plangent synth washes, "Santa Cruz", on a label he named after his financial situation. After a few more releases including 12"s from Brighton's indie stalwarts Arthur and Hip Optimist (aka one half of Lamb, Andy Barlow), Harris' relationship with Fatboy Slim (better known as ex-Housemartin/ex-Beats International Norman Cook) paid handsome dividends with the dancefloor-filler "Everybody Needs a 303" (1995), which was named after the Roland bass machine responsible for the squelching "acid" sound on the record. Its hedonistic feel made it a favourite at the Heavenly Social's legendary lager 'n' poppers bacchanalia, where it fitted alongside similar records by the Chemical Brothers and Sam Sever, prompting some journalists to label this new sub-genre "amyl House".

A far better name for this blend of hip-hop, House and guitar feedback was provided by Skint's fortnightly shindig at Brighton's Concorde club, Big Beat Boutique. The club was not only a showcase for Skint records like Hardnox's "Coz I Can" or Fatboy Slim's "Going Out of My Head", but a place where Lee Perry's dubscapes, The Tubes' preposterous art-rock extravaganza "White Punks on Dope", Aphrodite's jump-up Jungle and AC/DC's testosterone orgy "Whole Lotta Rosie" all got down and boogied on the same dancefloor.

This same eclecticism carried over to Skint's vinyl output which included the hip-hop cut-ups of DMC mixing champion Cut Le Roc, Harris' own loony tunes released under the name Midfield General, the remarkable ghost-town hip-hop of graffiti artist Req and Bentley

Rhythm Ace's uncategorisable capers in pop's junkyard. After the success of Fatboy Slim's **Better Living Through Chemistry** and Bentley Rhythm Ace's self-titled album and as Big Beat garnered more and more column inches in the mainstream press (even, shockingly, in the US), Harris signed a distribution deal with Sony.

Despite this deal with the corporate devil, Skint continue to release genre-defining records like Midfield General's *Omen*-sampling "Devil in Sports Casual", Fatboy Slim's awesome "Rockafeller Skank", Space Raiders' "Glam Raid" and Lo-Fidelity All-Stars' **How to Operate With a Blown Mind**. With the chart success of Fatboy Slim's **You've Come A Long Way Baby** (1998) Skint became the most inappropriately named label in dance music.

◐ Various Artists Brassic Beats Volume One   Skint, 1996

A nearly perfect overview of the label's first year including such essential tracks as Fatboy Slim's "Everybody Needs a 303", Bentley Rhythm Ace's "This Is Carbootechnodiscotechnoboooto", Req's "Razzamatazz" and Cut Le Roc's "Hip Hop Bibbedy Bop Bop".

DJ Spooky

Whilst the music that came from Britain's Ambient scene was as fluffy and cuddly as a Guatemalan sweater, New York's take on Ambient was as grimy and edgy as the Big Apple itself. Filled with dissonance, feedback, speeded-up hip-hop beats, dub basslines and bits from *musique concrète* records, "illbient" (as its practitioners called it) was crucially connected to the art world and made grand theoretical claims on its own behalf. Illbient DJs were probably more comfortable working at an installation than at a traditional club and the post-industrial holocaust their backwards orchestral records and bass pressure created was certainly more thought-provoking than rump-shaking.

The scene's prime mover was Paul D. Miller who took his *nom de disque* – DJ Spooky That Subliminal Kid – from William Burroughs' *Nova Express*. While Spooky's mixes of hip-hop, Iannis Xenakis, Techstep Jungle and Indonesian gamelan don't live up to the feats of his namesake who controlled his surroundings by manipulating tape loops, they are occasionally impressive audio portraits of what architect Rem Koolhaas has called "the culture of congestion" which take the term "soundclash" literally.

Moving to New York from his native Washington DC, Spooky started his own parties and art events at loft spaces throughout Manhattan and Brooklyn where the logic of the sound sculpture replaced the drugged immersion of the chill-out room. His first recorded work was the flurry of blurred beats, "Nasty Data Burst (Why Ask Why)", which appeared on the Bill Laswell-curated collection of experimental hip-hop, **Valis 1: The Destruction of Syntax** (1995).

More chaotic hip-hop deconstructions appeared on his own illbient compilation, **Necropolis: The Dialogic Project** (1996), and his debut album **Songs of a Dead Dreamer** (1996). Rarely more than high-falutin' Trip-Hop with an identity crisis, these records couldn't possibly carry the heavily theoretical baggage that they came with. Even more over-conceptualised was **Viral Sonata** (1997), the terminally unengaging dronescape dotted with hopelessly dated Ambient clichés which he released under his own name.

More successful was the **Synthetic Fury** EP (1998) which sounded like one of Spooky's DJ sets when he was on. The duet with German bass terrorist Panacea on the title track was the best thing he's ever done and the rest of the EP ditched the post-structuralist "play of signifiers" shtick in favour of a play of textures and rhythms. Despite the ridiculous concept of **End of Utopia** (1998), Spooky's contributions to this compilation of Down

Tempo beat collage marking the impossibility of Thomas More's ideal society managed to evoke images rather than theories. **Riddim Warfare** (1998) was still self-obsessed, but collaborators Kool Ke?? and avantist Arto Lindsay never let Spooky disappear up his own. Maybe the collaboration with Metallica on the *Spawn* soundtrack (1997) actually taught him something he didn't already know.

⊙ Synthetic Fury EP   Asphodel, 1998

Grooving almost as hard as it thinks, this is not only Spooky's most accessible work, but his best.

Suburban Base

G rowing out of Dan Donnelly's Boogie Times record shop in Romford, Essex, Suburban Base ranks alongside Reinforced and Moving Shadow in breakbeat's holy trinity of labels. Starting in 1990 with Kromozone's "The Rush", Suburban Base hit its stride with the boss' own "Dancin' People" (1991) which was credited to Q Bass. With a heart-attack synth riff not altogether different from Joey Beltram's "Mentasm" riff that kicked off the darkside sound and an insistent piano riff during the bridge, "Dancin' People" seemed to express Hardcore's speed-limit death drive long before Darkcore came into being.

Even before it fully embraced the darkside, Hardcore was all about the intensity of experience and perhaps no track expresses this delight in sensation as well as Sonz of a Loop Da Loop Era's "Far Out" (1992). With a wonderfully sloppy scratching intro, producer Danny Breaks invented skratchadelic delirium with "Far Out"'s carnival ride of sound effects. Follow-up records like "Peace & Loveism" (1992), the **Flowers in My Garden** EP (1993) and "R Yeah" (1993) continued the sonic rush with furious tempos, promiscuous sampling and galvanising keyboard riffs. Austin's Derrick Morgan-sampling "Rude Boy" (1992), Krome & Time's "Manic Stampede" (1992), which was just that, and Run Tings's "Something to Dance to" (1992) were in the same vein, but the child-like joy in discovery went too far with Smart E's "Sesame's Treet" (1992) which dragged rave's gratuitous drug references unceremoniously into the playground.

When Darkcore destroyed rave's sandcastles, Suburban Base kept up with DJ Hype's brutalist Belgian reconstruction of The 45 King's "The 900 Number", "Shot in the Dark/Weird Energy" (1993) and the drowning diva wails of D'Cruze's "Want You Now" (1993). The label's most effective exploration of the dark side, though, was Boogie Times Tribe's "Dark Stranger" (1993). A collaboration between Donnelly and D'Cruze, "Dark Stranger" picked up on Acid House's ambiguous equation of physical ecstasy and drug apocalypse with its "Girl, I'm starting to lose it" sample.

As hip-hop and ragga took Jungle out of the shadows, Suburban Base led the way with the rhythmic minimalism and bad bwoy vibes of Q Bass & Skeng Gee's "Gun Connection" (1993), DJ Hype's immortal "Rrrroll da Beats" (1994) and DJ Dextrous's "Time to Move" (1994). Marvellous Cain's "Jump Up" (1995) gave this new style a name and Suburban Base artists like Remarc, Dream Team, Swift and Pascal used classic hip-hop breaks and samples to bring back some of Hardcore's energy without any of its gurning naïveté or misplaced optimism.

○ **Various Artists A History of Hardcore:**
Moving Shadow & Suburban Base Joint, 1995

The selection isn't quite as good as it should be, but this is still an impressive collection of tracks from two of the finest breakbeat labels.

Technical Itch/
Decoder

Quite possibly the hardest-working men in the Jungle business, Mark Caro and Darren Beale have churned out dozens and dozens of tracks of substantial quality over the last few years while their colleagues brag about spending three weeks of fifteen-hour days tweaking the drums. Emerging out of Bristol's Hardcore and indie scenes, Caro's Technical Itch and Beale's Decoder projects have explored the more industrial side of drum 'n' bass.

Caro and Beale have both been making music since the early '90s, most notably Beale's Orca and Coda projects who released tracks such as "Valley of the Shadows"-like "Superpod" in 1993 for the Lucky Spin/DeeJay labels. The duo released numerous underground breakbeat records on labels like Ibiza and Force Ten as well as recording straight-ahead Techno as Alph Proxima. A union with Bristol's Ruffneck Ting label produced Decoder's bass-heavy "Deep Down" (1996), but, by and large, the duo languished in obscurity until they signed to Moving Shadow and Hardleaders. Technical Itch's "Can't You See/Contents of Thoughts" (1996) was somewhere between rolling and raving, while Decoder's "Circuit Breaker/Life" (1996) had more breakdowns than a two-hour Sasha DJ set.

The bludgeoning "Think" drums and distorted Martin Luther King Jr. sample of Technical Itch's "The Dreamer" (1996) and the kamikaze bass swoops of Decoder's "Fog/The Difference" (1997) showed that Caro and Beale were astute observers of inner city decay. Technical Itch's "The Virus" (1997) and Decoder's "Twister/Quake" (1997) explored the same territory, but with more machine-venom, while the

Decoder EP, "UXB/NuGen" and the inaugural release on Peshay's Elementz label, "Fuse/Tension" (all 1997), all featured electrical shorts,
twitching nerves and suffocating basslines.

Even more mechanical were the Secret Methods records –
"Domain" and "Animation" (both 1998) – released on Caro's own Tech
Itch label. After engineering Peshay's solo album, Caro and Beale
released Decoder's cavernous "Vapour Dub" (1998) in advance of the
Dissection album (1998). Broadening their tonal palette to include
'70s spy-and-kung-fu-funk, Caro and Beale tried their best to show
that drum 'n' bass hadn't been cornered in a dark alley by the villains
from *Tekken* and *Doom* and that there was still a way out of this Techstep cul-de-sac.

⊙ Decoder Dissection   Hardleaders, 1998

Coming at the end of a year when some of drum 'n' bass' biggest names
released absolute duds, this felt like a defence of the genre's relevance,
even if it was over-produced.

Me Favourits "

Thievery Corporation

Abstraction might be an intellectual pursuit, but the blunted beat
brigade has largely dumbed down the mental aspect of abstract
hip-hop by suffusing it with dope smoke and glossy textures. Perhaps
the *sine qua non* of Down Tempo as air-headed groove is the Washington DC duo, the Thievery Corporation. Typically for producers
who run a bar called the Eighteenth Street Lounge, obsess over
bossa nova records and wear immaculately pressed suits, the Thievery Corporation are concerned with style over substance.

Rob Garza and Eric Hilton met in DC in 1995 and soon started marking tracks together. The title of their debut, "2001 a Spliff Odyssey" (1996), said it all and, despite the cool Dennis Alcapone sample, the record was exactly the overly lustrous dub you'd expect. "Shaolin Satellite" (1996) was slightly funkier and managed to drop its poses once in a while, but "Universal Highness" (1996) again got the jazzy ambience/dirty textures ratio all wrong and sounded like cocktail music for the Stepford Wives.

With tracks like "Foundation" and "Manha", their debut album, **Sounds From the Thievery Hi-Fi** (1997), was just too damn elegant and knew it. The **Encounter in Bahia** EP (1997) was the exotica of Martin Denny and Les Baxter in well-tailored suits, while "Halfway Around the World" (1997) was the perfect soundtrack for slumming hipsters in their thrift-store finery. A night in their bar embalmed on CD, **Eighteenth Street Lounge – The Soundtrack** (1998) collected more smoking-jacket schlock masquerading as the cutting edge.

⊙ **Sounds From the Thievery Hi-Fi**   Eighteenth Street Lounge, 1997

Trip-Hop without the "trip" and not much of the "hop" either, but if you'd always wished Kruder & Dorfmeister could be less challenging, then this is for you.

Tranquility Bass

Mixing up Acid Trance, House, breakbeats, acoustic basslines and reggae samples before such eclecticism was even the gleam in the eye of a British dance mag editor, the Los Angeles-based Exist Dance label run by former Cal Arts students Tom Chasteen and Mike Kandel was an unsung pioneer of sampladelia. Originally released in 1991, High Lonesome Sound System's "Champion Sound" echoed Hardcore's bracing anything-goes spirit without touching its googlish loved-upness. With a couple of breakbeats rumbling around, an acid b-line, a human beatbox, some dancehall toasting, a processed Middle Eastern voice and instrumental flourish, a dub bassline, some TR-808 handclaps and a few hiccoughing squiggles for good measure, "Champion Sound" had nearly as much detail as a Bomb Squad production for Public Enemy.

Tranquility Bass' "They Came in Peace" (1993) was a not-quite Ambient, not-quite Trip-Hop collage of the dawn chorus, strings, new age synth washes, UFO samples, lugubrious breakbeats, a walking double bassline and woodwinds that proved that there was more to California than DJ Shadow. Equally low-key were the seminal "Cantamilla" and "Mya Yadana" (both 1993) singles, but Chasteen soon tired of the music biz and retired to Tucson, Arizona. After releasing the 5/18/93 album (1994) on Instinct Records, Kandel and Tyler Vlaovich (whose Tylervision had releases on San Francisco's Silent Records) relocated to a small island off the coast of Washington to bury themselves in Kandel's prodigious record collection and indulge in psychedelics.

The result of this two-year exile was Tranquility Bass' **Let The Freak Flag Fly** (1997). Part Brian Eno, part Country Joe & the Fish, part Stevie Wonder, **Let The Freak Flag Fly** appended Woodstock Nation's unwashed anarcho-syndicalism and lysergic visions to a thoroughly contemporary samplescape that was at times playful and at times completely disengaged. **Beep!** (1998), an EP of remixes featuring a reconstruction by Fatboy Slim, didn't make things any clearer.

While Kandel was flying his freak flag, Tom Chasteen had a change of heart and re-launched Exist Dance with the slowed-down Jungle breakbeat of "Ramp Up/Drill Down" (1999).

⊙ **Various Artists From Heaven**   Exist Dance, 1993

Largely unacknowledged acid-fried cut-ups that were the immediate
pre-cursors to Down Tempo and Big Beat.

Tricky

The first anyone outside of Bristol's Knowle West housing estate
heard of Adrian Thaws was on Massive Attack's second single,
"Daydreaming", in 1990. The Tricky Kid introduced himself with the
lines, "Trouble and strife, ain't no sunshine in my life/Wiseguys get
protection when they carry a knife". Unlike most American rappers
who throw around similar couplets with glee, Thaws uttered his rhyme
with a narcotic drawl that suggested that the spliff was his only
escape from an adolescence of petty crime that included charges for
robbery and assault.

Bristol's network of after-hours blues dances, ska clubs and hip-
hop shows provided Thaws' other escape route and he eventually
became a peripheral member of Massive Attack in 1990. In addition to
"Daydreaming", the Tricky Kid also contributed some rhymes to "Five
Man Army" and "Blue Lines" on their debut album, **Blue Lines** (1991).
It was his rap on the title track that foreshadowed the direction that
he would take for the rest of his career: "Even if I talked to you, you
still would not know me/Tricky never does, Adrian mostly gets lonely".

Indeed, he felt alienated from Massive's core trio and Tricky went
solo with "Nothing's Clear" (with some production by Portishead's

Geoff Barrow), his ska-like, *Betty Blue*-sampling contribution to **The Hard Sell**, a 1991 compilation of Bristol music in aid of sickle-cell anemia. With the encouragement of his flat-mate, ex-Pop Group and On-U Sound rabble-rouser Mark Stewart, Tricky recorded "Aftermath" (1994) in 1992 with money he blagged off of Massive's manager. With a guitar riff sampled from Marvin Gaye, slurring flutes and the baby-doll blues of singer Martina, "Aftermath" had a psychotic atmosphere to match the panicked confusion of Tricky's rambling "How can I be sure in a world that is constantly changing?"

"Aftermath" sat unreleased for two years until Tricky released it on his own after his cousin heard the track. After Island Records heard it and agreed to re-release it, he recorded "Ponderosa" (1994) with production by Howie B. Another torture chamber of disorienting samples,

"Ponderosa" was even better than its predecessor and set the scene for his debut album, **Maxinquaye** (1995). Along with **Blue Lines**, **Maxinquaye** was one of the most important albums of the decade. Not only did it create an audacious sound world out of painfully slow tempos, foggy atmospheres and Isaac Hayes and Shakespears Sister samples, but it stands as one of the more remarkable interrogations of the myth of black masculinity. Tricky's no sweet-talking love man – "Are you sure you want to be with me, I've got nothing to give/I won't lie and say this loving's best" – his girlfriend cuts his "slender wrists" and he's equally comfortable quoting effete dandy David Sylvian as he is quoting Cypress Hill. Meanwhile, Martina sings the cover of Public Enemy's anti-military, testosterone-filled jailbreak tale, "Black Steel in the Hour of Chaos".

While it avoided any hint of "supergroup" smugness, his Nearly God project with Björk, Neneh Cherry, ex-Special Terry Hall and Stereo MC vocalist Cath Coffey seemed to just drag along with the quicksand beats and dancing-with-gravity-boots tempos without ever making them signify. His perverse taste in covers continued with Siouxsie & the Banshees' "Tattoo" and its non-LP b-side, Slick Rick's "Children's Story", but **Nearly God** (1996), released on his Durban Poison imprint, was as detrimentally off-the-cuff as its two-week recording time suggested.

Pre-Millennium Tension (1996) was Tricky's "proper" follow-up to **Maxinquaye**. The production was even bolder and less compromising with tempos slowed down to a crawl and samples re-arranged and re-manipulated until they sounded as bloodshot and fucked-up as Tricky himself. Unlike the first album, however, his paranoia sounded merely self-indulgent rather than delirious and mesmerising, and **Pre-Millennium Tension** often sounded like he was moaning about his break-up with former flame Björk.

Finding time to record after his appearance in Luc Besson's *The Fifth Element*, he released **Angels With Dirty Faces** in 1998. Less petered-out hip-hop than hallucinogenic Tom Waits and deracinated

New Orleans hoodoo, **Angels With Dirty Faces** was another step forward into an oblique sound world of scraping guitar noise and murky swamps of bass distortion. Once again, though, his lyrics – about the perils of fame and how much the record industry sucks – were the words of a star whining about his mistreatment. Perhaps his work with hardman Mad Frankie Fraser and hardwoman Grace Jones will keep him in check.

⊙ Maxinquaye   Island, 1995

Tricky says he thinks bomblike and there's no evidence here to suggest that he doesn't.

Ultimate Dilemma

One of the few blunted beat labels that wouldn't get wiped out of existence with a single flick of DJ Premier's musical wrists,

Ultimate Dilemma was started in 1995 from the fallout of Mo' Wax's RPM. The Brighton-based crew of AJ Kwame, Joe 2000 and Stef released a couple of singles like the slow and low cut-up "Food of My De-Rhythm" (1993) and the spaced-out "2000/Sorti Des Ombres" (1994) which featured both the bassline from reggae's famous "Stalag 17" riddim and French rapper Menelik before breaking up.

Kwame then started Ultimate Dilemma with Max Iousada and released The Runaways' (Kwame and Joe 2000) **Pathways EP** (1995). Misterjon's **Seachange** EP (1996) followed with "Gratis" which featured a hard, wooden drum break that combined electronica's obsession with tone colour and breakbeat's hyperspeed, lateral acceleration. Req's **Miracles** EP (1996) and Raymatics' **Universal** EP (1996) furthered the label's reputation for experimental Down Tempo productions. The Runaways' **Playschool** EP (1996), meanwhile, brilliantly reappropriated easy listening for new age b-boys with the oboe obbligato of "Finders Kreepers" – one of the few successful fusions of hip-hop beats and spy-movie atmospherics to appear in the wake of Portishead's appropriation of Lalo Schifrin.

Musical Dilemmas (1997) was an audio précis of the label's first year and featured a French sort-of remake of Dawn Penn's "No, No, No" by Melaaz in among tracks by ringers like Danny Breaks, Tek 9 and Peshay. Star of the show, though, was the title track from Req's **Miracles** EP, a strange conglomeration of jazz loops, stilted Electro effects and coarse drum programming. The Runaways' debut album, **Classic Tales** (1997), meanwhile expanded on the success of "Finders Kreepers".

Ultimate Dilemma managed to avoid the limitations of a genre whose *raison d'etre* is lethargy by reaching out to fringe hip-hop artists like The 45 King and Cyclops 4000 (aka Sir Menelik). UD released The 45 King's excellent **Lost Breakbeats** album in 1997, proving the label had a sense of history as well as a desire to raid its record crates. Cyclops 4000's "Macroscope" (1998), meanwhile, turned mouthfuls of verbiage like "indiscriminate use of antibiotics" into the components of a freaky, freaky flow and pulled off the same feat that Melle Mel managed when he made "sacrophiliac" sound dope.

Unlike the rest of that ever-growing sub-culture of charity shop *bricoleurs*, Jadell managed to make something remarkably groovy out of all those Black and White Minstrels and Max Bygraves records lurking in the country's Oxfam shops on "Brand New Sound" (1998) and had fun, fun, fun 'til Daddy took the Akai away. Jadell and The Runaways were part of the Down Tempo supergroup Common Ground which also numbered Tim "Love" Lee, Waiwan and Aim among its members. Although it seemed more of a publicity stunt than anything else, Common Ground managed to come up with a few good tunes and their album, **No More Heroes** (1998), was quite a reasonable survey of the end-of-the-millennium broad-mindedness.

○ Various Artists Musical Dilemmas　　　　Ultimate Dilemma, 1997

Although it was a bit on the harmless side, this was a fine survey of the label's first year.

DJ Vadim　*talented Vadim.*

For all the much vaunted non-specificity of blunted beats artists like DJ Shadow and DJ Krush, no one has pushed hip-hop further into the realm of abstraction than DJ Vadim. Inspired by both hip-hop producers like DJ Premier and Prince Paul and *musique con-*

crète artists like Pierres Henry and Schaeffer, this Russian émigré wages a war of attrition on rhythms and textures until they are left gaunt and threadbare. With beats made out of creaking doors and

static, Vadim's records are journeys into the dark heart of entropy and torpor.

The name of Vadim's label, Jazz Fudge, was a perfect description of his sound and his debut EP, **Abstract Hallu-cinogenic Gases** (1995), was com-prised of beats made out of molasses and morose keyboards. This sound of dope-induced lethargy con-tinued on the **Headz Ain't Ready** EP (1995) with its mordant vocal samples, bloodshot atmospherics and rigor-mortis beats. Even closer to the realm of Thanatos was Little Aida's Vadim-produced

"Confessions" (1996) which sounded like the last-breath response of the love object of Van Morrison's "T.B. Sheets".

Recruited by Ninja Tune, Vadim released the excellent "Non Lateral Hypothesis" (1996) which was chilled to the point of numbness and so slo-mo that it seemed as if it was wading through quicksand. With the sampled tag line, "Rap is something you do, hip-hop is something you live", "Aural Prostitution" (1996) preceded Vadim's debut LP, **USSR Repertoire** (1996), with a slightly more lively take on psychotropic beat collage. Featuring loops that decomposed before your ears, torpid breakbeats and all manner of magnified blips, bleeps and clicks, **USSR Repertoire,** however, was a universe away from the facetious quip-hop of his Ninja Tune labelmates. Tracks like "Live in Paris" and "Conquest of the Irrational" felt like Jungle 45s played at 33 rpm, but they worked because of details like scratching buried in the mix so that it sounded like a ghost wind shivering down your spine.

The **Revelations of Wrath** EP (1997) introduced Vadim's alter-ego, Andre Gurov. Despite the personality change, **Revelations of Wrath** was just as lugubrious and dysfunktional as his other records. Decent contributions to compilations by fellow travellers like Germany's Mille Plateaux and Japan's Soup Disk labels followed, but when artists like The Herbaliser, Oval and Reflection returned the favour by remixing tracks from **USSR Repertoire** on **USSR Reconstruction** (1998), the results were less rewarding.

Hooking up with New York rappers Anti-Pop Consortium, Vadim moved in a more explicitly hip-hop direction, albeit with his characteristically skewed sensibility, as The Isolationist. On **Orators of Advanced Thought** (1999), dark and moody production and some fine karate-chop scratching set the scene for the rapid-fire, almost a rhythmic flows of MCs Priest, Beans and M Sayid which treated 'your ears as [their] punching bag'.

◎ USSR Repertoire　　　　　　　　　　　Ninja Tune, 1996

Moody and paranoid beat hypnosis practised by one of the masters of
Down Tempo rhythmic psychedelia.

Wagon Christ/Plug

Inspired and validated by the nerdscapes of Aphex Twin, bedroom
musician loners like Luke Vibert were influenced by the sounds of
clubland without ever venturing near their social milieu. Without the
context, their music fol-
lowed no unwritten
rules about groove or
beat and flitted between
genres whenever it
seemed appropriate to
create a type of music
that was about sound
for sound's sake.

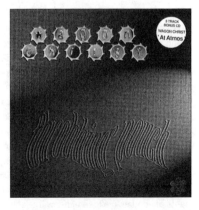

Vibert was a neigh-
bour of Aphex Twin in
Cornwall, where he
played bass in a Crass-
influenced punk band
before his friend turned
him on to the possibilities of electronics. Vibert's first album, **Phat Lab
Nightmare** (1994), was recorded as Wagon Christ (which was

inspired by a comic book character) and described a frigid and chilling vision of hi-pitched ambience. An album on Aphex's Rephlex label recorded with Jeremy Simmonds, **Weir** (1994), explored similar terrain and bore no relation to the Grateful Dead's rhythm guitarist who is the album's namesake.

Vibert switched gears for the **At Atmos** (1994) EP which ventured from ethnic soundscapes through Shakatak-on-mescalin jazz-funk to grating instrumental hip-hop. **Throbbing Pouch** (1995) was a funkier, but no less individual, take on Trip-Hop: "E-Z Listener" added to '70s cop show soundtracks that bizarre, off-key, piss-taking, sarcastic sound that µ-ziq turned into an art form; "Vibes" made a mockery of hip-hop shout-outs; "Pull My Strings" was a relatively straight, if deathlike, take on standard Trip-Hop; "Scrapes" was crammed to bursting with sonic minutiae; on "Throbbing Pouch" Vibert actually seemed to like what he was sampling and didn't heap scorn upon it.

As Plug Vibert applied the same techniques and attitude to drum 'n' bass. **Plug 1 – Visible Crater Funk** (1995) was constructed out of Electro beats chopped up into particles, scratchy atmospheres, remnants of academic experiments with electronic instruments and manically timestretched voices. **Plug 2 – Rebuilt Kev** (1995) was similarly "different", but with even more madcap mayhem, constructed as if breakbeats were Rube Goldberg mousetraps. Less nutty, **Drum n Bass For Papa** (1996) suffered a bit from drum 'n' bassers' irritating insistence on making artistic statements when they release albums.

Vibert's association with Mo' Wax began with the lacklustre **A Polished Solid** EP (1995), released under his own name. **Big Soup** (1997) was a sprawling two-hour plus not-quite epic of sonic clutter that was the audio equivalent of a boy who had not cleaned up his room in three years. More successful were remixes of Moloko's "Lotus Eater" (1996) and 2Player's "Extreme Possibilities" (1996), which was a classic of gratuitous timestretching, and the "Get Your Head Down" (1996) hip-hop one-off for Ninja Tune.

Allegedly, **Tally Ho** (1998) was conceived as a cheerful send-up of the "naffness" of British culture. The musical *Carry On* film never quite developed, however, as the album was mired in tinkly textures and chiming timbres that had nothing to rub up against.

◗ Throbbing Pouch   Rising High, 1995

One of the very few '90s albums to reference jazz-fusion without congealing into an unctuous blob of aspirational yearnings.

Wall of Sound

R un by football fanatics Mark Jones and Mark Lessner, Wall of Sound kicked off its breakbeat eclecticism with the piss-take Latin shenanigans of E-Klektik's "Maracana Madness" (1994). Mekon's exemplary "Phatty's Lunchbox" (1994) followed with dope-addled beats and atmospheres that helped solidify the Down Tempo template. **Give 'Em Enough Dope Volume 1** (1994) furthered the

Down Tempo agenda with tracks like "Blacker" by Ashley Beedle's Ballistic Brothers Versus the Eccentric Afros and Kruder & Dorfmeister's "High Noon".

Back to Mono (1995) followed with a collection of tracks by the label's artists like Mekon, Akasha and Artery (aka Jon Carter of Monkey Mafia). **Give 'Em Enough Dope Volume 2** (1995) featured not only the expected Down Tempo of the Mose Allison-sampling "Young Men" by Kruder & Dorfmeister and the abstract Electro of Mekon's "Last Breath", but tracks by Deep House guru Larry Heard and Junglist T.Power as well. Overlooked singles by The Wiseguys ("Nil By Mouth/Too Easy") and Ceasefire (aka Derek Dahlarge)

("Trickshot") (both 1995) followed, as well as a neglected album by Rootless, **Rotten Wood For Smoking Bees** (1995), which effectively grafted samples of acoustic guitars and wheezing old men onto hip-hop beats.

More fried hip-hop cut-ups appeared in the form of the Mad Frankie Fraser-sampling "Revenge of the Mekon" (1996) by Mekon, and The Wiseguys' "The Sound You Hear/We Keep On" (1996). The **Dive EP** (1996) introduced the world to the Propellerheads, while Les Rhythmes Digitales' **Liberation** (1996) made your acquaintance with the Human League's drum machines and other kitschy Electro-disco touches.

Les Rhythmes Digitales' awful pun, "Jacques Your Body" (1997), followed suit with more disco yuks, while The Wiseguys' **Executive Suite** (1997) knocked up hip-hop with loungecore smarm. Mekon met up with Philadelphia's favourite son, Schooly D, for "Skool's Out" (1997) (not an Alice Cooper cover). Akasha's **Cinematique** (1998), meanwhile, featured Neneh Cherry rocking out on a cover of Guns 'N' Roses' "Sweet Child o' Mine". Riding the old-school hip-hop trend for all it was worth, DJ Touche's The Wiseguys' "Ooh La La" (1998) stole a catch-phrase from a rapper stealing a catch-phrase from an old designer jeans advert, borrowed some wink-wink-nudge-nudge '60s teenbeat from Bentley Rhythm Ace and pilfered a snatch of driving flute funk to become a distillation of the past couple of years' worth of student dancefloor fillers.

⊙ Various Artists Give 'Em Enough Dope Volume 2 Wall of Sound, 1995

Perhaps not as eye-opening now, but putting Kruder & Dorfmeister next to Larry Heard next to T.Power next to Norman Cook was a radical move way back then.

DJ Wally

With a youth spent on the perimeters of New York's hip-hop scene, DJ Wally understands more than most that Trip-Hop ain't nothing but instrumental hip-hop and that it's been around since day one. Knowing that DJ Premier is fresher and wilder than any stoned-to-the-gills Down Tempo producer, Wally never lets his productions, whether Down Tempo or Junglist, stray too far from the wildstyle.

Born Keef Destefano in Queens, New York, the future DJ Wally would spend the bulk of his adolescence tagging derelict buildings and practising on the wheels of steel. Turning on to the Down Tempo and Junglist sounds coming out of England, Wally started his own Samz Jointz label in 1995 with the somnambulant beats of the **Posse Purple Fetish** EP. The **Mustard Plaster** EP (1996) followed in a similar style, but with more off-beat samples. With long-time associate DJ Swingsett, Wall released the **Kind Budz** EP (1996) which featured the insect-song and minor-key piano of "Space People" and the loopy "Bitchley's Kow Korn".

The piercing piano loop of his "My Bloody Valentine" appeared on Mo' Wax's **Headz 2** compilation (1996), while New York's Jungle Sky label released Wally's Junglist excursions "Big Apple Rinse" and "Toast" on the **Fuck Jungle** EPs (1996). At around the same time, Wally started barraging the Big Apple with gangstadelic Dope Dragon and Frontline 12"s as one of the residents of New York's Konkrete Jungle club.

Liquid Sky released Wally's debut album, **DJ Wally's Genetic Flaw**, to universal acclaim in 1997. Embodying New York's compression and pollution, **Genetic Flaw** was filled with industrial noises and layers of bass smog, not to mention a cheeky remix of Simon & Garfunkel's "59th Street Bridge Song". There were also old-school connections aplenty, particularly on the scratchy "Mr. Beaver Saves the Day" and "Last Chance to Comprehend".

Wally's hip-hop chops served him well in his incarnation as Pish-Posh on the Jungle wing of the Rawkus empire, Raw Kuts. With old- and new-school samples aplenty, Pish-Posh became New York's home-grown avatar of jump-up with tracks like "Get Ill" (1997) and "On Yer Feet/Are You Ready" (1998). **Up Jumps the Boogie** (1998) was Wally's Junglist mix album and featured his remix of Reflection Eternal's underground hip-hop classic "Fortified Live", and his own commentaries on New York's finest, "Corrupt Cops" and "NY Under-cover".

⊙ **DJ Wally's Genetic Flaw**   Liquid Sky, 1997

Walking the fence between detachment and funkiness, Wally created one of the few Down Tempo long-players that was more than just a cloud of smoke.

Wordsound

Florida might be the home of Bass Music, but nowhere is the low-end rumble as important as it is in New York City. Manhattan's grid has created what architect Rem Koolhaas calls "the Culture of Congestion" and the sound, texture and physicality of the low end approximates this phenomenal density of humans, things and cultures. While dub, with its pressure-cooker aesthetic and dirty timbres, is a perfect metaphor for the compression and pollution of New York, at the same time it is also where the bass and drums stretch out and breathe – a search for width in a city dominated by its skyscraping verticality. Operating out of a converted warehouse in Williamsburg, Brooklyn – a section of town that squashes Polish immigrants, Hasidic Jews and slumming hipsters into a deteriorating Hispanic neighbour-hood across the East River from Manhattan – the Wordsound label explores dub's double meaning of grimy paranoia and horizontal space.

Run by journalist S.H. "Skiz" Fernando, Jr., Wordsound is the urban soundboy label *par excellence*. Making connections between King Tubby, Bill Laswell's avant-funk, the hip-hop psychedelia of the

Jungle Brothers and Prince Paul, Middle Eastern trance music and Down Tempo's disengagement, Wordsound's inaugural releases, the **Red Shift** compilation and Scarab's **Scarab** (both 1994), explored the universe that exists in a puff of smoke. Wordsound's "Crooklyn Dub Consortium" of producers – Sub Dub, Roots Control, We, HIM, Dr. Israel and Spectre – went even further into the heart of the bass on **Certified Dope Volume 1** (1995). Tracks like We's "Second Hand Science" and HIM's "Chemical Mix" turned dub into the sound of the urban underbelly, while Dr. Israel's awesome "Saidisabruklinmon (Nobwoycyantess)" joined the dots between Edie Brickell, a dancehall in Kingston, Ofra Haza and do-or-die Bed-Stuy.

Recording as Spectre, Fernando's occasionally stunning excursion into hip-hop's dark side, **The Illness...** (1995), laid the foundations for the label's release of De La Soul producer Prince Paul's ultra-scatalogical hip-hop skit writ large, **Psychoanalysis (What Is It?)** (1996). Wordsound's best hip-hop flava-ed release, though, was **Subterranean Hitz Volume 1** (1996) which, as Spectre himself put it, was an album for "castaways on the vast oceans of the mind". Featuring such deranged beat desecrators as the X-ecutioners' Rob Swift, New Kingdom's Scotty Hard, Prince Paul and Afrika "Baby Bam" from the Jungle Brothers, **Subterranean Hitz** was a refreshing reminder that Brits did not have a monopoly on abstract hip-hop and that there had been instrumental hip-hop since Kool Herc first stole electricity from the New York City Parks Commission.

The second volume of **Subterranean Hitz (1997)** was equally successful, while the **Shake the Nations** (1997) double-disc compilation collected the highlights of the label's first three years. The vinyl-only Black Hoodz imprint was responsible for fine EPs by Dr. Israel and Truck Stop and the utterly messed-up **Smoke It Exact** EP (1998) by Spectre and hip-hop lunatic Torture. In 1999 Black Hoodz released the even more bizarre, but thoroughly essential, **Crazy Wisdom Masters** EP of outtakes from the Jungle Brothers' **J Beez Wit The Remedy** sessions.

Wordsound artist **Dr. Shehab** started his own Baraka label in 1997, releasing the rootsical drum 'n' bass of Dr. Israel's Brooklyn Jungle Soundsystem among

other projects, and proving that the Wordsound virus is spreading.

◉ Various Artists Crooklyn Dub Consortium: Certified Dope Vol. 1   Wordsound, 1995

Some of the New York underground's finest artists interpreting dub as a harbinger of illness.

◉ Various Artists Subterranean Hitz Vol. 1   Wordsound, 1996

Trip-Hop that takes the term literally and drags instrumental hip-hop deep into the bowels of New York's grim underbelly.

µ-ziq

With rhythms that sound like Zimmer frames clattering down staircases, a worldview that seems to see everything from a caustic window and tunes that veer from prehistoric Ambient to planet-rocking Electro-phonk at the drop of a hat, Mike Paradinas is the Willem de Kooning to Aphex Twin's Jean Dubuffet. Paradinas is no modernist, however, as his music cares little for its materials or processes and concerns itself only with a play of textures that expresses nothing but irony, if it bothers to communicate at all.

After dropping out of an architecture course at the same university that spawned Aphex Twin, Paradinas released his debut album, **Tango 'n' Vectif** (1993), on Aphex's Rephlex label. With titles like "PHI*1700 [u/v]" and liner notes and Ambient noises from a time long before the dawn of the modular synthesizer, μ-ziq's **Tango 'n' Vectif** was the precursor of the current fetishisation of old-school electronic music pioneers like Pierre Henry and Morton Subotnick. It was also one of the first records to view rhythm purely as texture without even a nod to its traditional functions of providing a foundation and shaking booty. **Bluff Limbo** (1994) was more of the same, but without as much of the play between fuck-off analogue misanthropy and archaic gentility that made the first record so fascinating.

After a brutal, merciless remix of indie miserablists The Auteurs, Paradinas released knowingly cheesy Electro/E-Z listening pastiches as Jake Slazenger and Tusken Raiders for the Clear label. Slazenger's **Makesaracket** (1995) album was a combination of Bontempi organs, sarcastic O'Jays samples and laboured funk beats that felt like a send-up of the kitsch culture of working men's clubs and Butlins discos. "Roy Castle" (1995) may have had similar influences, but the contrast between the grain of the trumpet sample and the crushing beats made it the best, and most irony-free, thing he's ever done.

"Roy Castle" appeared on the third μ-ziq album, **In Pine Effect** (1995). The album had its moments ("Old Fun #1" came across like

Bernard Herrmann and avant percussionist David van Tieghem jamming inside a Casio keyboard), but the pan-stylism meant that there was little to grab hold of. His **Spatula Freak** (1995) album as Kid Spatula for Jonah Sharpe's Reflective label moved away from the unkempt-facial-hair-and-lab-coat ambience of his first two records towards a more contemporary and crystalline application of aural tincture.

The flood of Paradinas product continued unabated in 1996 with **Expert Knob Twiddlers**, a collaboration with Aphex Twin and the second Jake Slazenger album, **Das Ist Ein Groovy Beat Ja.** He also unveiled his Gary Moscheles persona with **Shaped to Make Your Life Easier**, which had some grooves, but tried way too hard to be funny. **Lunatic Harness** (1997), his fourth µ-ziq album, more or less followed the blueprint created by **In Pine Effect**, but with an attitude that suggested that maybe he had a modicum of regard for his audience after all.

◉ Tango 'n' Vectif   Rephlex, 1993

The base materials may not have been too dissimilar from Aphex Twin's **Selected Ambient Works**, but they were presented without his control-freak over-programming which made for an album that sounded like the Saturday morning cartoon version of Karlheinz Stockhausen.

Some, Freestylers,
Massive Attack

Chemical Brothers

Prodigy

and

Garage - House - Drum'n'Bass -
Hardcore - Rap - Techno
Cele Niai fatue style - ...d

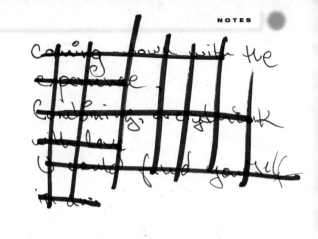

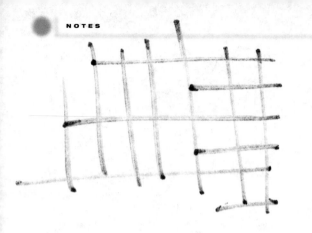

Stay in touch with us!

ROUGHNEWS is Rough Guides' free newsletter.
In three issues a year we give you news, travel issues, music reviews, readers' letters and the latest dispatches from authors on the road.

I would like to receive ROUGHNEWS: please put me on your free mailing list.

NAME . . . .

ADDRESS . . . .

Please clip or photocopy and send to: Rough Guides, 1 Mercer Street, London WC2H 9QJ, England

or Rough Guides, 375 Hudson Street, New York, NY 10014, USA.

ROUGH GUIDES: Travel

Belgium
& Luxembourg
THE ROUGH GUIDE

ROUGH GUIDES: Mini Guides, Travel Specials and Phrasebooks

MINI GUIDES

Antigua
Bangkok
Barbados
Big Island of Hawaii
Boston
Brussels
Budapest
Dublin
Edinburgh
Florence
Honolulu
Lisbon
London Restaurants
Madrid
Maui
Melbourne
New Orleans
St Lucia

Seattle
Sydney
Tokyo
Toronto

TRAVEL SPECIALS

First-Time Asia
First-Time Europe
More Women Travel

PHRASEBOOKS

Czech
Dutch
Egyptian Arabic
European
French

German
Greek
Hindi & Urdu
Hungarian
Indonesian
Italian
Japanese
Mandarin Chinese
Mexican Spanish
Polish
Portuguese
Russian
Spanish
Swahili
Thai
Turkish
Vietnamese

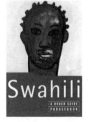

AVAILABLE AT ALL GOOD BOOKSHOPS

ROUGH GUIDES:
Reference and Music CDs

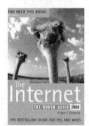

AVAILABLE AT ALL GOOD BOOKSHOPS